Other Books by Elisabeth Young-Bruehl

Freedom and Karl Jaspers' Philosophy (1981)

Hannah Arendt: For Love of the World (1982)

Vigil, a novel (1983)

Anna Freud: A Biography (1988)

Mind and the Body Politic (1989)

Freud on Women (1990)

Creative Characters (1991)

Global Cultures (1994)

The Anatomy of Prejudices (1996)

Subject to Biography (1999)

Cherishment

A Psychology of the Heart

Elisabeth Young-Bruehl
Faith Bethelard

THE FREE PRESS
NEW YORK LONDON SYDNEY SINGAPORE

THE FREE PRESS
A Division of Simon & Schuster Inc.
1230 Avenue of the Americas
New York, NY 10020

Book Design by MSPACE/ MAURA FADDEN ROSENTHAL

Manufactured in the United States of America

10 9 8 7 6 5 4 3 2 1

Library of Congress Cataloging-in-Publication Data
Young-Bruehl, Elisabeth.
    Cherishment: a psychology of the heart / Elisabeth Young-Bruehl,
    Faith Bethelard.
        p. cm.
Includes bibliographical references.
    1. Love. 2. Psychoanalysis. 3. Freud, Sigmund, 1856–1939. I. Bethelard, Faith.
II. Title.

BF175.5.L68.C54 2000
158.2 — dc21

                                                                            99–046500
ISBN 0–684–85966–1

The illustration on page 115 is from Lincoln, Andrew, William Blake's Songs of Innocence and Songs of Experience. Copyright © 1991 by Princeton University Press in conjunction with the William Blake Trust and the Tate Gallery. Reprinted by permission of Princeton University Press.

The illustration on page 161 is from a photograph by Jerry Cooke Inc. Reprinted with permission.

Contents

Illustrations

Preface

What we offer in this book is a way of thinking about a basic human need—a need for affection, for the kind of love we call "cherishment," a love that goes heart to heart, telepathically. We offer a way of thinking about how the need for cherishing affection appears first in the relation between a preverbal infant and the infant's caretakers and then, from this beginning, in all other human relations. You already know from your own experience, your own need, what we are going to be talking about: cherishment, affection. You will have your own definition. It will be tacit in your immediate associations to the words "affection" and "cherishment," what sprang to your mind as you read them. But you will also know that it matters a great deal *how* we all think and talk about a basic human need, so we hope you will find it good to be reflective about what you already know while reading what we have to say. After all, each person's reflective thinking and talking about such a basic need shapes both how its fulfillment is sought and how fulfilling it for other people is done. Similarly, we have found in our work as therapists that how you think about an infant expecting affection or cherishment shapes how you respond to a patient—someone who is still feeling infant needs—and how you cultivate the relationship you and your patient have.

xi

We work in this book with concepts from Freudian psychoanalysis, and with the whole remarkable history of psychoanalytic treatment—by which we also mean psychotherapy, as the various kinds of psychotherapy are all the offspring of psychoanalysis, derived from its insights. But psychoanalysis, until very recently, has not had a place in its conceptual storehouse for this "cherishment." Among the contemporary psychoanalysts who have been emphasizing their patients' very early childhood experiences with caretaking, or with traumatizing lack of caretaking, cherishing affection (under different names) has become a topic. The current discussion is exciting and inspiring. But still, it seems to us, contemporary psychoanalysis has not come to the way of thinking and talking presented here.

We have worked with psychoanalytic concepts, but as newcomers. Both of us started to train for clinical practice in midlife, after other kinds of experience and work. So, we do not have a large fund of clinical expertise. But we also do not have the debts and baggage, distortions and controversies of old hands. We have the advantage of being childlike, but not naive; capable of being astonished at how human beings—ourselves included—are in therapy, but also capable of freshly relating our astonishment to "the literature," and to the contributions of our teachers. Our teachers, however, are not just psychoanalysts. We bring to our clinical work and to this writing the literary, philosophical and spiritual traditions in which each of us has steeped, traditions that, we think, can help psychoanalysis open to the concepts and the words it needs to talk about cherishment. And to talk in a more cherishing language!—not the caricaturable scientific jargon that has crusted up over the heart of psychoanalysis.

We have tried to play freely in this book with many ways of writing: memoir, dialogue, theoretical exposition, poetry, meditation, travelogue, joke, essay, dreamtext, anecdote, and vignette—

everything but footnote. We have tried to create a literary form that presents our discovery process and the conversation in which that process was born and grew up. The journey we took talking about "cherishment" was not down a paved, curbed road; we were more like the journeyer in Walt Whitman's "Song of the Open Road," learning to be in every way we could receptive:

> *I inhale great draughts of space,*
> *The east and the west are mine, and the north and the*
> *south are mine.*

So, the journeybook we have made does not have the simplicity of a map. It will require your imagination and something like the kind of listening that an analyst once described as "with the third ear."

For the reflective journey we invite you to take with us in this book, our guiding sign has been a figure called "Inner Truth" from the ancient Chinese book of wisdom the *I Ching*. It looks like this (calligraphed by our friend the Chinese painter Ying Li):

The *I Ching* comments: "The hexagram consists of firm lines above and below, while it is open in the center. This indicates a heart free of prejudices and therefore open to truth." Openhearted receptivity is, we will say, cherishment.

Please note: Throughout *Cherishment*, we have written about patients we have seen in psychotherapy and psychoanalysis, often citing their words. But no patient has been presented under his or her own name, and all details that could possibly identify the patients have been disguised. Also, when we discuss our patients with each other, we use the pseudonyms we have used here, and we are careful to protect each patient's confidentiality in our conversations, as we would in a case conference or in any other professional context. In the two instances where we have used a patient's text, we have done so with the patient's permission.

Chapter 1

Discovering Cherishment

Times of growth are beset with difficulties. They resemble a first birth. But these difficulties arise from the very profusion of all that is struggling to attain form . . . So too the superior man has to arrange and organize the inchoate profusion of such times of beginning, just as one sorts out silk threads from a knotted tangle and binds them into skeins. In order to find one's place in the infinity of being, one must be able both to separate and to unite. . . . It is important to seek out the right assistants, but he can find them only if he avoids arrogance and associates with his fellows in a spirit of humility . . .

—"DIFFICULTY AT THE BEGINNING," *I CHING* (3)

Our long conversational journey began as a short trip. On December 3, 1995, my friend Faith Bethelard and I went to New Haven to celebrate the Centenary of Anna Freud's birth. The Child Study Center at Yale University was hosting a meeting of psychoanalysts from various American cities and a group from the Anna Freud Centre in London. I had been invited to address the gathering in my capacity as Anna Freud's biographer.

The weekend was to include many lectures, receptions and dinners, but the event we anticipated most eagerly was a case conference. A young American analyst was going to summarize a treatment he had concluded with a little girl, six years old when they began, and the Anna Freudians were going to respond, discuss, reflect. We would hear from the elders who dated their affiliations with Freud's daughter from the war years, and from the ones who were, like us, trainees of trainees, psychoanalytic grandchildren. The whole history of child psychoanalysis, represented by some of its most talented living practitioners, would reverberate, and we had been invited to partake in it. Having breakfast in the hotel dining room before this event, Faith and I were feeling like pilgrims at a shrine. And that Sunday morning, while we were in a state of deep expectation, we fell into a conversation.

Faith and I had had many psychoanalytic shoptalks in the preceding two years, while we had both, in the middle of life's way, set about training to be clinicians. Having sent her daughter off to college, Faith was starting a clinical psychology doctorate that had her doing therapy several days a week, first at a community mental health center and then in a hospital outpatient clinic. After twenty-some years as a professor and a writer, I was working at the Institute of Pennsylvania Hospital and training at the Philadelphia Association for Psychoanalysis. We shared a clinical language, which we spoke like eager emigrants as we mapped out the vertiginous tangle of our experiences in mental health. Getting oriented, acclimated, we were making a transition from being bookishly fluent in psychoanalysis to mixing it up with real people. Topics theoretical and technical had challenged us, but "What do you think I should do?" went through most of our talks like a drumbeat. That morning in New Haven had an entirely different feeling, though; we were not struggling to learn, not driven to *do* (hoping to do no harm). We simply came upon an emotional clearing and stood still there, wondering.

The conversation began on a familiar enough plane: a project was up for consideration. Faith, sipping her tea, staring out the window at the New Haven harbor, told me that she had been thinking about writing her dissertation on how therapy works; what are the various views existing in our business on "therapeutic action"? She laughed at herself for the audacity of this idea, knowing that the literature on therapeutic action is enormous, but even more, knowing that her own work as a psychotherapist was so new that she had, and would have, only a beginner's experience to draw on. "But," she said, "there is my analysis—and that's a lot of experience!"

Faith told me that it had fascinated her to look back on the course of her own psychoanalysis, because it had had such distinct phases in it, and in each one such different shifts and changes had come about. A year into it, for example, she had found herself suspended in a peculiar state: "dreamy neediness," she called it. And while she was there, dreamily needy, her analyst took his summer vacation and she went off for two weeks in Bermuda. On a day when the Atlantic weather was gray and heavy, she passed up the beach and stayed in her cottage, reading and staring out the window at the ocean harbor below.

Her book was Michael Balint's *The Basic Fault*, and she was in a chapter called "Primary Love." Balint—born, we later learned, on December 3, 1896, a year to the very day after Anna Freud—was a Hungarian psychoanalyst, a student of Freud's friend Sandor Ferenczi. Best known for ideas about infants that were novel in the 1920s, Balint had held that newborns live in a condition of relation to people that is profoundly influenced by the undifferentiated quality of fetal existence, life in the "harmonious mixup" of baby in mother, like fish in water. Our first bonds after birth are, Balint suggested, ones in which we have no sense that others might have wishes and expectations that are not our own, so there is no need for seeking power or making effort. A newborn is in a harmonious condition of passive expectation. If the unconditional dependence of primary love is disturbed more than it must be by the normal demands of living and growing, the baby responds desperately. In a baby who is unwanted, physically or emotionally neglected, abandoned, attacked, hatred is born, aggression springs up. A "basic fault" is a failure to feel primary love or an unrepaired, even irreparable, rupture of it.

Faith told me how she had floated past Balint's complex technical terminology, pulled by the current of his sensitivity to the emotional life of babies and his conviction that he was exploring an infant experience—the primordial infant experience—that psychoanalysis had neglected. Fundamentally, Balint said, each human being wants to return to "an all-embracing harmony with the environment, to be able to love in peace." With the phrase "to love in peace" reverberating in her mind, Faith halted at a nearby passage, an aside Balint had whispered to his reader.

Before going further, I wish to refer here to some clinical and linguistic observations of T. Doi (1962). According to him, there exists in Japanese a very simple, everyday word, *amaeru*, an intransitive verb, denoting "to wish or to expect to be

4

loved" in the sense of primary love. *Amae* is the noun derived from it, while the adjective *amai* means "sweet." These words are so common that "indeed the Japanese find it hard to believe that there is no word for *amaeru* in the European languages." Moreover, in Japanese there is a rich vocabulary describing the various attitudes and moods that develop if the wish to *amaeru* is frustrated or must be repressed. All these attitudes are known in the West, but they cannot be expressed by simple words, only by complicated phrases like "sulking or pouting because he feels he is not allowed to show his wish to *amaeru* as much as he wants to, thus harboring in himself mental pain, possibly of masochistic nature," etc. etc. Doi adds that according to his information, the Korean and Ainu languages have equivalent words, as possibly has the Chinese.

From this passage, the two phrases written by this unknown Japanese psychoanalyst, T. Doi, jumped out and lodged in Faith's memory. She gave them to me by heart in New Haven: the one that translated *amaeru* as "to wish or to expect to be loved," and the one about frustration as "sulking or pouting because he feels he is not allowed to show his wish to *amaeru* as much as he wants to, thus harboring in himself mental pain, possibly of masochistic nature."

During the rest of that vacation in Bermuda, Faith could see herself in the mirror of these phrases from the East. She wrote wildly in her journal, day after day, about her expectation to be loved and how it had been so inconsistently met when she was a child, leaving her in a state of great anxiety, sometimes sulky, in mental pain. At that juncture in her analysis, she realized, her expectation to be loved was all directed to her analyst: "dreamy neediness" was her *amae* tuned on him. She was hatefully angry at feeling so needy. The bewildered questions that all people have when a therapy or an analysis has really engaged them gripped her: "What can be happening to me?" "What *is* this?"

The mysterious Japanese psychoanalyst, then, made an appearance in a dream she had on returning home, returning to her analyst. T. Doi was a Japanese beetle, shimmeringly blue-green.

> I dreamt that from my bed I saw a large creature come in through the window. I couldn't imagine how it got in through a crack. Its feathered wings were folded, but I could see it was a peacock. It looked very unfriendly, and I had feared that it would find me. So I got down under the covers, but just as I did it was all over me —walking on my face and head, with just the thin sheet between us. And then it latched onto my head and took hold just like a tick. I was very afraid. Finally, I got it away from me by brushing it frantically off my head. But when I looked onto the bed where it went, it had become a harmless little Japanese beetle.

When she told her analyst this dream, feeling again in its "watery colors," her associations went to the theme of attachment, and she talked about her intense attachment to her daughter—how could any mother endure the loss of her child? Then about being frightened of attachments, frightened of becoming attached to her analyst. She wanted to brush him, as the peacock, out of her head. But she herself was also the peacock, beautiful and dangerously angry. Attacking as it was, though, the peacock could also metamorphose into the harmless Japanese beetle, which reminded her of an Egyptian scarab, symbol of death and rebirth, spiritual regeneration. This redeeming presence was the theorist of *amae*, T. Doi.

Almost a year earlier, Faith had told me about her Bermuda sojourn with *The Basic Fault*. I had a vague recollection, too, of having responded at that time with ruminations on the mother tongue of psychoanalysis, German, and on how oddly scientific Freud's everyday expressions had become in the English of the

Standard Edition. I had also wondered then if a word for "the expectation to be loved," for *amae*, was embedded in Freud's simple adjective *anlehnung*, "leaning on," which Freud's translator James Strachey had rendered with the esoteric "anaclitic." An anaclitic type of love is one that involves, literally, leaning on, touching on, being dependent on, a person. It is the opposite of a narcissistic love choice, in which a person loves himself or herself in another person. Back then, I had had one of my characteristically scholarly responses. Everything in its linguistic and historical context. Speaking from the library in my head.

But when "the expectation to be loved"—Doi's *amae*—came to my ears again in New Haven as Faith presented it to me again, I heard it differently. I heard it in my feelings. My own expectation to be loved reached up inside me like two small beseeching hands about to go around my mother's neck. Faith interpreted the difference correctly: "You see, you have been in your analysis to that same point, your own neediness is painfully exposed, so you recognize it in Doi's word, *amae*. " We wondered at the simple power of the phrase, "the expectation to be loved."

After reflecting a little while in silence, Faith came back to the start of our conversation. "I have such a strong intuition now that there is some kind of deep connection between this *amae*, this expectation to be loved, which sits like a kernel in everyone's self, and how therapy works. That's what I want to write about. *Somehow*, the therapy—the tie between you and your analyst—has to reach deeply into that core expectation, beneath all the defenses you've erected around it, and release its warmth to go like rays throughout you, relax you, grow you, allow you to feel again the expectation of love—from your therapist and, slowly, *somehow*, more generally."

"I know what you're talking about, and I also know that this is not the way—not any of the ways —'therapeutic action' is talked about in the psychoanalytic literature. Many writers speak of some kind of 'corrective emotional experience' happening in therapy, along with interpretations and reconstruction of the patient's past, but you are talking about restoring a capacity for emotional growth, reconnecting with a basic expectation." Even then, we both sensed that Faith's intuition pointed toward something elemental, elementary, but also something hard to express in words—certainly hard to express in psychoanalytic words.

There was a long pause in our talk. Finally, as we were walking over to the Child Study Center and the case conference, Faith said: "Be the scholar and tell me, Elisabeth, is it true that there is no word in the West for wishing or expecting to be loved in this way? I never found it—the experience had to go on through dream language in my analysis. And is Balint right that psychoanalysis does not speak about *amae?*" I couldn't answer. But I had an uncanny feeling that we were standing by a great silence. The silence is a condition, expectant baby loving, which is wordless because it is preverbal. But the silence is also a condition in the listeners to childhood, the psychoanalysts, of being wordless because of a story of repression. Psychoanalysis has not let the expectation to be loved into its theory, although it has certainly let it into its therapy. And in "the West" and contemporary Western languages, more generally, there is also a barrier keeping *amae* out; there is a critical, even condemning, attitude toward dependency. Even the word "dependency" has negative connotations. Sharing as they do the general cultural admiration for activism and autonomy, psychoanalysts would not speak positively of an ability to be dependent or to be an expecter of love.

Amae. Amaeru. How could we translate this noun and this intransitive verb into everyday English, much less into psychoanalysis? Since that conversation in New Haven, Faith and I have pondered the language problem again and again. Sometimes we just use the Japanese words, having asked an East Asian Studies colleague for the correct pronunciations: *ah-mah-eh* and *ah-mah-*

eh-ru. But more often we use an old English noun—unfortunately, one without an intransitive verb—that is, we have come to think, closest in meaning and emotional tone to *amae:* "cherishment." For the verb, we use "getting cherished," or "expecting cherishment."

"Cherishment" derives from the French *cher* ("dear") and the Latin *caru,* which comes from *caritas,* a word that means love, but of a special sort: benevolence, well-wishing, presuming goodwill. *Caritas* has a history in the Christian concept of charity, too, but "cherishment," as we use it, does not imply any moral obligation to give love or be altruistic; cherishment is spontaneous affection. It also does not imply any saintly transcendence or asceticism or selflessness, but is located right in the roil and broil of emotional life, in the growth and development of a self. And, besides, it is not so much about giving love as it is about receiving love and being able, because receiving, to be benevolent, kind, considerate, indulgent. When you come to think that the precondition for giving is receiving, or talk about how a baby wishes to be wished well, expects to be cherished, to get cherishing, it is natural to say "That child has cherishment" or "That is a well-cherished child" or "There is a child who wants cherishing." We now easily think of cherishment as the emotional equivalent of nourishment. Soul food.

When our language questions first arose, we felt very awkward with them, just as we felt reluctant to speak without qualification, as Balint and Doi had, of "the West" and "the East," for these abstractions have such complex cultural and political histories. We also became aware that evaluations of cherishment change as historical conditions change. Many contemporary Japanese do not have the same appreciation for *amae* that Takeo Doi and his generation had, before the recent Westernizing trend in Japanese family life, and many contemporary Americans are exploring cherishing child-rearing ideas and practices without a specific lexicon. So, as we have built up our understanding of "the expectation to be loved," we have stopped relying on existing dictionaries. *Amae* is, all at once, an instinct, a need, an emotion, an attitude, a behavior, a philosophy, and what might be called a cultural mood; there is no translation for it.

Further, we slowly learned that the only way to be able to speak about cherishment was to become receptive to it and to become more consciously cherishing, to cultivate in others and ourselves what we call cherishment consciousness. Now we know that to talk about cherishment one must follow the principle held to be fundamental in both Eastern and Western aesthetics: as Dante expressed it, *Chi pinge figura, si non può esser lei, non la può porre.* ("Who paints a figure, if he cannot be it, cannot draw it.") If you cannot expect love, you cannot give it—or get it!

Walking to the case conference that day in New Haven, Faith and I had no vocabulary or expressions of our own as we do now, but we were in a strangely pre-tuned state, like concertgoers who, still soaked in sound, go out into the city with remembered music playing on through the chatter and bustle of the street, the traffic charging by. When we settled into our chairs at the Child Study Center, we were both listening—we could feel each other listening alike—to an *amae* story. When we heard how the six-year-old patient had brought her analyst a snack, making it plain that she herself needed a snack from him, we heard this as the currency of her frustrated baby wish for indulgent, sweet love. My wish and your wish must be one! She was imploring, sulky and pouting. The little girl's story was a story of thwarted expectation, *amae* unfulfilled and desperately seeking fulfillment.

The Anna Freudians at the conference, old and young, went over the little girl's gesture, its meaning, the analyst's response, the role in her life of her mother's eating disorder, the general question of whether or not it is ever a good idea to eat snacks a child offers—all with loving attention to every detail. But they spoke in a language, the lucid, the illuminating language of Anna Freud, which had no words for *amae* in it. To us, as we reflected on the conference later, it seemed, however, that their whole conversation was an *amae* conversation: each of them was expecting to be loved, appreciated, listened to. Cherished. At the celebration of Anna Freud's birthday, they were playing out their wish to be an Anna Freud family, bundled safely in her devoted spirit, her legacy, and far from the contentiousness and faction that so frequently, so typically, mark meetings of psychoanalytic colleagues. They were all having a conversational snack together, even though psychoanalysis itself does not have a conceptual language to present the need they were satisfying for each other. The talk went lapping and rippling quietly around the room and they—we—were fishes in its water.

"Why don't we go find the Japanese beetle?" I suggested to Faith when our train pulled into 30th Street Station, Philadelphia, at the end of that day. I didn't want to let go of the conversation— I needed it. "T. Doi must be in the library. The Psych Lit database is not exactly a place you would expect to find a sage or a sage's everyday word, *amae*, but maybe there will be a clue." She offered to run a computer search the next morning, for she knew that I, the one with the library in my head, have no skills fit for contemporary library technologies. Thus our "research" phase began.

GOING EAST, AND WEST

Takeo Doi, trained as a psychiatrist during the War in Tokyo, and then just after the War in America, had felt fortified by reading Michael Balint's work, just as Balint had by reading his. While Doi was slowly formulating his ideas about *amae*, he had come across an essay collected in Balint's *Primary Love and Psy-*

choanalytic Technique. "As I was reading it," Doi remembered, "I gradually realized with surprise and pleasure that what the author referred to with the forbidding name of 'passive object love' was in fact none other than *amae* . . . His remark, too, that 'all the European languages fail to distinguish between active love and passive love' seemed to me to underline still more strongly my conviction that the existence of an everyday word for passive love—*amae*—was an indicator of the nature of Japanese society and culture."

An epistolary conversation began between the two men in 1962, and then they met—just once—in London. "I had the good fortune," Doi wrote in his restrained, polite, deferential English, "to discuss the matter with him personally when I went to London in 1964. I was furthermore delighted that he honored me later by citing my work in his last book, *The Basic Fault.*"

Balint died suddenly of a heart attack on December 31, 1970, just at the time when Doi, after some twenty years of reflection, felt ready to publish his *Amae no kozo*, translated soon afterward into English as *The Anatomy of Dependence.* This book was instantly a best-seller, going through twenty-five printings in its birth-year, and launched a whole intellectual movement in Japan. For two decades, "*Amae* psychology" was virtually synonymous there with Japanese national consciousness.

Among anthropologists, we discovered, there is now a voluminous literature on *amae.* Japanese child-rearing has been studied extensively, with European and American anthropologists marveling—sometimes marveling enviously—over how Japanese mothers have indulged their babies, particularly their sons. Debates have arisen: Doesn't indulgence produce spoiled children, children who cannot separate from their parents, boys who have overbearing senses of privilege and prerogative with respect to women? *Amae* has also become the measure, in this literature, of how Japanese society has been changing since the end of the

War, and of how Western child-rearing assumptions have been adopted in many Japanese households, particularly in the last decade.

Anthropology has had an extended period of reflection on *amae*. But the conversation that Takeo Doi and Michael Balint started was never so fruitful for psychoanalysis. "Amae psychology" did not become part of psychoanalysis in the West. Occasionally, a European or American psychoanalyst would come forward to say, as the British analyst J. O. Wisdom did in 1987, that *amae* has "not been sufficiently acknowledged in the West." But this claim has never really been argued except by Takeo Doi himself, who was invited for the first time in the same year, 1987, to address an International Psychoanalytical Congress.

At the Congress—the 35th such Congress, held then in Montreal—Doi made a number of specific suggestions about how the psychology of *amae* could permit reformulations of some of the most vexed and difficult psychoanalytic notions, particularly narcissism and identification. He turned his attention to therapy by presenting *amae* as "the kernel of transference," by which he meant that when a patient replays in analysis and with the analyst childhood love feelings, those love feelings are not just the erotic feelings Freud had emphasized, but the even earlier expectation to be loved. Given her intuition about *amae* and therapeutic action, Faith was not surprised to find Doi suggesting that "*amae* constitutes the underlying unconscious motive in seeking psychoanalytic treatment," no matter what specific illness or dilemma or crisis the patient may present. And then, in the treatment, *amae* is always there as the person seeks cherishment and, eventually, seeks to be cherishing.

Pulling the threads of his brief lecture together, Doi concluded with a grand hope modestly phrased: "Somebody might raise an objection that I have overemphasized the universality of the concept of *amae*, that I have tried to explain too much by it.

Certainly I have related the concept of *amae* to many psychoanalytic concepts that are usually dealt with separately. But it is not that I have simply equated them all. My point is that if the concept of *amae* can be related in a meaningful way to other psychoanalytic concepts not usually related to one another, that fact could only suggest that it can unify them into more satisfactory theory. I shall be happy indeed if this paper contributed toward this end."

Only two instances of Doi's wish being fulfilled have come about. In May 1997, there was a conference of American and Japanese clinicians and anthropologists speaking on "Amae Reconsidered" at the annual meeting of the American Psychoanalytic Association. Earlier there had been a symposium of researchers, published by the journal *Infant Mental Health* in 1992. This symposium connected Doi's work to the emergent trend within psychoanalytic studies of infancy that has been stimulated by Daniel Stern's book *The Interpersonal World of the Infant*, a trend called interpersonalism. Both the Japanese and the American contributors stress the interpersonal nature of *amae*—that is, they view it as a love *between* baby and mother, interactional. How a baby relates to and mentally represents its mother cannot be understood apart from how a mother relates to and mentally represents her baby, her expectation of the baby's love. *Amaeru*-ing is a mutual pleasure.

This kind of adapting of Doi's work to an emergent trend is very important, and instructive about how psychoanalysis itself has been changing in recent years. Stern has pioneered, for example, in doing treatment with mothers and babies together—couples work. In theory, more and more attention is being paid by analysts to mother-child relations in the first years of life, and to the ways in which both patients and analysts may be re-creating together their individual stories of mother-child interaction. This is territory that Freud did not survey. But, making Takeo

Doi into a contemporary interpersonalist or intersubjectivist theorist does not really address his aspiration to be a revisionist of *Freudian* theory; nor does it hear his hope that a more satisfactory psychoanalytic theory might grow from a cross-cultural conversation of the sort he and Michael Balint had initiated.

As we read our way through the anthropological and psychological writings generated by *amae*, Faith and I found ourselves imagining that unfinished, hardly begun conversation. We found ourselves having it, playing with it. "You be Takeo, and I will be Michael," I joked with her one evening while we were talking about Balint's background in the Budapest School, where infant research was undertaken in the 1920s that has lost none of its relevance for today.

Playing Michael, I prepared to weave notes on the experiments with psychoanalytic technique initiated by Michael's colleagues, especially Sandor Ferenczi, into my spring 1996 undergraduate lectures. I wanted to track the Hungarian concern with "primary passive love" up into the work of émigré Budapest School analysts in America—like Franz Alexander, who originated the phrase "corrective emotional experience," and in Great Britain, where the pediatrician-analyst D.W. Winnicott so creatively adapted "primary love" into his work with mothers and babies. Faith filled up her journal with *amae* images from her therapeutic work, from everyday life and from the history of art, her original field of training. As Takeo, she wanted us to be able to see *amae* everywhere, breathe it in. She wanted to find this Japan in "the West," and find ways to present it in English.

While we were getting to know each other better in these conversations, Faith admitted to me—shyly, as though expecting my disapproval—that she was accustomed to think in visual images of situations because she had been taught to do so by the *I Ching: The Book of Changes*. When she was in her late teens, she had begun to educate herself with this ancient Chinese book of trigrams (three-line figures), hexagrams (six-line figures) and commentaries. It, we came to think, is an *amae* book, a book built up over centuries on a base of preverbal gestures—moving around the lines that make up the book's original trigrams to divine the meaning of situations, which were later interpreted or glossed in the Chinese language.

Faith had been reluctant to tell me how thoroughly she has been involved since her adolescence with the *I Ching* because she had often been teased and taunted. "People who have no idea what the book is take you for a fortune-teller or some kind of cult member or a flake. I was afraid you would be judgmental." I certainly did not feel critical of Faith's education—it awed me. But I did feel very ignorant of her teacher, this book. So Faith showed me how to read the sixty-four six-line figures, or hexagrams, of the *I Ching*, which represent all the situations that may ever come up in life. A reader can seek their counsel in judging the "right conduct" for any situation, and also inquire of the hexagrams what the deeper meaning or the heart—the *Tao*, the Way—of any situation is. It's a book you interact with; you ask things of it, coax it, and interpret its care-taking replies. But Faith seldom actually consults the book, because she knows it by heart. I was stunned to discover that by the time she was nineteen she was able to recite, like a Homeric bard, the two hundred and fifty pages of the text and was quite at home in the four hundred pages of materials explicating the text. She has a whole world in her head. When she feels safe, her talk is woven through with images and phrases from the *I Ching*.

Learning from Faith, reading the *I Ching* commentaries, so beautifully translated into English from the German of Richard Wilhelm, and studying Carl Jung's appreciation of Wilhelm, I was drawn as she had been by the idea that all of life, all people, all situations, *are* the interplay and complementarity of the two principles that underlie the whole hexagram system. These two principles are The Creative, Heaven (six undivided Yang lines) and The Receptive, Earth (six divided Yin lines), which look like this:

Everything is driving, powerful, expansive, untiringly strong Creativity, which needs taming, at play with holding, sustaining, inclusive, perseveringly open Receptivity, which needs to be devoted. I was moved to hear from Faith how this philosophy had been generated around the original hexagrams in the twelfth century B.C.E. by the legendary sage King Wen and his son the Duke of Chou, when they were imprisoned by the last Shang emperor, isolated and always under the threat of execution. This was their book of insights into the misery of their times, the horrors of a tyranny, and it was the book of their expectation that change would come. They believed that redemption was in the nature of things and could be expedited by a superior person, a wise prince, one who cultivates kindness. Kindness—the human-heartedness, or *jen,* so much discussed in all of the later Confucian commentaries on King Wen's book—is the primary virtue in the *I Ching.*

Slowly, as we talked about The Creative and The Receptive in the Chinese philosophy of change, we asked ourselves: Is this Receptivity, in its play with Creativity, is this cherishment? Is this *amae?* Is this primary love and care-taking devotion?

While we pondered this question, with its suggestion that

there may be words or pictures for *amae* that are not translations in the dictionary sense, but other ways of saying *amae*, I also came to understand more about why the cherishment conversation we had started meant so much to Faith. She identifies herself with King Wen, and "cherishment" gave a name to her expectation that King Wen's "Joyous Lake" of conversation could be the antidote to life in the court of any form of tyrants.

> A lake evaporates upward and thus gradually dries up; but when two lakes are joined, they do not dry up so readily, for one replenishes the other. It is the same in the field of knowledge. Knowledge should be a refreshing and vitalizing force. It becomes so only through stimulating intercourse with congenial friends with whom one holds discussion and practices application of the truths of life. In this way, learning becomes many-sided and takes on a cheerful lightness, whereas there is always something ponderous and one-sided about the learning of the self-taught. (58)

While she was teaching me about the *I Ching*, Faith asked me about the books that had been my friends when I was young, the books toward which I had turned for nourishment. I told her that in college I had had teachers who convinced me that any educated person should know ancient Greek. Immediately, I had felt at home in the *Introduction to Greek* textbook because the first sentence by a classical author that I was asked to translate had captured my whole desire: *To sopho xenon ouden*, wrote Antisthenes, "Nothing is foreign to a wise person." The next one was by Aristotle: *Koina ta ton philon*, "The goods of friends are held in common." To this day, I enjoy advising myself in Greek—my conscience speaks it. And I easily become didactic in it. "Look," I told Faith in a little tutorial we held on the similarities of sensibility so evident in her Chinese mentors and my Greek ones, "look, how the same word, *philophrosune*, means kindliness and friendliness. The word literally means loving-mindedness, an emotional state. It's cherishment, isn't it?"

The whole of ancient Greek literature had become my pasture when I was a graduate student in philosophy. But I also began to travel intellectually around the ancient Mediterranean, and spent months of wisdom-quest on a super-serious essay linking the philosopher Heraclitus to the world in India of the Vedantic Upanishads—my first excursion into texts of the *I Ching* commentary's vintage. The books to which I always returned, however, were the epic poems *The Iliad* and *The Odyssey*. "These," I told Faith, "are poems in which there is everything—nothing was foreign to Homer. They have in common with the *I Ching* both the idea that throughout the cosmos everything changes, cycling, rising and falling, and the idea that all the situations of human life can be represented as variations on fundamental forces. War and Peace. Strife and Love."

It wasn't until six months later that Faith had time to read the Homeric epics through systematically in Robert Fitzgerald's wonderful translations, propelled both by my descriptions and by her memories of an earlier trip to Greece—and especially to Delphi—during which she had felt strongly that there was something in Greek culture that she needed, something that belonged to her because of her mother's Greek lineage. But when she first acquired the Homeric texts in the winter after our conversation began, she behaved in the manner familiar to her and let *The Iliad* fall open, as though consulting it on chance, like the *I Ching*. She found before her eyes one of the most beautiful cherishment images in any literature.

Hearing her magnificent and doomed son Akhilleus as he cries in pain at the death of his friend Patroklos, the water nymph Thetis rushes from her deep sea cave to comfort him, taking his head between her hands. A *pietà*. Before Akhilleus goes into the battle where he will kill Hektor and then be killed himself,

Thetis indulges him with brightly shining armor and an immortal shield made by the smithy god Hephaistos, to whom she tells her story, lamenting:

> *Our son, bestowed on me and nursed by me,*
> *became a hero unsurpassed. He grew like a green shoot;*
> *I cherished him like a flowering orchard tree,*
> *only to send him in the ships to Ilion*
> *to war with Trojans.*

(18:436FF)

There was our word, "I cherished him." The idea began to grow in us that *amae* might be in the early languages of the West, the languages at the root of Western civilization. Many 19th- and early 20th-century European philosophers and philologists— Richard Wilhelm among them—who had sponsored a renaissance of Greek traditions in modern European thought, had worked with the idea that Greek culture was the childhood of the West, as modernity is the adulthood of the West, recapitulated in each adult reaching maturity. Such an evolutionary philosophy is quite specific to that modernist historical moment, but maybe it points to something individuals and cultures do have in common: elemental *amae* feelings can, in both individuals and cultures, including languages, get covered up, transformed, obscured, over time. *Amae* can also get contorted inside individual and cultural forms that are contradictory; forms suggesting, for example, as the very patriarchal *I Ching* does, that Yang is in "superior men" and Yin is in inferior women, while at the same time saying, on a deeper level, that both Yang and Yin are universal, in both men and in women, and "spontaneous affection" is common to all people. *Amae* needs archeologists—feminist archeologists.

Out of our play with our favorite books came our first feeling that these familiar texts—both achieving their written form during the 800 to 500 B.C.E. period of cultural flowering that the German philosopher Karl Jaspers has named "the Axial Age"— were going to teach us not only about cherishment but about how to speak what we were learning. They were going to be our Japanese.

THE BOOK AS A BABY

Through the winter and spring after our New Haven initiation, Faith and I kept up this Takeo and Michael, East and West, hexagrams and epics conversational play, renewing it with each episode in our psychotherapeutic work that seemed to be "an *amae* moment." Clinically, we were listening for how the desire to be cherished appears in the transference. But everywhere our *amae* ears were like fishing nets pulled along behind us as we went from our homes to our clinics, to classes taken and classes taught, gatherings of friends, workshops, movies, museums, business trips.

We started a common notebook—"the goods of friends are held in common." In it we put reflections, but also stories. A friend told us about her eighteen-month-old daughter, a child who was right in the midst of that exciting transition from one-word exclamations to two- and three-word sentences. One evening when the child was suffering from a bad case of diaper rash, her mother left her diaperless, distracting her and calming her by cooing "Honey, honey," words the mother reserved for moments of great intimacy. The child was impressed, obviously, because later, when she had to have a diaper put on again, she cuddled up to her mother saying "Honey, honey." And the next day, when she had to leave her mother to be delivered to her day

care by her father, she waved, smiling, and said "Bye-bye, honey."
A perfect cameo of how cherishing, received, becomes cherishing given.

Slowly, as our notebook grew, we came to the idea that we would use it to write . . . *something*. Considering cherishment, we were often in the position Freud described so well in one of his last fragments (23:275): "I find myself for a moment in the interesting position of not knowing whether what I have to say should be regarded as something long familiar and obvious or as something entirely new and puzzling." We wanted to convey both our wonderment and our sense of familiarity. Also, we wanted to picture cherishment—to show it, draw it with all kinds of stories—but at the same time to explore its implications for psychoanalytic theory and therapy. A task of representation and a task of exposition.

Finally, we decided to assemble at my office our notebook and all the books and papers we had been reading, and make a work schedule to launch the writing, which we imagined as our conversation continued by other means. We had agreed just to see what would happen, to set out, and to give it up if it seemed that we were either reinventing psychoanalytic wheels or losing what seemed precious to us in the conversation by writing it. Our first working session, our first scheduled conversation, was set for a Wednesday afternoon. I arrived in a strange state.

Between my first analytic patient and my own analysis that morning, I had an hour to use for looking up in the Standard Edition of Freud's work all the instances of the word "anaclitic." I felt compelled, even as I was trying to get away from psychoanalytic language, to test my old idea that "anaclitic object choice" reflected an *amae* level of feeling. Following the Index around, I came upon the associated phrase "affectionate current of love," which Freud had contrasted to "sensual current of love." Particularly striking was a passage about the two currents in a 1912 essay "On the Universal Tendency to Debasement in the Sphere of Love" (11:180):

> The affectionate current is the older of the two. It springs from the earliest years of childhood; it is formed on the basis of the interests of the self-preservative instinct and is directed to the members of the family and those who look after the child. From the very beginning it carries along with it contributions from the sexual instincts—components of erotic interest—which can already be seen more or less clearly even in childhood and in any event are uncovered in neurotics by psychoanalysis later on. It corresponds to the child's primary object choice. We learn in this way that the sexual instincts find their first objects by attaching themselves to the valuations made by the ego-instincts, precisely in the way in which the first sexual satisfactions are experienced in attachment to bodily functions necessary for the preservation of life.

Freud called "the affectionate current" an ego instinct, not a sexual instinct, and described it as the original guide for all love relations—or "object relations," as analysts say when they are stressing how the lover mentally represents or makes a mental object of the beloved. Yes, I said to myself, this "affectionate current" is "the expectation to be loved" and it is the ego's drive. It is a self-preservative drive in the sense that it pushes the ego to develop: the child attaches herself to the caretaker who will preserve her, perpetuate her newborn pleasures and make her ego strong, so it becomes possible for her eventually to care for herself and for others. Cherish me! means Make me pleasurably safe, make me strong! Tend this green shoot! The expectation is not sexual, but it comes to involve the sexual instincts and to lay the conditions for their later development and for sexual object relations.

I had this simple thought, and then, in rapid succession, one thought after another came rushing through my mind. Telegraphic. Bursting like firecrackers. I could hardly grasp them, they made little or no sense to me. Dizzied, dazed, I wrote down a cluster of phrases and went off to see my analyst.

On the preceding Sunday night, I had had a dream that I had intended to relate on Monday morning, but had not. And not on Tuesday either. Instead, I had rattled on during those two sessions about how the anxiety and suspense surrounding my decision to commit myself to this piece of writing with Faith had finally abated, so that I could go ahead. I was full of reflections on an exhibition I had visited a week before at the Museum of Modern Art, "Picasso and Portraiture," and on what kinds of forces move an artist along from one preoccupation, one painting, to the next. I sounded like a biographer—of someone else.

Wednesday I came back to the dream. It had a reference to Picasso in its single image:

> **There was a kind of a keyboard with all white keys, but not rectangular, more square, like white kitchen tiles, like white teeth. Milk teeth. A hand reached out and slowly stroked along these keys, making them soft and pliant, a lovely feeling. As I woke up, I understood that these keys were my genitals, and I said to myself, with some embarrassment, "Well, I will have to tell this dream to J [my analyst]."**

At the Picasso show, a curator's careful note had explained quite psychoanalytically that the portraits of Nusch Eluard and Dora Maar in which these women had huge, frightening teeth, jaws like vises, repeated a *vagina dentata* image that Picasso had also used in other periods of fear and debasement of his women. The rigid jaw was described as a "rictus," a word I had never seen before. When I related my dream fragment to my analyst, I called the white keyboard a "rictus." And I said that in the dream I had been turned into the woman who preceded these two in Picasso's life: Marie-Thérèse Walter, who was softy beautiful, round; who had a baby girl named Maya. Picasso's *amae* woman. I was this woman, and I was also Picasso.

When I arrived at my office in the middle of the day, I was exhausted, but I took out the little piece of paper on which the morning thoughts were written and explained them all to Faith. Suddenly, I knew what each of the cryptic phrases meant and methodically went through them as though they were lecture notes. Afterwards, Faith asked me "What happened to you?" To my surprise, I told her that I had had a dream in which I was both The Receptive and The Creative. I used this *I Ching* language, not the one that I had used with my analyst: I was both the Yin woman and the Yang man.

Then I went on to tell Faith that bursts of thoughts come to me now and again, under very specific conditions, so that, if I am able to catch them, whole sections of manuscript are forecast. Out of a questioning, anxious state, feeling unloved, even rejected, struggling tensely to stay on an even keel, to avoid depression, a resolution comes to me. I relax, as I did in the dream. And in the relaxation, I am flooded with ideas. They are my relief. I can sustain such a creative surge in my thoughts, such a growth spurt, and the disorganization it produces, only if I feel safe, receptively ready. This was, we agreed, my version of turning into a harmless little Japanese *amae* beetle: a condition of expecting cherishment. "But you write books out of it!" Faith laughed.

So, by that summer day in 1996 we had Faith's dreamy encounter with Takeo Doi, my morning of automatic writing, and six months of conversation to make into a little book. At the very beginning of the writing, we produced passages of exposition and passages of memoir, pieces of case studies, anthropological reflections, meditations on the *I Ching* and the Homeric epics, excursions into the history of psychoanalysis, conversations real and imaginary that others have had. It was "mixed grilled vegetables" as my friend from graduate school Jerome Kohn commented when he read some of our pieces and urged us to consult his favorite essay by the philosopher Michael Oakeshott, "The Voice of Poetry in the Conversation of Mankind."

But then something very interesting began to happen while we continued to make the transition from talking to writing-and-talking. First, I became the narrator, our initial effort to write together and to speak as "we" having felt to both of us too merged, not reflective enough of our very different personalities and ways of thinking and talking. We had to assert our distinctness in order to be able to listen to each other more freely. This done, we noticed that the conversation changed. We had a third, we were a triangle. The writing—both what actually came to be on paper and the idea or image of the book—became like a child that we were parenting. A green shoot. We returned to this baby metaphor again and again, and linked it to how our friendship had begun several years before as a collaboration over teaching a whole classroom full of college-age green shoots.

The book made demands. It was a very greedy, eager baby, wanting our time and attention and thought, preoccupying us, getting into everything. And it pulled us, with its clamoring, into a second order of conversation: to the conversation about it and its form and content, we added one about us and our creativities, our book-parenting styles, which had turned out to be so very different and not always easy to harmonize. From our different creativities, we were always searching for common ground, complementarity. We became self-conscious, self-reflective, in relation to each other and to the baby.

The book similarly gave us a common world, an in-between-us, to link our concerns and our reflectivities. We discovered that our most basic task was to arrange ourselves in relation to this work so that we could do what we are writing about: cherishing.

We—Faith in her way, and I in my way—cherished the book as it grew; this sharing then became our understanding of what our ways of cherishing have in common, and so of what cherishing is generally. The cherisher says to the cherishee: "I care for your growth; I am good to you that you may grow; and it is good and pleasurable for me that you grow as is *your* want—so I will help you know your want."

When friends cultivate a common ground together, they are like coworkers with a common work, teachers and students with a common discipline, patients and therapists with a common conviction. The talking people develop together has in it, as Michael Oakeshott so beautifully shows in the essay Jerome Kohn gave us, all kinds of discourses—practical, moral, scientific, poetic—and these commingle in the conversation:

> In a conversation, thoughts of different species take wing and play around one another, responding to each other's movements and provoking one another to fresh exertions. Nobody asks where they have come from or on what authority they are present . . . There is no symposiarch or arbiter; not even a doorkeeper to examine credentials. Every entrant is taken at its face-value and everything is permitted which can get itself accepted into the flow of speculation. And voices which speak in conversation do not compose a hierarchy . . . As civilized human beings, we are the inheritors, neither of an inquiry about ourselves and the world, nor of an accumulating body of information, but of a conversation, begun in the primeval forests and made more articulate in the course of centuries. It is a conversation which goes on both in public and within each of ourselves.

As our conversations got longer, broader, more crowded with entrants, we found ourselves on a third level: we had been talking about cherishment, then we had talked about how we were each talking about cherishment, and finally we found ourselves talking about how the conversation was changing us by cherishing us. As we grew, it grew; as it grew, we grew. A series of dreams that Faith had had at the beginning of the writing suddenly made sense to her.

She had begun reading Homer's *Iliad* out loud, chapter by chapter, and talking about it with the people in a discussion group she attends, where she had also recently heard a presentation on Michelangelo. She told her colleagues that she was thinking about the transition from oral to written poetry, and that she was, generally, thinking about herself as someone who was exercising her voice, making a transition from talking to writing, which was a "coming unhidden, coming to light." As she said this, she felt a desire to go to the Metropolitan Museum in New York to look at one of her favorite paintings, Rembrandt's "Aristotle Contemplating the Bust of Homer." Promptly, funnily, she got there in a dream that night:

> **In the Museum to see "Aristotle Contemplating the Bust of Homer." There were partitions up, couldn't see it. But then looked around the partitions, and the painting was in animation. Aristotle was dressing in his robes, colorful, deep colors, purples, blues. Then people pushed forward to see the painting; there were some French women viewing with me.**

As Faith associated to this dream, it flowed into one from the night before in which a lamp had turned into a sculpted male, a Greek figure, who began to move. He came to life, was animated—literally, en-souled, given an *anima*. The French women watching Rembrandt's painting were Simone Weil and Rachel Bespaloff, two French writers whose essays on *The Iliad* Faith had recently received from me, read and loved; in their essays, they were animators of *The Iliad* for modern readers. Both of Faith's dreams were variations on the motif of Pygmalion.

And then, with her usual artistry enhanced by more art-historical free associating, Faith's unconscious produced another dream, a single magnificent revisionist image:

Woke up having dreamt the image of Michelangelo's Sistine Ceiling hands. Just God's and Adam's hands. But the hand was female. Mine.

She was aware when she awoke of being embarrassed that her hand had been audaciously in this painting—so she could not even remember whether her hand was God's or Adam's. But then, when she reflected on the ambiguity, she realized that she had been both The Creative and The Receptive in her image. She could see in this dream and the whole series how she was becoming animated as she let herself talk about herself with me and let herself contemplate and be receptive to Homer, who symbolized for her a person completely attuned to his world, receptive to it in every detail, infinite detail.

Those dreams of Faith's expressed her wish to be able to take in everything that came her way in her life—no partitions keeping her from seeing. She was doing what we have since observed our patients doing when they begin to grow in therapy, when their need for cherishment can be expressed. "Developmental dreaming," we call it. Dreams begin to supply images of the dreamer coming to life, animating, images of the sort that also make up what Freud called "the ego ideal," the wished-for self. In our conversations, dreams became the means, along with analytic work, of considering and relating the changes in ourselves. We were being created, while creating.

I, not as prolific or as witty a dreamer, registered our conversation chiefly in one dream, which used only the baby metaphor to which I had grown accustomed:

> **In an airplane that was sitting at the airport, awaiting takeoff, a young woman got up from her seat and came toward the crew. She cried out to them for help, and they realized that she was about to give birth to a baby. They very efficiently made the front seats into a couch, and one of them delivered the baby. When this woman—the midwife—put the baby on her bosom and patted it, I recognized her as Katerina Anghelaki-Rooke. Then I somehow knew the young woman was me the summer I first visited Katerina on Aegina, almost fifteen years ago.**

My unconscious had me on a couch—very analytic—being delivered of a baby by a Greek poetess, my old friend, on my way to Greece. Remembering that summer, I had an image of myself sitting on a rickety canvas chair in an olive grove, cicadas noisily everywhere, reading Sigmund Freud's *The Interpretation of Dreams* and anticipating the start of my first go at psychoanalytic training that fall, 1983, in New Haven, the site of the beginning of my conversation with Faith. I associated to the training analyst I saw then, Hans Loewald, who, in addition to being my analyst was one of the psychoanalytic writers whose reflections on the mother-infant duo meant most to me. So I knew that our conversation baby was my psychoanalysis continued, continuing. *Amae* as the kernel of the transference.

The collection of metaphors and images we were making worked on us. That is how a psychoanalysis works, too: a collection of metaphors is made by the patient and the analyst together; experiences past and present are registered in them; and then, like water, they wear away your stone. That was the poet Lao-tse's favorite metaphor, rendered in Stephen Mitchell's

beautiful translation of the *Tao Tê Ching*, a collection of poems
contemporary with the *I Ching* commentaries:

> *The gentlest thing in the world*
> *overcomes the hardest thing in the world.*
> *That which has no substance*
> *enters where there is no space.*
> *This shows the value of non-action.*
>
> *Teaching without words,*
> *performing without actions:*
> *that is the Master's way.*

(43)

The ancient Taoist texts themselves are known to permeate
the consciousnesses of their contemplators and awaken them into
pliant receptivity. "Receptivity," we thought, is really a much
more suggestive way than "expectation" to interpret the *amae*
concept. Not just "expectation to be loved," but receptivity to
love or cherishment. And lack of receptivity, we came to think, is
the condition that stops growth cold, that petrifies the open-
handed baby inside people and in their projects.

Thinking along these lines about how our conversation was
changing us, we decided to make a review of our patients, noting
the kinds of stoniness or growth stoppage we had encountered
working with them. We wondered whether we could sketch a
psychopathology, a catalogue of mental illnesses as states of unreceptivity. Getting expansively theoretical, we synthesized
Freudian descriptions of the neuroses with Takeo Doi's "amae
psychology" descriptions of the neuroses—West meets East in
the domain of psychopathology.

Out of our initial conversations and the growth spurt of setting out to write, the baby book's theory took shape. During the first year of writing, which we gradually made into chapters two, three and four of this book, we explored the interplay of ego instincts and sexual instincts as the basic human instincts. We argued that this early theory of Freud's is a more satisfactory basis for psychoanalytic theory than the instinct theory to which Freud turned in his later years, which features a dualism of the life instincts and the death instinct. The ego instincts and the sexual instincts seem to us to be The Receptive and The Creative in conscious and unconscious psychic life, so that we were, in effect, describing the early Freudian psychoanalysis that is, we think, a very Chinese philosophy. As a place where East meets West in a general psychology of normal development, the psychoanalysis we have written about has this *I Ching* beginning:

> Affection as the essential principle of relatedness is of the greatest importance in all relationships in the world. For the union of heaven and earth is the origin of the whole of nature. Among human beings likewise, spontaneous affection is the all-inclusive principle of union.

From this beginning, we think many features of the psychoanalytic landscape look different. We described the ego ideal as the main product of the ego instincts, and compared this to the superego as the psychic structure stemming from the sexual instincts in their development. The ego instincts seem to us to follow what we will call the Growth Principle, while the sexual instincts fit themselves—more or less—to what Freud called the Reality Principle, which tames the sexual instincts, teaching them limits and realism. The Growth Principle does not teach limits to the ego instincts, it shows them pathways, teaching self-preservation through relatedness, reciprocity. As we envision it and, as Freud insisted, psychoanalysis explores being with others for sex and pleasure, but also being with others for cherishment and growth.

GROWING UP IS HARD TO DO

In retrospect we realized that this year of intense work, on the book and with our patients, in which we loosened up and became so much more pliant and receptive in ourselves, had brought us, eventually, to theoretical clarity but also to a great deal of turbulence and confusion and questioning. We had gotten ahead of ourselves. We could see where we were going, we had a vision, but we did not know how to integrate it into our lives, how to take it into our worlds, how to work with it outside of the relationships we had with our patients and outside of our own conversation. We were like patients who have gotten to the point in a therapy where their problems are clear and they share with the therapist a working image of a future. They can see that it is no longer necessary for them to be ill in the old way, but the old way is still the only way. A time of "working through" has to come.

Becoming more receptive, we had become more troubled— and more permeable to the troubles of people around us. We had not developed the means to assimilate in ourselves or in the conversation the flood of experiences and ideas that had come over us. And our conversation, then, took on yet another form. It became explicitly therapeutic. We had to help each other. And we specifically had to help each other with making our ideas worldly, with taking them—and the book—out into the world. With working through.

When we could get our bearings on what had happened to us, we concluded that after a receptivity spurt, as after a physical growth spurt, comes a constriction, a period of getting used to your new shape. All that you have taken in mingles with all that holds you back—all your history of cherishment neediness—and getting a new balance takes time and lots of effort. We were like adolescents who had suddenly discovered in the mirror that we were transformed. Big receptivity had meant big change. And our book, too, was in its adolescence, no longer a baby but an awkward half-child-half-adult thing with no clear identity. We knew, too, that by putting so much of our attention to receptivity, to Balint's "primary passive love" and Doi's *amae*, we had tipped our thought away from The Creative. Trying to speak to a silence in psychoanalytic theory about "the affectionate current," we had neglected "the sensual current" and the interplay of these two currents.

The adolescence of our book threatened to be like contemporary adolescence: very prolonged. But once we got some perspective on it, realizing that our book was like a teenager, clamoring and sulky, demanding parental patience, competing for our attention, we gave it guidance. "The book is about cherishment," Faith reflected one evening over the telephone, "but the book is also about our creative processes, individually and together. We have to make that more explicit, and we have to let the chapters follow our creative course over time, while they are following the topical outline, the developmental outline that presents cherishment's growth over the life course, from infancy to adulthood. We have to present our ideas, but also make it clear when and how we came to them. They are not doctrine, they are our reciprocity and the reciprocity we want to establish with our readers. Everybody in discovery mode." So, the fifth and sixth chapters of the book were focused on adolescence and on adulthood, and both contain our reflections on how cherishment develops over time into adult relationships, how it goes out into the world in its mature forms. Adolescence repeats the cherishment story of infancy, not in the closeness of the child-and-caretaker duo, but rather out in the world, in the search for adult relationships.

We converged on and through this big organizing thought of Faith's. And as we analyzed it, we realized that it had grown up from a desire she had not been conscious of: she wanted the book to be like an *I Ching* hexagram, in six chapter parts. Unconsciously, she had wanted her book to be like her teacher-book and reflective of what her teacher-book had given her, what she could give in a teaching-book. In an adult way, she had done a version of what the little girl did who received her mother's "Honey, honey" and then, having identified with the cherishing, reciprocated with her smiling "Bye-bye, honey."

After I thought for a while about this dynamic in Faith's creative life—her way of hearing a cherishing language and then speaking it, symbolizing in it—I told her that I thought we should take her symbolizing impulse right to its logical conclusion: we should interpret the six-chapter hexagram we had planned, consult it, ask it what it had to say for itself, and for us. I wanted to treat our book the way Carl Jung had treated the *I Ching* when he was writing an introduction to Wilhelm's translation of it. He considered the book "a method for exploring the unconscious," and I wanted to consider *Cherishment* both as an offspring, a green shoot, of King Wen's book and also as "a method for exploring the unconscious." So I suggested that we survey our six chapters, interpreting them as either Yang or Yin lines—that is, as lines of The Creative and The Receptive, heaven and earth, male and female, to see exactly which hexagram we were making and where our next development would lead.

This chapter, the first, the bottom line, we felt as a strong undivided line, a Yang line, arching under the whole territory of our conversation and creativity, representing a principle of movement and development. A birth, a creative thrust. The second chapter is the whole territory, too, but in the medium of theory building and focused on infancy. The middle two chapters about our therapy work are divided, yielding, listening, receptive. They are Yin lines, representing the principle of rest; representing *amae* moments rising up like peaceful pauses inside wild storms; representing earth. "The earth in its devotion carries all things, good and evil without exception." Chapter 5 about adolescence is a developmental Yang line, again a creative thrust, and we agreed that Chapter 6, on adulthood, the top line, the one we had planned but not yet drafted when we made our survey, should also be a Yang line. Thus we arrived at the sixty-first *I Ching* hexagram Inner Truth. This is made up of two trigrams, the top one being The Gentle, the eldest daughter—as I am—in the family of the primary trigrams, and the bottom one being The Joyous, the youngest daughter, which Faith considers her sign, as she is a youngest daughter. Inner Truth is a hexagram of two females, sisters, who meet around a receptive center—an image of creativity organized around a core of receptivity.

And the Inner Truth section of the *I Ching* also contains an image of mother-child cherishment, about which the commentary says "This is the affection of the innermost heart—to which it immediately juxtaposes an image of adult friendship or comradeship, implying that the two cherishment forms are invisibly connected:

> *A crane calling in the shade.*
> *Its young answers it.*
> *I have a good goblet.*
> *I will share it with you.*

This refers to the involuntary influence of a man's inner being upon persons of kindred spirit. The crane need not show itself on a high hill. It may be quite hidden when it sounds its call; yet its young will hear its note, will recognize it and give answer. Where there is a joyous mood, there a comrade will appear to share a glass of wine.

With Inner Truth as our guide, we set out on a working August vacation to Greece, to Homer's place, where we intended to draft the last chapter and to begin revising and refining the five underneath. This was to be a journey into the wider world, an odyssey. Our curiosity about how the last line would evolve, and how we would evolve with it, how our adulthood line would unfold, put us back into the frame of mind that we had been in the year before when we had originally recognized an ideal for ourselves and our work in Lao-tse's *Tao Tê Ching*, such a close cousin to the *I Ching* philosophically. Faith copied the poem about water wearing away stone into our notebook, and then another, quoted below. These poems went with us to Greece, to remind us there of the journey we had made already, through all the seasons since we first collected that Japanese beetle in New Haven, T. Doi.

> *Know the male,*
> *yet keep to the female;*
> *receive the world in your arms.*
> *If you receive the world,*
> *the Tao will never leave you*
> *and you will be like a little child.*
> *Know the white,*
> *yet keep to the black:*
> *be a pattern for the world.*
> *If you are a pattern for the world,*
> *the Tao will be strong inside you*
> *and there will be nothing you can't do.*

(28)

Chapter 2

Amae in Infancy and After

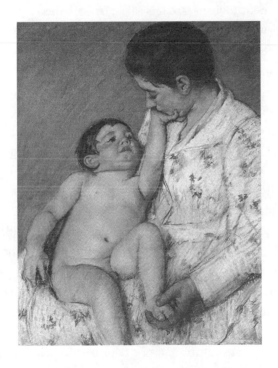

You road that I enter upon and look around,
    I believe you are not all that is here,
I believe that much unseen is also here.

—WALT WHITMAN, "SONG OF THE OPEN ROAD"

*T*he winter in which Faith and I began our conversation was wild. Week after week, the weather was a box of surprises. But when the January "Blizzard of '96" struck, Philadelphians were truly stunned. Getting six feet of snow off the city's roads and buildings was a huge communal drama, in which the people on my street had to play their little Victorian character parts.

Built in the early 1890s like much of Germantown, the original Quaker section of Philadelphia, my street is brick-paved and very narrow. The city's gigantic snowplows cannot get onto it. So the neighbors had to form a shovel brigade and get the snow into trash cans, then haul the cans over to the designated snow dumps, in order, slowly, foot by foot, to uncover the buried cars and, finally, the bricks. There was much joking about how my walk should be the first one cleared in case anybody needed psychoanalysis while we were working. "I suppose I could lie on a Freudian couch for my aching back," the high school teacher next door mused, "I certainly could not in a million years do it for my head—much as I might need it!" My patients flickered into my thoughts while I shoveled on: the one who would be pacing at home, feeling sulky and bereft; the one who would be imagining an adventurous cross-country ski trip to arrive triumphantly at my door; the one who would be elaborately blaming the weather on me . . .

The neighborhood banter about my strange profession was good warm-up for getting into my liberated car, inching up the still very slippery street, and then heading cautiously off to launch the spring semester's lecture course, "Freud and Freudians," with a room full of shivering young skeptics. Psychoanalysis is a hundred years old now, I wanted to tell them, and a diluted, often distorted version of its theory has permeated our culture to an incalculable degree; but it is also now, as a therapy, in its infancy all over again and struggling in a hostile climate. This is a little-known story, which I hoped to convince them is very pertinent to them and their future.

Most of my students come with mixed but mostly negative feelings about Freud, and these feelings turn out, they discover, to be like the negative feelings they have developed about adult human beings in general, and about college. Freudian psychoanalysis, they think, is a cold, forbidding affair. A snowstorm in which some desperate crazy person lies on a couch and tries to get rid of suffering by suffering somehow the austere frozen silence of The Analyst. But, on the other hand, they have the impression that there is something deep about psychoanalysis, something from which they could learn a great deal more than they do from the pop psychological therapeutic culture all around them, which they know to be superficial and stultifying. Similarly, they expect the majority of classrooms to be chilly, dispiriting places where education is dispensed in an impersonal, official way by adults. Criticism is the norm. Anxiety is the feeling state. In their student spaces, by contrast, they expect fun, supportiveness, and affirmation. But, they also think that classrooms could be, might be, part of their growth and self-discovery, and that teachers might be, like, you know, like, uh, Real, whatever.

For years, I have worked on trying to field all these mixed feelings. So my teaching practice has been geared to making Freudian thought friendly, to translating past its off-putting technical language and the stereotypes about how analysts behave. On my good days, I can make a classroom atmosphere that is humorous, easy, *gemütlich*, not in any way intellectually unrigorous, but also not scary. When Faith and I began to talk about cherishment, though, I shifted in my sense of why my students' feelings were so mixed and what I could do about it.

Faith, who was auditing the class with some of her fellow doctoral students, kept me posted through the semester on how my effort to put some of our cherishment ideas into my lectures was playing. Referring to an opening night conversation she had with a young man named Eric, who had sat down next to her, shyly, and been thrilled that she remembered him from when she graded his freshman papers, Faith reflected: "Eric wouldn't want you to cherish him individually. He knows he must once again sit in a hall with seventy-five others while he is, as he joked, 'waiting for Enlightenment.' But he certainly would want your warmth and affection to wash over him. He is more than willing to struggle with the texts—even to spell 'cathexis' and 'anaclitic' correctly, as he finally did!—but the bottom line would be his expectation that you make him feel special to you, because all your children are special to you. He would hope that you loved . . . well, not exactly him, but . . . what am I trying to say? . . . his once-and-future self, his ideal of himself."

With that, Faith had, as she so often does in our conversations, jumped right from a feeling state to a key concept. She imagined Eric wanting me to cherish his sense of who he might become—his "ego ideal," in Freudian language; she imagined him wanting me to promote his growth into his ego ideal. Wanting to be cherished in this way is the precondition for the learning to cherish that goes on in adolescence, building on the foundation of childhood learning. Most of my students, young and older, want to be people who are able to give to others what they hope to get from cherishers, and the students who do not envision themselves as cherishers are very obvious in their unhappy self-enclosure. The classroom—like what the *I Ching* calls a Joyous Lake—should be a place for promoting this take-and-give process, which wears against self-enclosure. So when my teaching assistant had to go rushing out to Colorado in March to be with her daughter, who was dangerously toxemic after giving birth prematurely, we talked about this terrifying crisis in class. For weeks, I wove into the lectures news bulletins from Colorado about little Max and capsule histories about how the conditions of neonatal hospital care have changed since the end of the Second World War.

Here, I told our students, is the heart of what psychoanalysis is: psychoanalytic child researchers alerted obstetricians to the importance of the earliest parent-child interactions, and rigid hospital policies were gradually revolutionized. Pediatric wards have been opened, so parents can now stay overnight, visit whenever they can. Newborns are no longer separated from their mothers. Max was getting what is known as "kangaroo care" rather than being isolated in an incubator, untouched, unheld; and his parents were getting to be his parents, his holders and cherishers, rather than being sent away to wait while he fought for his life under strictly medical supervision. Over the course of the semester, Max and his mother both recuperated, and our students shared his family's joy and relief. But many of their comments made it clear that they were also relieved for themselves, in their identifications with Max. Caring, they felt cared for themselves through the image of caring that came back to them from Colorado.

"Cherishment is fundamentally about safety," Faith said to me after a class devoted to Freud's intricate case study of the Wolf Man, a patient who was born sickly and later, after much more trouble, had a little bit of almost every neurosis in the Freudian book. Children who get damaged or feel damaged can become detached from their expectation to be indulgently loved, as the Wolf Man did. If they find themselves later in a safe and cherishing place—like a psychoanalysis, or even a class about psychoanalysis—their expectation reawakens. They can grow receptive again. "But no wonder psychoanalysis is so frightening," Faith went on. "It is frightening to reawaken. And it's so much easier to think that psychoanalysis would be just more damage, more hurt, more trouble. Or to think that psychoanalysis is just an indulgence—as though being indulged were a terrible, shameful, weak thing!"

"You know," I said, after reflecting a while on her words, "Takeo Doi thought it is an ego instinctual, self-preservative or self-developing drive for love—indulgent love—that brings people to a psychoanalysis, and we can certainly see that need as what brings students to pull for cherishment in a class about psychoanalysis. But if we are going to understand more about how this baby drive expresses itself in infancy, or later in adolescence, we should ask how Doi came to this understanding. How did he come to his feeling for infant *amae?*" What were his own *amae* needs, and how did he expect caretakers and those they care for to fit together? We decided to wander through all of Doi's writings, to study *his* development, listening.

THE WORDS TO SAY *AMAE*

Woven delicately through Takeo Doi's articles and books, we found a very discrete autobiography in which he recalled beginning to think about *amae* after the Second World War. His reflections eventually began to yield succinct formulations like this one, which is virtually a summary of Doi's early papers: "*Amae* itself is an emotion that is constituted tacitly. It is telepathic, prelinguistic, and does not need the medium of language. It is communicated directly from heart to heart."

When he traveled to America to pursue psychoanalytic training soon after the war, leaving his own country and culture for the first time, Doi had felt disrupted and displaced. Unsafe, unwarm, the fledgling psychiatrist longed for the familiar *amae* of his everyday life at home. While visiting American colleagues, he was asked if he was hungry—and he found the question astonishing. Japanese hosts would simply have served their guest. In another home, he was asked before dinner what he would like to drink, and then, when he answered, how he would like his drink mixed. After the meal, which he was so relieved to find involved no decisions, he was asked whether he would like coffee or tea, with milk or without, with sugar or without. Again, a Japanese would simply have served the guest. The Americans, eager to please, told Takeo Doi to make himself at home and help himself to whatever he needed. A feeling of displeasure, even revulsion, rose in him. A Japanese host would have made it clear that his guest would never need to help himself.

The cascade of trivial decisions exhausted Takeo Doi and made him feel uncared for, even though he realized that his hosts intended their questions as attentiveness. He wondered if the Americans needed their multifarious choices to reassure themselves of their own freedom. And he suspected that his hosts were not as considerate or sensitive to others as the Japanese. "As a result, my early days in America, which would have been lonely at any rate, were made lonelier still." When he got home, Doi began to think that his patients, too, suffered from various kinds of frustrations of their need to *amaeru*. They were not in their element, like Japanese travelers in an emotional America.

As he was considering the idea that expecting indulgent love is peculiar to the Japanese and to their language, Doi mentioned it to the head of his psychiatry department in Tokyo. The professor put his reservation very starkly. "I wonder, though—why even a puppy does it." Presuming on someone's love seemed to the psychiatrist-in-chief so universal a phenomenon that it would be strange if only the Japanese had a word for it. But this was precisely Doi's point. The peculiarity of the Japanese is not that they *amaeru*, as all humans—indeed, all animals—do, but that they have a word for it; it is in their lives in a way that has a language. They value it.

On his second trip to America, a decade before he met the Hungarian émigré Michael Balint in 1964, Takeo Doi had another conversation with a displaced person. While presenting a paper on language and psychology to a group of American clinicians, he discovered in his audience Frieda Fromm-Reichmann, a refugee from Germany who worked with psychotics, particularly at Chestnut Lodge in Rockville, Maryland, which is the setting for *I Never Promised You a Rose Garden*, a famous account of her work by a former patient. While my students were reading and discussing *I Never Promised You a Rose Garden* in my class, I told them how Dr. Fromm-Reichmann was struck by Doi's reflections on *amae* because she had, as Doi recalled, "perceived that the word *amaeru* suggested an affirmative attitude toward the spirit of dependence on the part of the Japanese."

Dr. Fromm-Reichmann was herself a person whose clinical practice rested on the idea that her patients had to learn to express their helplessness and to recognize how their early-childhood dependency needs had gone unmet, and often hypocritically unmet—unmet by people who denied and lied, who said that everything was fine when it definitely was not. She was, in Doi's experience, not American in her attitude. On a stint at the National Institute of Mental Health in 1961, he reached a conclusion he had suggested earlier and had shared with Fromm-Reichmann: "I frequently observed interviews with patients and their relatives conducted in rooms with one-way mirrors. I began to feel that, generally speaking, American psychiatrists were extraordinarily insensitive to the feelings of helplessness in their patients. In other words, they were slow to detect the concealed *amae* in their patients."

Doi tried to formulate for himself what distinguished his own attitude toward his patients from the one he found prevailing in American hospitals. He suggested that "the criterion of self-reliance that was assumed in psychoanalysis and psychiatry was admirable and undoubtedly indispensable as a goal to be achieved by the patient, but when it became not simply a guiding principle in the course of the treatment, but something to which the doctor conformed unthinkingly, it tended in effect to abandon the patient in his helplessness and even make it impossible to understand the patient's true state of mind."

"Frieda Fromm-Reichmann shared Takeo Doi's feeling," Faith observed. "He wanted therapists, and parents, to protect their children, but not by promising them a rose garden, not by pretending that the world is not dangerous and painful. Not by saying 'You always have choices—help yourself!' That would be false indulgence." "Yes," I agreed. "What they called for—in the terms we are working with—was not a prefabricated vision of independence but acknowledgment of the child's, and the patient's, helplessness and then indulgent tending *of their growth*. You give the help that helps them not need help."

Doi adjusted his clinical care to his critique when he returned to Japan. "In working with neurotic patients in Japan, my attention was called to the singular phenomenon that these patients almost invariably present themselves as quite helpless, a feeling which usually becomes intensified in the course of treatment, along with a development of hypersensitivity about what the therapist might feel or think about them. One might say that the patient develops such a sensitivity toward the therapist because the therapeutic situation promises help but does not give him the kind of help he wants. I subsequently realized that his initial helplessness and subsequent sensitivity really refer to the wish to be loved or to be taken care of."

"Do you think there has ever been a patient who didn't fear at the beginning of treatment that the therapist would be critical? who wasn't hypersensitive to the therapist's caring tone?" Faith asked me one early spring day. After all, patients come because they have failed, so they think, and they are critical of themselves, often harshly critical. Their expectation to be loved comes under a blanket of expectation to be rejected. They have rejected parts of themselves. We began to think of thwarted *amae* as expectation of rejection. Unreceptivity, closing down of parts of the self, internal growth stoppage, which then is expressed as stopping the growth of others. Envy, hatred—these are expectations of rejection.

As we read along in Doi's essays and books, we could see that his thoughts had turned to how *amae* is thwarted, too, but his process was very slow because his struggle for a way to talk about his *amae* concept was so complex. The first step he had had to take on returning to Japan was to stop speaking German. Japanese psychiatrists were trained to listen to their patients in Japanese, but take their notes and make their diagnoses in German, which had been the chief language of psychiatric diagnosis since the turn-of-the-century work of Emil Kraepelin. It was only when Doi began both to hear *and to feel* his patients in Japanese that the peculiarly Japanese *amae* vocabulary struck him. "You know," Faith remarked after considering this struggle of Doi's, "feeling alienated in a language is somehow crucial to discovering or rediscovering, reexperiencing, an *amae* state. In therapy, most people come in speaking a language of expectation of rejection, words they feel hard-hearted inside of—and this is rather like speaking the language of a dominant culture, speaking like a slave. Or like someone enslaved to acting like a master."

In his developing reflections, Doi emphasized certain characteristics of the expectation to be loved to which his word cues alerted him. *Amae* is associated with infancy. The intransitive verb *amaeru*, "to depend on or presume upon another's love," has the connotation "to bask in another's indulgence'" and it always invokes the sense of sweetness from the related adjective *amai*, sweet. But the root experience of getting cherished is preverbal: even before a baby can fully identify its mother and father cognitively, the baby seeks their sweet indulgence. And getting cherished retains this early ego, preverbal quality in the sense that there is no *amae* vocabulary for asserting "I love you." The Japanese do not think that the deepest connection between a lover—infant or adult—and a loved one needs a declaration.

In his first writings, Doi sometimes referred to *amae* as a "silent emotion," and he felt that its silence might explain why so many languages have no word for it. Getting cherished is done, not spoken about. Similarly, responding to a baby's or an adult's desire for cherishing is essentially a matter of picking up on silent and sometimes symbolic cues, not hearing words. You have to "get it."

As being cherished is initially preverbal, so it usually remains outside the public domain, even hidden from it, protected from it. Public displays of affection are not encouraged among the Japanese. Parents do not embrace or kiss their children in public, especially as the children grow older. Lovers and married couples do not show affection before others. The word *amae* retains from the period of *The Tale of Genji* some of its associations to coyness, coquettishness, even private toying with public conventions.

Amae is not only rooted in infancy, but always makes reference to infancy. The English word "love" does not conjure up the infant's love of her mother, and we do not have a word that specifically designates babylove. That is why psychoanalysts have invented terms like Balint's "primary love" or his teacher Ferenczi's "passive object love." We would also find it strange to be reminded of babylove while speaking of love between adults, whether in relationships of mentorship or friendship or romance or marriage. Even when popular songs are entitled "Baby Love" or seductions launched with "Hey, Sweet Baby," we do not think consciously of babies. If we think of babylove at all, we do not understand it as the ever-present foundation of all love. Rather, we conceptualize babylove as the love left behind by adolescents in their first excursions outside of the family and transcended by adults in both their passions and their family-founding loves. The idea that an adult's capacity to love might require a capacity to reexperience babylove would seem shocking, as might the idea that lovers need to reexperience being receptively cherished in order to be cherishers.

From Doi's perspective, people in the West are so anxious "to banish dependency need from the adult world" that they have almost succeeded in banishing it from the child world as well. Childhood dependency is acknowledged in studies of development, but then quickly set aside—as it is acknowledged in manuals of parenting with the recommendation that it be overcome as quickly as possible. Psychologists in the 1950s started using the mechanical word "attachment" to indicate a child's first bond with its caretakers, but the term studiously avoids any emotional coloration. Attachment theorists like John Bowlby were intrigued by the work of the Budapest School researchers on "clinging" behavior, but that word seems to have disappeared in a wave of anxiety about its dependency connotations. "Dependency" is a negative word, and the recent coinage "co-dependency" is more than double the trouble. Independence is valued. "Autonomy" is a plus. "Vulnerability" only means danger, it does not imply "receptivity." Prolonged dependency equals being spoiled, being entrapped, no matter what the dependency is actually like; the judgment is *tout court*. No distinctions are made between growth-promoting dependency and growth-inhibiting dependency.

The American psychiatric community that Doi found so alien nearly fifty years ago now knows a condition called Dependent Personality Disorder (DPD)—but not one called Independent Personality Disorder for people who are incapable of dependency. The very name of the Dependent Personality Disorder, which used to be "passive-dependent personality," obscures the childhood situation, which was at least acknowledged in the original Freudian designation, "oral character": it is a child whose oral stage, whose period of dependency, is a story of starvation or of harmful feeding, of being *unable to depend* in a healthy way, who later becomes unable to act independently, who cannot move without asking for instruction, help, orders, or some form of food. But DPD sounds accusatory, as though it named the recalcitrance of a spoiled person.

While we were reading around in the anthropological literature on *amae*, Faith came across a young Japanese-American's reflections on Doi's work that captures well this complex of attitudes toward dependence. During her childhood in Japan, Carla Bradshaw was taken by her Japanese grandmother to early morning public calisthenics sessions. As is customary, she was carried on her grandmother's back. But one morning a friend of the grandmother's said mockingly: "Such a big girl to be on the grandmother's back! Look! Your feet nearly touch the ground." Carla became suddenly aware that she, at age five, was almost as tall as her diminutive grandmother. "I had felt so nurtured by her that I had indulged in a fantasy with her of still being nearly an infant. It was not until this friend mocked me in her kindly but critical way that I realized what a comical scene we must have presented. I do not recall that my grandmother was shamed or embarrassed by her friend's comment. Rather it was I who felt some shame and stopped indulging myself in this way. I do not know when I would have stopped riding on her back or when she would have begun to object, but I suspect that she would have allowed this until I was ready to stop on my own." In the West, a five-year-old might be carried as a special treat or game, but if a parent or grandparent made the ride a matter of course, alarms about "developmental arrest" would sound.

Doi was also impressed that among psychoanalysts discussions of dependency needs have focused on severely disturbed or deeply regressed patients, that is, on people who are held to be arrested in their infantile dependency or cast back into it by later traumas. Even Michael Balint, with whom Doi felt most akin, developed his notion of primary love in the context of a psychopathology. Balint held that primary love, as an infant-mother relationship, is fundamentally different than any adult relationship, and that when the early relationship is re-created in an adult relationship—as it is re-created in the psychoanalytic transference—it is pathological. As Balint wrote in *The Basic Fault*, referring to a patient's efforts to seek gratification in the psychoanalytic situation:

> In my view, all these processes happen within a very primitive and peculiar object-relationship, fundamentally different from those commonly observed between adults. It is definitely a two-person relationship in which, however, only one of the partners matters; his wishes and needs are the only ones that count and must be attended to; the other partner, though felt to be immensely powerful, matters only insofar as he is willing to gratify the partner's needs and desires or decides to frustrate them; beyond this, his personal interests, needs, desires, wishes, etc., simply do not exist.

No possibility is acknowledged here that mutuality or equality in adult love might involve, in crucial part, the lovers being able to shift gracefully back and forth the roles of wisher and gratifier of wishes—cherishee and cherisher, in our words. There is no sense in Balint's words that giving and taking can be equally gratifying roles or that flexibility in role-playing is itself gratifying. And no sense that such healthy flexibility might be learned first in infancy, prepared there, played there. Balint did not appreciate that the baby is a gratifier of wishes, too—first and foremost a gratifier of the mother's wish to love the baby, to enjoy the baby's beauty, to have a lovable baby, to be smiled at, cooed at.

The common Western attitude toward babylove—that it is babyish and that it is pathological if it appears in adult love—is reflected in the various efforts that have been made to translate *amae* and *amaeru*. Most of them sound dismissively negative. One scholar catalogued a number of English vernacular possibilities for *amaeru:* "to be babied, to act like a spoiled child, to coax, to be coquettish, to request favors, to avail oneself of another's kindness." Another suggested "to desire to be pampered," and another "to seek the goodwill of others . . . flirt with, take advantage of, or butter up." Being a baby who is getting cherished seems so hard to talk about that one translator even suggested that *amaeru* should be rendered "to play baby." None of the scholars we read have even tried to translate the wonderful noun *amaekko*, which describes a child or an adult who likes to be indulged—someone who might, in the West, be judged a spoiled brat!

FREUD'S BABY AND DOI'S BABY

The tour that Faith and I took of Takeo Doi's writings made us want to conduct a comparison of The Baby as imagined by Doi and by Freud, to ask in the medium of such a comparison more about why psychoanalysis has been silent about cherishment. We began where both men began, with the simple observation: human babies go through a period of helplessness and dependency longer than that of any other animals. Freud called this "the biological factor," and held it responsible for the most important developments of later life because it creates the need to be loved. "The biological factor . . . establishes the earliest situations of danger and creates the need to be loved which will accompany the child through the rest of his life," Freud noted (20:154), un-questioningly subscribing to precisely the idea that Takeo Doi found so astonishing, so Western. In Doi's view, the need to be loved is a biological given at birth, even in puppies, and not something created in response to anxiety and danger.

When Freud considered the human infant's dependency need, he saw something that stood in the way of *development*. If babies did not have to rely on their parents for the satisfaction of their basic needs for food, warmth, shelter, their development would not be impeded; but as it is, they start off in a condition Freud called "primary narcissism," which means that while they are being supplied they do not send libido, their erotic instinct, out into the world to invest it there, but keep it within. When they later do send libido out, they invest it in their suppliers and then have to resolve or dissolve those bonds, the bonds of the Oedipus complex. Primary narcissism, Freud said, would not ex-ist "were it not that every individual goes through a period of helplessness and dependence on fostering care, during which his urgent needs are satisfied by agencies outside of himself and thereby withheld from developing along their own lines."

For Doi, babies enter into relatedness with their caretakers as soon as they can mentally keep them in mind; for Freud, so-called "object relations" with the caretakers are formed only when primary narcissism can be left behind, that is, when infants are no longer helpless and dependent. From Takeo Doi's per-spective, there is no such condition as primary narcissism. Care-fully and succinctly, Doi drew the contrast between his view and Freud's:

> Against [Freud], I propose that dependency need should be thought of as an independent drive, distinct from the aggres-sive or sexual drives, from which develops the need to be loved. In psychoanalytic terminology, the sexual and aggres-

sive drives are usually referred to as id impulses, whereas I believe that dependency need should be thought of as deriving
from the ego; that is, it corresponds to the ego instincts in
Freud's early formulations.

[1969:236]

Many contemporary "object relations" analysts agree with Doi
in rejecting the notion of primary narcissism, as do many infant
researchers. But those who do agree with Doi do not say, as he
does, that what *is* primary is *amae* and that *amae* is an ego instinct.

We began to wonder why Freud himself had given up his
early interest in the ego instincts—the self-preservative ones, like
hunger—and submerged the contrast he had drawn between the
ego instincts and the sexual instincts. Our question took us back
to texts written prior to the 1914 essay "On Narcissism," including the 1912 essay that we had visited soon after our conversation
began in New Haven, "On the Universal Tendency to Debasement in the Sphere of Love." There, the ego instincts give rise to
"the affectionate current" of love, which Freud contrasted to
"the sensual current":

> The [affectionate current] springs from the earliest years of
> childhood; it is formed on the basis of the interests of the self-
> preservative instinct and is directed to the members of the
> family and those who look after the child. From the very be-
> ginning it carries along with it contributions from the sexual
> instincts—components of erotic interest—which can already
> be seen more or less clearly even in childhood and in any
> event are uncovered in neurotics by psychoanalysis later on. It
> corresponds to the child's primary object choice. We learn in
> this way that the sexual instincts find their first objects by at-
> taching themselves to the valuations made by the ego-in-

stincts, precisely in the way in which the first sexual satisfactions are experienced in attachment to bodily functions necessary for the preservation of life.

For a brief period, Freud was imagining The Baby as, from the beginning, relating ego-instinctually or affectionately to its first objects, its caretakers, and then relating to them out of sexual instinctual drive on the basis of the earlier relating and evaluating. First affection, then eroticism. But after 1914, when he shifted over to emphasizing how the sexual instincts eventually reach outward, overcoming primary narcissism, the ego instincts faded out of consideration. The "affectionate current" was redefined as any part of the sexual current that becomes "neutralized" or desexualized; it was no longer a separate, primordial current. In biographical terms, this shift can be understood in light of Freud's quarrels with two of his early supporters, Alfred Adler and Carl Jung—both of whom, so Freud thought, tried to repudiate Freud's sexuality emphasis and concentrate on the ego instincts. Freud was defending his sexual theory turf, and so strenuously that he himself practically repudiated the ego instincts. It was a theoretical psychodrama.

Faith and I talked a good deal about this historical theater of ideas, but our attention always returned to the question: Why not both? Why not acknowledge the object relatedness of both ego and sexual instincts, and acknowledge that the two forms of object relatedness are different, come about differently, even though they intertwine? This would be obvious, at least for adult love, if we were speaking a language like Greek that has two broad families of words for love: the *philia* words for the adult affectionate current and the *eros* words for the sensual, or sexual, current.

What Doi himself wanted as a theorist was nothing less than "to do with the concept of dependency what Freud did with that of sexuality." That is, he wanted to show this ego-instinct, cherishment, manifest in the whole continuum of human life from infancy to adulthood, as Freud had shown the id-instinct sexuality on the same continuum. To carry out his plan, Doi suggested that the object relations that arise initially from the expectation to be lovingly cherished come from the ego. But he was also going much further and suggesting that *all* object relations come from the ego—which is, we think, an unnecessary leap, one that was also unnecessary when Adler and Jung took it, each in his own way. It seems to us simpler and truer to our experiences with affectionate and sensual love to see object relations forming to serve both self-preservative cherishment needs *and* sexual needs. The balance and interplay of the two sorts of bonds make all the difference in different personalities and styles of love.

It does make sense, we think, to speak of the "primary narcissism" of the sexual instincts. The sexual instincts are, at least partially, autoerotic before they reach out as the child becomes physically and mentally able to be erotically engaged with others. But the ego instincts—encompassing not just the basic need for hunger satisfaction that Freud stressed but crucially "the expectation to be loved"—are other-related from the start, they *are* in relatedness, as sucking mouth is to breast in hunger satisfaction. Through the course of human development, sometimes the affectionate current prevails, sometimes the sexual; and in different individuals, all different kinds of mixes of the two emerge. But we think it can be said as a general rule that those who do not get and give affection—*both* get *and* give affection—are rudderless on the sea of sex.

While we were comparing Freud's baby and Doi's baby and talking through these ideas—which are the theoretical foundation for all that we have to say about cherishment in therapy, in daily life, and in culture through the rest of this book—Faith and I began imagining The Baby who is both, who is a Freudian sexual pleasure seeker and a Doian cherishment getter and giver.

Creating this synthetic vision, we knew we were going to ignore the fact that Freud, after he abandoned his idea that the ego instincts and the sexual instincts are the two basic human instinct types, went on to speak instead of the life instinct, Eros, which included both the ego instincts and the sexual instincts—and "the death instinct." But we agreed to leave the complicated question of "the death instinct" aside, to come back to it if our picture of The Baby could not encompass what Freud was trying to point out with his later speculation. So, instead of wrestling further with Freud's second instinct theory, we turned our attention to a historical reading tour of the Freudian followers, where we looked for consideration of the possibility that the emerging ego establishes object relations as it strives for its own development, guiding as it does the sexual (and perhaps also aggressive) instincts. Then we turned to contemporary infant research to meet The Baby who is imagined there, too, a baby who is biologically programmed to "fit" with its mother, who has an inborn capacity for interactivity, mutuality and reciprocity with her.

The day we met to launch this next stage of our journey, Faith set her notebook in front of me. "I brought you two snapshots of where the developmental line of cherishment can lead," she said. "I thought we could keep these endpoints in mind while we talk about babies, babyhoods." On one page of her notebook, she had copied an excerpt from a biography of Leo Tolstoy.

> As a man of seventy-eight, the author of *War and Peace*, depressed, was writing in his journal, remembering his mother, who had died when he was two: "Felt dull and sad all day. . . . I wanted, as when I was a child, to nestle against some tender and compassionate being and weep with love and be consoled . . . become a tiny boy, close to my mother, the way I imagine her. Yes, yes, my Maman, whom I was never able to call that because I did not know how to talk when she died. She is my

highest image of love—not cold, divine love, but warm, earthly love . . . Maman, hold me, baby me!"

"You can hear the hope for sweet indulgence—'Baby me!'—and the association with warmth," Faith said, "and you see this inconsolable loss, the incredulous depression, right into old age." And, then, for contrast, she had copied an 1863 letter Walt Whitman wrote to his mother after spending grueling months working as a nurse in the Civil War hospitals, caring for the soldiers. He, the well-cherished child, was able to celebrate himself in his loving-kindness:

> I try to give a word of cheer to everyone [on the ward], then confine my special attention to the few where the investment seems to tell best, and who want it most. . . . Mother, I have real pride in telling you that I have the consciousness of saving quite a number of lives by keeping the men from giving up, and being a good deal with them. The men say it is so, and the doctors say it is so; and I will candidly confess I can see it is true, though I say it myself. I know you will like to hear it, mother, so I tell you.

We pondered these images from two of the greatest philosophers of cherishing fellowship and community in the nineteenth century: one who was always failing his highest image of love and despairing, and one who achieved the serene, cheerful accepting relationships with the many people invoked in his *Leaves of Grass:*

> *And these tend inward to me, and I tend outward to them,*
> *And such as it is to be of these more or less I am,*
> *And of these one and all I weave the song of myself.*

It is in infancy that this fellowship is first experienced, which Whitman could then envision and establish in his life, while Tolstoy could never quite put the personal practice to his theory. Its first manifestation comes as a baby suckles, satisfying hunger, but also beginning almost immediately to improve sucking skill in tandem with the mother's helping and with her smiling, her coaxing. Their coordination, in turn, binds them more closely, constitutes their emotional intimacy, their cherisher-cherishee bond. The baby's suckling also stimulates the mother's milk flow, usually it arouses her, and generally it pulls her into closeness with her baby. Skin to skin. Cherishment is from the start a conversation in the most literal sense of the word—a kind of taking-turns-with, *con-versare*, building familiarity, in body language before language. The ego, as Freud used to say, is first a body ego.

The way we imagine the baby highlights an emerging ego seeking the means for its own growth, which is experienced as pleasure in and from its first objects, its caregivers. Such pleasure enhances the baby's growing ability to form stable mental representations of the caretakers, to remember and expect them in their absence. A baby loves fulfillment of her wishes and, as she becomes able to hold onto objects mentally, she loves them as fulfillers of her wishes. Anna Freud spoke of "need objects" preceding "love objects," but this sounds as though only physical needs such as hunger are involved at birth. Like her father, Anna Freud was presuming that we should not speak of love or expectation of love until the baby is capable of holding object representations clearly in its mind. Similarly, Anna Freud's contemporary Margaret Mahler, who so brilliantly tracked the baby's "separation-individuation" from its primary caretaker—its "hatching" from a symbiotic, primary narcissistic state—also assumed that "object constancy" is the precondition for object love. But both women were thinking along the Freudian developmental line of the *sexual* instincts slowly leaving a primary narcissistic state and finding objects. They did not work with a concept of ego instincts.

But if you believe as Doi does that a baby has an emergent

ego instinct for self-preservative cherishment, which we would also call a drive for development, it makes rich sense to say that when a baby first begins to explore her surroundings—visually and by touch in the weeks right after birth—then she also begins to grow in relation to her mother's face and body, in and through her mother's initiatives and responsiveness. The mother is like an ego outside, encouraging the emergent ego inside. For their pleasure and for the exercise of their capacities and especially for relatedness with her, closeness, the baby will *amaeru*. When a baby coos and coaxes and cuddles—when she is *amaeru*-ing—she is soliciting more of the stimulation, the babytalk and smiling and touching and kissing she has been receiving from her caretakers. In the exchange, perception improves, memory enriches, motor control increases, communication builds, eventually into speech. Comprehension spreads over space and time. These ego functions develop in the experimental relations an infant has with its own body, others, and things. The mode is playful. It *is* play. And this play may be what the turn-of-the-century German psychologists and students of animal behavior used to call *Funktion-lust*, pleasure in exercising capabilities, or what an American analyst named Ives Hendrick named the "instinct for mastery."

On the side of the mother or the first caregiver (who may be the father) there is also an ego interest, for which the Japanese also have a word: *amayakasu*. The caretaker's ego interest is in the child's development; she or he wishes the child well. Cherishment or benevolence is directed toward the child's growth, which means, initially, that the caretaker cultivates in the child his or her capacity to be receptive to cherishment. The caretaker is the teacher, playfully. From her child's good development, then, the caregiver gets her satisfaction—and the pathologies of motherhood and fatherhood are pathologies of being unable to sponsor good development.

D. W. Winnicott was one of the pioneers among psychoanalytic theorists who turned attention to a mother's cherishment and how it enwraps a baby. He noticed, for example, that when her baby is born a "good enough mother" experiences a few weeks of "primary maternal preoccupation" so intense that it is like a "normal illness." In a reawakening of her own *amae*, she is in an empathic "heightened sensitivity" to the baby that involves a temporary withdrawal or dissociation from the rest of the world. "She feels herself into her infant's place, and so meets the infant's needs." "The important thing, in my view, is that the mother through identification of herself with her infant knows what the infant feels like and so is able to provide almost exactly what the infant needs at the beginning, which is a live adaptation to the infant's needs." The cherisher knows, through identification based on the experience of having been a dependent baby, what the baby needs, and this initial caring then grounds the normal caring after this intense period, when the baby is more able to give signals, make its needs known.

When we look at the first year of life, we see it as the first period in which the ego instinctual drives are ascendant—a period of huge growth and development and a period of intense affectional relatedness. The ego's drive is expressed primarily in expectation of cherishing care—feeding, holding, cleaning, cuddling, kissing. In Freud's scheme, based on his libido theory, this is "the oral stage." And certainly it is. But the baby's orality is *both* affectional and erotic, in proportions that vary through the period and varying from one individual baby to the next. Toward the end of the first year, the erotic—and aggressive—usually emerges more and more clearly, so that Freud's colleague Karl Abraham used to distinguish two oral stages, the earlier one more passive and the later, toward the end of the first year, more active—or, as he said "oral sadistic." The baby is a biter, with teeth.

In the first year of life, babies are in a growth spurt, a green shooting, fed by the Human Growth Hormone as the later libidinal surges are fed by the sex hormones. But they are also still echoing the fetal state that the analyst Phyllis Greenacre once described as "a life of comparative ease, relaxation, and passivity." A condition in which the capacity for and rate of growth are greater than they will ever be again. Toward the beginning of the second year, this echoing relaxation and passivity give way to the ego-instinctual surge expressed in the child's get-up-and-go, in the joy of walking, of being in a body that can *do;* and a little later there is the joy of communicating in language. Toddlers are "hatching," as Margaret Mahler puts it, from their more dependent bond with their mothers and then "practicing" for independent movement and individuated exploration of the world.

Here the expectation of love is explicitly an expectation for supportive growth: it is "Grow me! Watch me go!—and be right behind me so I can come back to you!" But this moment of explicit expectation of growth-promotion is also the most vulnerable time in childhood for the ego; vulnerable in both the sense of opened up and the sense of dangerous. This is when the child, the explorer, is most *actively* receptive, taking the world in by gulps.

While this ego-instinctual surge is peaking, the sexual instinctual comes forward in the child's struggle with the mother or primary caretaker over control. This is a struggle that comes to focus, in Freud's libidinal scheme, around the child's anal pleasure-seeking and the parent's toilet-training and body-disciplining. Frequently, in this time of struggle, popularly known as the "terrible twos," the ego's drive for development and cherishing gets thwarted. It suffers from any of a multitude of forms of noncherishment, and frequently from caretakers feeling challenged, even overwhelmed, by the child's growth and activity. There can be an ego-developmental pause, a slowdown, while disciplining, often punishing, prevails. The child goes into a condition we think of as a kind of ego dormancy, a first latency that is an ego latency, not the sexual latency or slowdown that Freudians locate between the ages of about six and ten. Many types of inhibitions and many later learning problems have their origins here, and so does ego precocity, or an uneven development of the ego, consisting of dormancy in much of it and a kind of artificial brightness or protective intellectuality elsewhere. If a child is in ego dormancy when its Oedipal period begins, around age three, the sexual instinct goes running on relatively without the ego's guidance or evaluation, and balance is very difficult to recover. The oral and anal forms of the sexual instinct then play a huge role in the Oedipal period, which is full of regressions or reversions to very infantlike behavior.

The oral, anal and phallic-genital stages, which Freud described as moving from autoerotic narcissism to object-relatedness, are universal, as is the libidinal upsurge at puberty. Similarly, as Jean Piaget and many other students of "the child's sense of reality" have shown, there are preprogrammed stages of development for the ego's functions, like cognition and memory. But the ego's drive for development and its capacity to develop are reality-influenced to a very high degree. All of the theorists who consider pathologies of ego growth and integration, and psychotic ego fragmentation, note that traumatization is involved: harsh realities of abuse, illness, extreme deprivation, loss, disappointment—what we would call summarily lack of cherishment—can overwhelm the normal stage-by-stage unfolding of the ego drive.

In the history of psychoanalytic theory, much of the impetus for thinking this way about ego pathology came from the work of the prewar Budapest School and from work done just after the Second World War by the Hungarians in exile and those they influenced. For example, Rene Spitz, an infant researcher who trained first under Ferenczi and later under Jean Piaget, showed that children living for long periods in institutions suffer a generalized slowdown of ego development when they are adequately but uncherishingly tended. "Hospitalism," Spitz argued, is a disease of childhood: six-month-old babies, who are just becoming able to form stable object representations can experience what Spitz called "anaclitic depression," and what many contemporary clinicians call "attachment disorders." Similarly, children suddenly and shockingly separated from their caretakers close down, become unreceptive, as though they have given up on growing. Winnicott later spoke of "environmental deficiency diseases" in his effort to draw attention to children's cherishment needs. Similarly, Anna Freud and her colleagues, who ran nurseries for children whose parents were occupied with the war effort in London, had observed that sudden separations and lack of relationships froze their young charges in their ego-developmental courses. From work like this eventually came the important reforms in the way pediatric wards are run that the students had learned about.

Freud wrote about the growing child's Pleasure Principle meeting—often colliding with—the Reality Principle. All libidinal desire, all unlimited child wishing or imagining of erotic satisfactions, must succumb to limits—although the limitless state may be re-created, revisited, in dreaming, fantasizing, or other unworldly conditions close to what Freud called "primary narcissism." But we have found ourselves thinking that the ego instincts, too, have a principle, a Growth Principle, that pushes them. Then cherishment is their Reality Principle, the shaping, refining, tending, cultivating of the ego's drives; while absence of cherishment produces arrest, distortion, fragmentation. As we found ourselves noting again and again while we talked over this territory, thwarting or harshly frustrating the expectation to be loved provokes expectation of rejection, hatred, and envy. Rene Spitz put the whole story in a sentence: "Infants without love . . . will end as adults full of hate."

Satisfying the ego's interests allows the ego to develop its ability to guide and influence the sexual or erotic desires and the aggression they involve. The ego models its self-cherishment on its having been cherished, while the caretaker is acting as an auxiliary ego to the emerging ego. There is a process of identification with the caretaker, or with the cherishing relationship itself, that is central to the ego's development: "These tend inward to me," as Whitman said. A child forms what psychoanalysts call an "ego ideal" on the basis of its own *amae* feelings and its first identifications with cherishers. A "what I want to be, how I want to grow." The ego ideal of an adult, then, comes to include the experience of growth through cherishment. As Faith wrote one day in our notebook: "I have been thinking that we should define maturity as the condition in which a person is able consistently and carefully to sponsor other people's growth—knowing that she wishes that sponsoring for herself and knowing that sponsoring comes to those who sponsor."

OTHER WORDS FOR *AMAE*;
THE INFANT IN THE ADULT

To have time to pull together these conversations about our Freudian-Doian Baby, Faith and I traveled together to Washington, D.C., to attend a conference over the Veterans Day weekend. In anticipation, Faith had a dream:

> I had seen an image in the Art and Archeology library at Bryn Mawr that I wanted to get for *Cherishment*, and I was returning to get it. The image was on the cover of a journal, but I didn't find it on the big wooden tables where I expected it to be. Instead, it was on the floor of a small room—like a storage closet: there was a lot of food on the shelves—my favorite things. I wondered if the food belonged to Antonia [one of my Bryn Mawr friends], and I was also concerned that I might not get the chocolate I

wanted. The image was of a serene Venus holding a baby in the crook of her right arm.

Faith was herself in this dream, engaged in her creative work; but she was also the greedy baby, close to the floor, wanting to be indulged her favorite foods, wanting an unaccustomed treat of chocolate, and worried rivalrously that the food belonged to someone else—another of alma mater's children, a big sister. At first she interpreted the image she was seeking for *Cherishment* as a suggestion that we should advance our talk about the interplay of ego and sexual instincts beyond infancy: the image was an ideal of herself adultly sexual—a Venus—holding her own growth principle, her babyself and babylove, on her arm, cherishingly.

Provoked by Faith's dream, we spent our first day in Washington thinking not about childhood development, as we had originally planned, but more about adults, and about the child in adults. We came back to Tolstoy and how he, working out of his depression, had written *War and Peace*. But as we talked, Faith began to look at her Venus and baby image differently, realizing that the important part of the image was its adjective, "serene," which we had used for Walt Whitman in his period as a war nurse. She had been looking for something serene, therapeutic, in the midst of the scene where the baby was confined, frustrated, competitive, and greedy. Something in the logic of this thought drew us across the Mall to visit the Vietnam War Memorial. We did not anticipate the memorial as a serene place—it is, after all, a war memorial—but that is what it turned out to be, and that is what it turned out we needed. We and all the other visitors.

At the memorial, there was a long line of people waiting to walk down the slope that gently puts people into that sage, dignified, welcoming space. Many vets in insignia-covered jackets; many families, with parents and grandparents pointing to the Wall and giving little histories to their young; many tourists from other countries. A Japanese couple carrying their toddlers on their backs made us smile in recognition. A group of Vietnamese stood hesitating at the entrance, and then went down the walk, wiping tears from their faces with pale yellow handkerchiefs.

"Your uncle was killed when he was only nineteen," an American mother told her gangly adolescent grandson, a boy too young to have known his uncle, her son. "You put his photo here, and then we will make a rubbing of his name to take home." People clustered around them while they worked, looking at the photograph, asking the woman about her son, remarking that the grandson looked like him. "He is my daughter's boy, and she looks like my son. They both took after their father." We could see the boy glow awkwardly receiving all this cherishing, and we felt how it would be challenging for him to carry his uncle's name home as part of himself, after his *rite de passage*. He took his grandmother's arm shyly when they walked on.

"This," Faith said, as we paused again at the point of the V, people pressed around us, reading the names, looking at the offerings left at the foot of the wall, "this place is the war's *Iliad*. We are in the *amae* moment; the battle, the hatred, is suspended, and held off by this wall."

"I know what you thought: she is a Thetis, mourning her son."

"Yes, I did."

As we headed up the exit walkway, Faith turned to look back: "I've never been to a monument that is receptive like this. It allows—it invites, people to be emotional together, and they—we all—have made a monument of our emotions within the monument."

As we walked back along the Reflecting Pool, fragments of conversations in many tongues drifted through the graying air. It began to rain lightly. A little girl, entranced with the raindrops rippling on the Reflecting Pool, broke loose from her family and began throwing pebbles to make her own watery design, screaming in delight—in French—that the pebbles made pee pee. Her people chuckled and her father gathered her up. We all sought shelter under the awning of a souvenir stand, where even the T-shirts and caps and scarves were multilingual.

"I remember how it was when Jennifer learned to speak," Faith said. "She just gloried in having words, played with them, sang them, shouted them like that. There was a time of enormous joy in rhyming. But I think she also felt a kind of constraint. Words are different than the touching and stroking of *amae*. They supplant the bodily *amae* language, and I think she felt nostalgic for the days when she just pointed at things and awaited my reaction. Maybe what poets do—or novelists like Tolstoy—when they experience everyday language as a constraint is to retreat into the earliest feelings, into the expectation of cherishment, the cherishment core, and then translate themselves from there back into words. Not that words "express" the feeling, but *feeling* the feeling expands people's relations to their words, opens them, makes them receptive."

"That's the way you experienced the memorial," I said, and added: "The architect is from a Chinese family, Maya Lin. She must understand about hexagrams, about The Receptive."

"That's the way I experienced the *Iliad*, too, remember?"

Waiting for the rain to stop, we went traveling in our memories back to the time in our conversation when, excited, delighted, we had discovered and acquired an *amae* lexicon from Homer; a gallery of images; when we had become convinced that the Japanese are not alone in their *amae* words and culture.

It was early in the summer, while we were just beginning to think in terms of the ego's drive for cherishing and for development, that Faith began to read Robert Fitzgerald's translations of *The Iliad* and then *The Odyssey*, one book a day, out loud, ritualistically. Astonished by the poem, the world of the poem, she would telephone me each day to register the treasures. One busy afternoon at my outpatient clinic, her excited voice was recorded on the answering machine: "Oh, my God, the death, the destruction! The ramming of spears into stomachs, the legs cut in half with swords, the bodies felled like trees. Unrelenting. And then the poem breaks into scenes of such tenderness and delicacy. It's hard to believe the same poet composed in these two modes!" She was hearing in the poem the great alternating chords of aggression and . . . not aggression and sex, Thanatos and Eros, but these two, sex-and-aggression and cherishment. What she had discovered about the poem was what we had just felt at the memorial: how there can be serenity, rest, peace, inside war.

Faith had kept a log of the peaceful scenes so that she could revisit them. I became curious and got the Greek text from the library. Perhaps, I thought, there is a cherishment vocabulary in these scenes. I was anticipating the *philein* ("to love") compounds that I knew were thickly woven through the poem and that any student of Greek knows as an astonishing feature of the language. In Greek, you can love practically any object with a specific word. There are twenty-three columns of compound words made with *philo-* prefixes in the huge Liddell-Scott lexicon!

After many pleasant hours of reading, calling up the language out of the recesses of my graduate student memory, I came to a conclusion that thrilled us: there is an *amae* concept conveyed by the many verb forms of *trephein*, a verb as everyday and simple as Takeo Doi's *amaeru* and one that specifically refers to infancy, unlike *philein*.

At its broadest, the Homeric *trephein* simply means "to raise," or "to rear," or "to get to grow or increase," and it can be used of plants and animals as well as children, in transitive and also intransitive ("to get raised") forms. Nouns came from it in later Greek: a *trephomenos* is a child of less than five, one still being raised among women, a nursling not yet ready to go to school. A green shoot, a leaf of grass. For older children and for adults, the *trephein* vocabulary gives way to *philein*. It is as though the words say you have to be raised cherishingly in order to be able to be affectionate, to love affectionately. The same is not so for erotic love and all the *eros* words.

The verb *trephein* can also mean "to nourish," and all of our English words containing *trophe* come from this meaning, like "atrophy." The Romans rendered the further meaning of "to tend, to cherish" with *colere*, the Latin word from which descend all the *cultus* group of words for *cult*-ic and ritual cherishing and *cult*-ivation or educational cherishing. "*Cult*-ure" depends on educational cherishing; *cultura anima* is cultivation of the soul or cherishment of the soul.

The *trephein* words are practical, but they can carry a deep emotional charge, as they do in the *Iliad* scene where Thetis, responding to Akhilleus's grief over his friend Patroklus, rushes to his side from the sea cave where she lives, lamenting to her water nymph companions as she goes (and we'll quote her here with the *trepho* form translated into a "cherish" form):

> *Sisters, daughters of Nereus, hear and know*
> *how sore my heart is! Now my life is pain*
> *for my great son's dark destiny! I bore*
> *a child flawless and strong beyond men.*
> *He flourished like a green shoot, and I [cherished] him*
> *to manhood like a blossoming orchard tree,*
> *only to send him in the ships to Ilion*
> *to war with Trojans.*
>
> (18:56–62)

Thetis cradles and comforts this huge warrior, most celebrated of the Akhaian military men, and then goes to get him new armor and a shield, even though she knows they will not protect him from his dark destiny.

71

While I was considering all the passages in *The Iliad* where the *trephein* vocabulary appears and then comparing them to *The Odyssey*, I noticed something that Faith and I found odd—or odd to us, twenty-five hundred years removed from this culture, and dependent on my amateur abilities in its magical language. Most of the passages in which the cherishment vocabulary appears are not about mothers and their children, like Thetis and Akhilleus, but about warriors who were adopted as children. Except for Telemachus, Penelope's and Odysseus' son, also called a "green shoot," most of the cherishing Homer describes is bestowed on a wanderer or an orphan or an illegitimate child or a nursling. Sometimes mortals are cherishingly raised by the gods, as Erkhtheus, founder of the city of Athens, was by Athena.

The most extended invocation of cherishment comes toward the end of *The Odyssey*, when Odysseus has returned to his home in Ithaca after twenty years of wandering. Standing disguised before his loyal wife, Penelope, Odysseus hears from her about Eurykleia, the woman who had nursed him when he was a child:

> *I have an old maidservant ripe with years,*
> *one who in her time [cherished] my lord. She took him*
> *into her arms the hour his mother bore him.*
> *Let her, then, wash your feet, though she is frail.*

> (19:354)

We puzzled over the way in which cherishment was concentrated in such fostering and adopting relationships, until it finally came clear to us. The expectation to be loved in this culture is an expectation to be loved by all who are loyal to your house and tied to you by bonds of hospitality, or what the Greeks called "guest friendship." Hospitality is cherishment in society. As you were indulged at home, so you will be in the world; and if you were deprived at home, the world will—the gods willing—provide. When he goes out into the world to look for his father, Telemachus, who, as Athena says of him, "was not born and [cherished] without the gods' favor," expects to be received like a son in the houses of his father's friends.

Like Takeo Doi's Japanese contemporaries, the Greeks received their guests without asking them to do anything, to make any decisions. If he was not immediately recognized, a guest was not even to say who he was and where he had come from until he had had his feet washed or been bathed and dressed, like a child, by the serving women in the interior of the host's house. He was then brought into the common spaces to be given food and gifts, and to tell his story. He received the cherishment first passively and then in an exchange of stories, in conviviality.

Akhilleus, the greatly cherished child of Thetis, expected to be received by his father's friends, men who had visited in his father's house and been visited by his father, but he was rudely disillusioned. With the Akhaians, he had gone to Ilion to fight the Trojans. But once there, the leader of the Akhaian troops, Agamemnon, treated him inhospitably, taking away from him a slave girl, Brisies, whom Akhilleus had been awarded for his bravery. Akhilleus became enraged and withdrew from the fighting. In his tent, he sulks and simmers—he is like the sulky, pouting, resentful child of frustrated *amaeru*, whom Takeo Doi calls *suneru*. He is a portrait of Freudian wounded narcissism, all turned in on himself. Finally, Agamemnon and a group of emissaries come to plead with Akhilleus, to offer him gifts and indulgence. Agamemnon himself, the offender, imagines how the hospitality enjoyed between his family and Akhilleus' will be restored:

> *If we return to Argo of Akhaia*
> *flowing with good things of the earth, he'll be*

my own adopted son, dear as Orestes
born long ago and [cherished] in bounteous peace.

(9:143)

Akhilleus, finally, begins to be cured of his wrath, but only after the loss of Patroklus, who had insisted on going into battle
with the Akhaians and died on the field at the hands of Hektor,
heir to the kingship of Troy. Akhilleus sponsors funeral games for
his friend, extending to all the warriors his hospitality—cherishing his friend and honoring him. In being hospitable, he begins
to overcome the breech of his hospitality expectation. But he
stays hard-hearted about Hektor, whom he has killed and whose
corpse he drags around Patroklus's pyre to avenge his friend's
death. He will not return the Trojan's body to his family.

The gods on Mount Olympus, most of them displeased by
Akhilleus' abuse of Hektor's body, call a meeting. It is a kind of diagnostic conference to determine whether Akhilleus is insane.
The case presenter is Apollo, who accuses the other gods of being
malevolent for letting Akhilleus be so insulting for twelve days:

> *This man has lost all mercy;*
> *he has no shame—that gift that hinders mortals*
> *but helps them, too. A sane one may endure*
> *an even dearer loss: a blood brother,*
> *a son; and yet, by heaven, having grieved*
> *and passed through mourning, he will let it go.*
> *The fates have given patient hearts to men.*

(24:39–49)

Even Akhilleus' patrons—Hera, Poseidon and Athena—yield to
Zeus' judgment that Akhilleus is mad and must be persuaded to

give the body of Hektor to the Trojans. So they agree to have Thetis summoned to be their messenger. She goes, again, to cherish her son—but this time acknowledging him as both a child and a mature man for whom sex would be a nourishment, a curative cherishment:

> *His gentle mother sat down at his side,*
> *caressed him, and said tenderly:*
> > *My child,*
> *will you forever feed on your own heart*
> *in grief and pain, and take no thought of sleep*
> *or sustenance? It would be comforting*
> *to make love with a woman.*

(24:130FF)

Hektor's father, Priam, guided by the god Hermes through the Akhaian lines to Akhilleus' tent, brings a royal ransom. Having agreed to the ransoming, Akhilleus receives his guest with the generous, cherishing hospitality he had shown to his companions at the funeral games. He provides sustenance. He even invites his enemy to sleep on his porch and lays out a bed for the old man. The gods, using his mother, Thetis, as their therapist, have cured him. They have taught him limitation by making him receptive again to his mother's cherishment. This is Homer's thought about the essence of peace.

No one knows who Homer was, or whether these magnificent poems were the work of one bard or more than one, perhaps a school. Some scholars, not believing that the cherishment sensibility in the poems could have been a man's—that is, not being able to understand the cherishment sensibility, but only to feel it—think the poems must have been written by a woman. But we, as we talked about them through the summer, left these questions of authorship aside and did what hearers and readers of the poems have done for centuries: experienced them as composed in and through a culture, as the voice of a people. We decided then to call it a "cherishment culture," and we started a long conversation about how a cherishment culture expects people to be cured of their disappointments. What is the cherishers' therapy? Also about what the cure might be for people who do not live in a cherishment culture—or have only oases of it, like the one we walked into at the Vietnam War Memorial.

"Remember that day when you called me up to tell me that you had found 'therapy' linked to all those cherishment words?" Faith laughed. "And I had the illusion for a moment that we were speaking Greek!" She had learned to speak the verb *therapeuein*, which means to attend to or do service for, to take care of or provide for, to raise, to foster, as well as to treat medically. But it also has another layer of meanings: to tend plants or land or animals or people, to cultivate. To cherish. As the Liddell-Scott lexicon notes, after its single use by Homer, the verb *therapeuein* was "then used in various relations, much like Lat. *colere*"—that is, like the Latin word that also translates *trephein*. *Therapeuein*, then, is the later Greek word, the Ionic word, that the Romans found equivalent to *trephein*. Right down at the Greco-Roman root of the West there is something quite Japanese: to cherish is to therapy.

Chapter 3

Cherishment in Therapy and Therapists

> ... Now it was I
> who formed your manhood, handsome as a god's,
> Akhilleus; I who loved you from the heart,
> for never in another's company
> would you attend a feast or dine in hall—
> never unless I took you on my knees
> and cut your meat and held your cup of wine.
> Many a time you wet my shirt, hiccuping
> wine bubbles in distress when you were small.
> Patient and laborious as a nurse
> I had to be for you, bearing in mind
> that never would the gods bring into being
> any son of mine ...
>
> —PHOENIX'S SPEECH, *THE ILIAD* (9:490FF)

*A*fter the exciting summertime in which we explored the cherishment words in *The Iliad* and *The Odyssey*, Faith and I often returned to the idea that Homer was portraying cherishment as therapy, therapy as cherishment. There are moments in which patients' needs emerge like the cherishment scenes in *The Iliad*: they leave the battles behind and surface from under layers of disguises and defenses; their expression feels like rest, reprieve, quiet release from tension. At such times, the patient is, often startlingly, receptive. Feelings can be spoken that could not be spoken in the preceding battles—and that cannot be spoken when battling begins again.

Such a moment marked Akhilleus' cure in the last book of *The Iliad*, during his meeting with Priam. And we think that the description of that moment penned in 1943, right in the middle of Nazi-occupied France, by Rachel Bespaloff, a Russian émigré, is among the most beautiful passages in Homeric scholarship:

> Suddenly it becomes plain that Akhilleus is just as much Akhilleus' victim as Priam's sons were. At the sight of the old king, to whom he has left nothing but the royalty of misfortune, the conqueror is struck dumb; he seems to come to himself and be cured of his frenzy. The old man's words arouse in him "the desire to mourn for his father." The killer is a man again, burdened with childhood and death. "He took the old man's hand and gently pushed him away. Both remembered . . ." Here, I think, comes one of the most beautiful silences in the *Iliad*—one of those absolute silences in which the din of the Trojan War, the vociferations of men and gods, and the rumblings of the Cosmos, are engulfed . . .

78

... During this strange pause arranged for him by destiny on the extreme edge of suffering, Priam delights in Akhilleus' beauty—the beauty of force. The soul, delivered from the bondage of events, substitutes the order of contemplation for the order of passion; it is a moment of sacred truce. Under the influence of grief, the atrocious reality had hardened into something stony; now it melts, becomes fluid and fleeting. Hatred is disconcerted and relents. The two adversaries can exchange looks without seeing each other as targets, as objects which there is merit in destroying. Thanks to this detachment, private life, the love of the gods and of earthly beauty, the frail and obstinate will of whatever defies death to flower and bear fruit—all those things that rage had trampled down—are reborn and breathe again.

What we have experienced in therapy, again and again, is this silence that Bespaloff analyzes: "Hatred is disconcerted and relents." And what this hatred is—behind all particular ingredients, all specific history—is an inability to be cherished or to be receptive to cherishment. Something stony, a hardening. A refusal of love or a loving gaze—sometimes even to the extreme of a belief that no love can be, that there is no love, anywhere in the cosmos. An idea equivalent to death.

In the terminology of psychoanalysis, these peculiar receptive moments we were talking about come when the patient has been in a "regression," an upheaval of revisiting early or earlier feeling states, and the therapist has been able to stand together with the patient on this "edge of suffering," sharing it. Some of the accumulated armor plating, the protections, shift, and the patients *see*. They gain "insight," to use the term for such knowledge; but "empathy" is the feeling term for what they gain. They come into relatedness. It is as though they suddenly have back their baby ability to feel into the world, into other people, into themselves. The word empathy is, of course, Greek: *pathos* is the word for feeling or emotion, so empathy is "in-feeling."

"IT'S A PROBLEM" —
A CHILD IN MOURNING

Faith and I knew in some half-conscious way before we knew consciously that empathy is the end as well as the means of our work as therapists. Exercising it arouses it in the patient. So we had learned six months before our conversation in New Haven even began, when a woman whom we will call Betsy had brought us to the topic of empathy, and shown us a receptive *amae* moment—initially because she brought Faith to tears.

Betsy is mildly retarded and partially deaf. Her speech is animated, sometimes pressured, and very "concrete"—that is, without many abstract nouns or complex syntactic relationships. She is always on anxious alert for fear of not hearing something. Her cherishment needs and her history could be felt and seen more immediately than is the case with people who have the ability to make more thickly complicated defenses. Faith's clinical journal for that year contains Betsy's story, and the story of Faith's initiation as a therapist.

> Besty first greeted me with a cocked head and downcast eyes, revealing a shy and timid nature. But she was also, I soon learned, excited to express herself and to be heard. I was not her first therapist. She had been in the system for a long time because of her mild retardation and hearing problem, and she had had numerous experiences with mental health professionals: therapists, psychiatrists, case managers, vocational counselors. Age forty, divorced for

many years from her husband—he also mildly retarded, abusive.

In the first two sessions I obtained some of her history. She stressed that she got very angry with her father when he visited her on Saturdays to take her on outings: she went into verbal tirades and then floods of tears in public. Betsy's mother had died five years before. Before her mother's death Betsy had lived on her own but near to her parents. Since that time she has been in this community so that she could be connected to the city services available here. The new community is "unfamiliar," she said, and she missed having neighbors who opened their houses to her, received her as her parents' child. "The people in my apartment building are not like me. I was raised as a good Jewish girl, and these people are into drugs and drinking and I feel afraid all the time."

It became clear that what Betsy most craved was to go home to her father, but he couldn't have her, she told me, because he "has a woman friend now and she doesn't like me much, and besides my father has a bad heart and it would be too much for him." I thought about her outbursts of anger whenever she was with her father and about the guilt that devastated her when she indulged these behaviors, and I knew that her frustrations, depressions and anxieties were about her thwarted expectation to be loved—there is that phrase from Michael Balint's book. An expectation that seemed to have died with her mother's death and left her with burning anger, confusion and tremendous loneliness.

After our two initial therapy sessions there was a mass transit strike and I did not see Betsy for three weeks. When she returned, she sat in silence and would only say that she was ill and that she was concerned about what I wrote in her chart. She then handed me a note—a summary of our work thus far:

I know I criticize myself. I know I want to go home to my
father. What else can you help me with?

Betsy did not speak for the remainder of the session.
She was clearly uncomfortable and held her head shame-
fully, but I had the impression that she was like a child
bursting at the seams with excitement while in the same
moment feeling naughty. When she got up to leave the
session early, I wrote her a note: "What do you want in
your life?" One hour later she telephoned to make sure
that we had an appointment for the next week.

Betsy arrived at our next appointment two hours early.
I had an opening and debated whether I should "indulge"
her and see her sooner or whether I should hold to the
therapeutic frame. It seemed wrong to have her wait so
long so I saw her after forty-five minutes. She was very
talkative in the session after she had announced herself
with: "I still criticize myself, but can you please tell me
more of what you mean." We began to explore her feelings of deficiency and she began to tell me how she "says
things that just come out of my mouth like I'm under a
spell, I can't help it and then I regret it and then people
turn away from me." I was remembering her silence from
the week before and knew that she had been struggling
with an expectation of rejection. Writing to me and keeping her mouth shut had felt safe.

In our meeting she answered my question about what
she wanted in her life by talking freely about how she
wanted friends and good health. She mentioned a woman
at the Vocational Center who might be a friend—a
woman like herself in age and religion—but she feared
that Ellen wouldn't be interested in her. So we practiced
inviting Ellen for coffee. Betsy began to express her fear
that she was "slow," telling me that one of her previous
therapists had told her that she was. Did I agree? She

laughed, telling me that another practitioner once told her—she thought—"You have knee problems"; but what he really said, she finally figured out, was "you have lots of needs." Then she asked me, "What do you think he meant?" I mentioned her difficulties with some of the practical matters of her life and also her sadness about her parentless condition. I explained that therapy was a way she could be good to herself, a place to practice talking. I said that I accepted her and was interested in her. Betsy mused out loud: "I wish a magic carpet could make it all different." Then she asked me if I minded if she took some Kleenex with her because, she told me, "I cry the whole way home after I leave you." I told her that I liked to spend time with her, too, and I felt sure as I did that this kind of supportive comment was right and rightly timed for who Betsy is—for her need problems.

That evening I felt depleted and fragile. I phoned Elisabeth, and she asked me how the work was going. I mentioned about the session with Betsy, and before I knew it I was in tears. Certainly I was despairing over Betsy's situation, her growing attachment to me and the nagging reminder that I was leaving in two months, but also—and I knew it with clarity despite my emotional upset—that I had tapped into Betsy's deep loneliness and it had overflowed into my own. I had the first stanza of Blake's "On Another's Sorrow" running in my head like a prayer for help:

> Can I see another's woe,
> And not be in sorrow too.
> Can I see another's grief,
> And not seek for kind relief?

I am in a major countertransference reaction with Betsy, wondering guiltily to myself if more clinical experience is going to take care of my "hypersensitivity," help me handle better the emotional demands of psychotherapeutic work. But I also know that this countertransference situation is unusual. It has, after all, been only six months since I took Jennifer to Boston for college—and since I began my own graduate experience; five and a half months since mother died so suddenly. The mourning is still going on, and Betsy's material allowed the feelings to surface in full force. I have to think about why I am so freely able to empathize with others, with their loneliness and suffering, but not with my own. No answers.

Betsy's next session began with a note:

> *Dear Therapist Faith,*
> *I try not to criticize myself. I've been waiting for an interview at the vocational center but I'm afraid to go there to work. What do you think I should do about the center? The woman told me I could go however often I wanted to. Could you help me with "relationship."*
>
> *Thank you, Betsy*

I tried to help her explore her fears and she began talking of her need for someone to guide her, help her with decisions, and instruct her so that she doesn't make mistakes. She said bewilderedly, "I need my parents or someone like that." Betsy then associated to an incident in junior high school when a gang of tough girls had made her get down on her hands and knees and behave like a dog, making fun of her as she did. She just could not understand that people would behave like that and hurt others so deeply. "I'm not like them," she said. She followed this with a criticism of herself for being so dependent. "I'm forty years old. This is wrong that I feel this way. I have to take care of myself." We ended that session with her telling me, "I like to talk to you. I feel calm after I do. You help me." She asked if I could write down some "relationship" instructions for her. I explained that I couldn't do that, and that relationships take time but that our having a relationship is a start.

The next session Betsy arrived two hours early and I was not able to see her. She told me that she had to come early because she was so depressed. The session began with a note:

> *Dear therapist Faith. Could you help me with my spend-ing. I'm trying to budget my money monthly. Also help me so I don't criticize myself.*
> *Thank you for your interest in me, Betsy*

"I have a problem with spending," she said. "I want things and then I know that it's not okay to buy them or to want them. You know, like candy bars. I shouldn't buy them but then I can't help myself from wanting them." "It's a prob-lem," she said repeatedly. After she went on a bit about her budget concerns, she told me about her body twitch-ing when she lies down in bed. "Shouldn't I, at forty years old, know myself and my body better?" She berated her-self for being a "late bloomer," claiming that others knew themselves while she was still learning about herself. Such a rage she was in!

While Faith was telling me about this session with Betsy, she remembered the last part of it—the key part of it, which she had found too painful to record. Betsy had continued to rail on at herself mercilessly for being a "late bloomer"—she was in a rage-ful regression—and then her associations had gone to how she had spent her Sunday. "I went to McDonald's by myself," she said, "and I got really angry and threw a donut. Then I got really depressed and sat in a park on a bench." Faith said to her: "It was Mother's Day, Betsy, do you think that was part of why you were angry and sad?" Betsy tried to fight off tears, saying she was too old to be upset about her mother's death. It had been five years, she argued. But then she admitted that she still feels her mother nearby. "It's a problem," she said, very quietly.

While Betsy was in this receptive state, Faith helped her to think positively about her mother's nearness. She understood that Betsy was a person who had had basically good mothering, parenting, but then had lost it when she was not developed enough to give it to herself. Betsy had, in effect, lost her mother when she was still a child and could not, during her period of mourning, securely relate to an image of her mother in herself, one set up by identification with her mother and her mother's cherishing. An illustration from one of Jennifer's children's books floated through Faith's mind: a protective bubble named "mother love" was around a child on her first day of school. "Think of her near to keep you safe, Betsy, like a guardian angel who protects you from harm." Betsy's spirit lightened and she left feeling joyful, saying to Faith as she went out the door, "How was your Mother's Day? Are you a mother?"

Betsy left in a joyful mood, protected by the permission she had been given to let herself be cherished by her mother-image in herself, bouyed by her ability to receive Faith's cherishment. But Faith, on the other hand, was cast right back into her own sadness. This, she came to understand, had to do with how she had taken on Betsy's feelings and with how unhappy she had been on the last Mother's Day she had spent with her own mother. They had been at odds with each other. Faith's mother, who had a gregarious, generous, glamorous side and a depressed, despairing, remote side, had been locked in a bad mood. "Elisabeth, don't you think forty-two years old is a little too old for me to be needing my mother?" she asked, mocking herself with Betsy's mantra: "It's a problem." I told her I thought she would be a much less upset therapist when she could do unto herself what she did unto her patients so well: help them admit their needs for love, stop being so self-chastising. "You need a candy bar, too." Betsy's self-criticism had become Faith's self-criticism. That was Faith's countertransference.

So, Betsy, the concrete thinker, had given us a whole vocabulary for the condition that Takeo Doi called psychological helplessness, and that we understand as the lack of receptivity to cherishment that results from lack or loss of cherishment. Much could be learned from her because she was so simple, so relatively undefended, because she wore her need right on her sleeve. The struggle she conducted with Faith was not, as it is with so many patients, full of anger and attack on Faith; certainly she struggled, understatedly, for Faith's time and attention, but most of her anger was directed at herself. Her *amae* moment about Mother's Day came when she finally relented and let herself feel her own need and frustration without self-criticism or fear of criticism.

Then Betsy's struggle went on at a deeper, older level. She came one day with the exciting news that her case manager had taken her for lunch at the McDonald's where she had often gone with her mother. She said: "I cry in public. What is that? I cry before my father comes and when I'm with him." Faith asked if she ever reminisced with her father about her mother. "No. Why, do you think I should explain to him why I'm sad, that I miss Mom?" Then, without much pause Betsy said: "It's a shame to need someone so much—it's like clothes cling on you. Do you know what I mean? I don't think that's an easy thing to overcome even after five years. Is it possible to be grown-up but still be a kid? I don't think that's right. How will the person move on?"

Betsy continued to criticize herself, but she was gentler about it because she could understand that her mother had been her protection—"it's like clothes cling on you"—and that she was replacing her with a shell of criticism. Without her mother, life was too hard, and she experienced herself as too needy, a

87

greedy kid insatiable for candy bars, without an ego. Alone, and rejected by her father as well, she could not let herself feel her ego interest; she had to constrict herself with criticism, becoming unreceptive. Not getting what she needed, she had become unable to receive what she needed. It was that constriction in her that emerged in the transference, and that Faith responded to countertransferentially. When we looked back on Betsy's therapy, we began to think of transference in terms quite different from Freud's.

RECEPTIVITY IN TRANSFERENCE: THE EGO-INSTINCTUAL STORY

Transference, the concept, came into psychoanalysis with the patient whom Freud called Dora in his 1905 case study of her. At age eighteen, she was brought to therapy by her father after she had shocked her family with a suicide gesture. No one would believe her when she complained that for four years her father's friend Herr K. had been making inappropriate advances to her. And no one knew how miserable she had become as she felt herself trapped in a tangle of adult passions—not just Herr K's for her, but her father's for Herr K's wife. Freud worked with her for three months, until she dismissed him as though he were one of her family's servants. Fired, he was left to ponder what had happened. His conclusion was one of his most important discoveries.

While he was analyzing her, Freud was unaware that she was recreating her history and her conflicts in her relationship with him. But retrospectively he saw that the roles played in her life by her parents and other figures were being rewritten onto him. He spoke of "new editions" of her neurosis. And he came to understand that this "latest creation of the disease" had to be fought in the analysis "like all the earlier ones." Dora's complex feelings for her father, and her complex feelings for Herr K., the seducer, were echoed in her complex feelings for Freud. But, Freud also saw, slowly, that her feelings for her mother and especially for Frau K. were transferred to him as well. In the transference drama, the analyst plays everybody. And it's not easy to know who you are at any given moment.

As an analysis proceeds, Freud concluded, all the *dramatis personae* and plots of the transference become conscious. As they are analyzed, the transference currents lose their force and their ability to determine the present. "Transference, which seems ordained to be the greatest obstacle to psychoanalysis, becomes its most powerful ally."

Interestingly and strangely, Freud did not write about transference again with anything like the clarity or the declarative certainty about its importance that he demonstrated in the Dora case. As he became more aware of the analyst's response to the patient's transference, which he named countertransference, he noted it, too, but Freud's followers were left to explore how countertransference can be used to understand the patient. Among Freud's contemporaries, Sandor Ferenczi, who described himself as "a specialist in particularly difficult cases," was the great explorer, the one who really developed Freud's understanding that analysis is, fundamentally, a conversation between the unconscious of the patient and the unconscious of the analyst—a conversation that is slowly raised to consciousness, on *both* sides.

Ferenczi's technical adventures were the focus of a good deal of controversy in his lifetime, and since then they have been rediscovered during every period of psychoanalytic reconsideration of technique. Freud became quite concerned in the early 1930s to rein Ferenczi in because he felt that his Hungarian friend was becoming too physical with his patients—touching them and allowing them to kiss him—and too self-revealing with them. But even though most analysts have agreed with Freud that Ferenczi went too far, everyone who knew him and his readers since could recognize in him a real cherisher and take seriously his credo about the importance of treating patients kindly and not repeating in the analysis the story of the patient's thwarted expectation to be loved: "Psychoanalysis has discovered that [neurotics] are like children and wish to be treated as such."

Because Ferenczi's work raised so many questions—and fears—about whether analysts should actively promote with restrictions or indulgences a reproduction of the painful past, neither he nor Freud wrote much about the transference phenomenon itself, about the ingredients of this "new mental structure" created in the analysis. But what little Freud did say seems to indicate that he thought of transference as a production of the ego. We interpret this to mean that a key part of the transference will be a repetition of how the ego itself came into being and developed—it will tell the ego's story; and that means to us that it is part of, a function of, the ego instinctual drive for cherishment.

What is emphasized in the psychoanalytic literature, however, is the sexual and aggressive content of the transference, how the analyst is erotically loved and hated as the paradigmatic figures of infancy were. Ferenczi, too, emphasized the sexual and aggressive content of the transference, but he also contributed the very important notion that the transference is, as he put it, "auto-symbolic." It is the process where the patient is able and has the desire—which we would say is an ego instinctual expression—to symbolize herself, tell her own story, a story she does not consciously know.

From our own experiences in analysis, as well as from working with patients, we know well the rich, always present Freudian picture of erotic and aggressive compulsion to repeat and transfer. But what we have learned to listen for now is the dimension of the transference that is the patient's childhood cherishment,

the patient's longing for *affection* and for *growth and development.*
We listen for autosymbolizations of how the patient as a baby was
or was not cherished, but more important, how the child was or
was not able to receive what she demanded and how she hopes,
still, to receive. There is in the transference both a hurt person
who needs repair and a knowing person who prescribes the cure
but cannot bring it about without the therapist. In a relationship
with a therapist, the patient can slowly resymbolize the past and
herself.

In her countertransference to Betsy, Faith was responding out
of her own cherishment story, and she knew it at the time. But
she knows it differently now, and much less self-critically, after
more time in her analysis, and after we developed—with many
thanks to Betsy—the cherishment lexicon. Faith recorded the
shift in an autobiographical reflection she wrote to show how an
amae moment can come through in a dream and its interpretation and reinterpretation, a process of resymbolization through
interpretation. Her vignette shows clearly how her analyst got
woven into her childhood cherishment story and then into her
resymbolizing process:

> My analysis began as a twice-a-week psychotherapy. Less
> than three months later, my beloved grandmother, age 94,
> died suddenly. Just prior to this event, my analyst had sug-
> gested that I consider analysis, but my grandmother's
> death and my increasing anxiety in the therapy relation-
> ship—my growing attachment to my analyst, which was re-
> flected in a hail of criticism of him for being so silent, so
> remote, so unresponsive and austere—allowed me to put
> the idea out of my mind. On the day that my grandmother
> fell into a coma, I was struggling before my analyst's eyes to
> hold in my pain, when he asked, "How would you feel if I
> were empathic to something you were upset about?" The
> question took me aback. I answered that it was a very

loaded question because I wasn't good at receiving in general. "In fact," I said, "I am afraid of intimacy." My analyst made a gesture with his hand implying mutual recognition, which led me to respond with, "I know this about myself, that is what is wrong with me and why I am here with you."

That evening I said good-bye to my grandmother. My mother and her brothers were all there. Nana appeared very frail and looked "babylike" to me as I kissed her good-bye and told her I loved her. In that moment, I thought, "Nana was good to me. I let her take care of me." And, in fact, she had been my chief caregiver when I was a baby because I, the third child born to my mother in three years, was a strain for my mother and a distraction to my father, who was so busy at work. My parents hired Katherine, an African American woman, to help with us, while my grandmother came to stay for weeklong visits throughout each year and for four months each summer at the shore. I was the most helpless child, so Nana and Katherine became "my team" while my mother's attention went to my sister and brother, who were stronger in their clamoring for attention.

In the weeks that followed my grandmother's death, my mourning reflections had a sweet quality to them. I contemplated how in the last dozen years of her life, our roles had reversed. Several times a year she would come to stay with me and I would take her to lunches and shopping for clothes, which she adored, since she adored looking beautiful and well cared for. Helping her in the dressing room at Bloomingdale's, buttoning and zipping, and unbuttoning and unzipping as she leaned on her walker for support, I would think about how she had indulged my every desire in childhood and how glad I was to have the opportunity to indulge her, to return the cherishment, when she needed me and was babylike. She had made me into a person who could cherish her.

A month after Nana's death, I did begin a psychoanalysis proper (four days a week), despite my continued struggle over how depriving I felt the analytic situation to be.
In the context of these events, I had the Sun Dream,
which I recorded in my journal:

> *I dreamt that I was at my session with Dr. R. I was waiting*
> *for him in his waiting room, but his office was an apart-*
> *ment on the 2nd floor of a city building. There was a little*
> *food shop on the next corner. He lived in this apartment too,*
> *and I was curious about the few things revealing his private*
> *life, though there was very little to notice. Dr. R. had told me*
> *that once a month we would make lunch at the apartment. I*
> *went to get some food next door. While I was there, I noticed*
> *that there was a very pretty black woman and several other*
> *customers. When I got back to Dr. R's. office/apartment, the*
> *black woman was there and I recognized that she was his*
> *wife because she was behaving very affectionately to him.*
> *For some reason my husband was coming to pick me up or*
> *he was already there. My therapy session was to begin, and it*
> *was going to be in a place with extremely bright sunlight*
> *flooding in. Dr. R. took sunglasses and then I did, too, but I*
> *remarked to him, "It's difficult to talk to people with glasses*
> *on." Then we were curled up on our sides, lying face to face.*
> *I said to him that I really liked how it felt to be close and*
> *snugly, and he said that he liked it too. I thought that my*
> *husband would be jealous, but I felt really warm with the*
> *sun and the snuggling and didn't care. I said to myself that*
> *the dream was not sexual but psychical.*

I awoke from the dream with my body tingling, warm.
It was so palpable especially because I have always, since I
was a child, felt a little chilly, chilled. I had never had such

a dream—a sense dream, a temperature dream—before. On the one hand, I felt exhilarated and excited to tell my analyst the dream, but on the other hand I was still fearful and mistrustful. I couldn't stop thinking about the dream, but when I got to analysis that day I couldn't bring myself to tell him, and instead spent the session talking about my daughter in greater length than I had previously. At the end of the session, as I was leaving, I said, "Oh, by the way, I had a dream about you." In my session the next day, he reminded me of the two things we had talked about the day before, Jennifer and the dream. I took this as an opportunity to continue my talk about Jennifer, until finally he said, "Why do you think you don't want to talk about the dream?" So I told him the dream with only a few minutes left in the session, certainly no time for associations, but I did say that I felt some anxiety wondering if he was the right "match" to me as a therapist. With only a minute left, he said to me, "What is interesting is that you felt warm and snugly, and liked it, but that it upsets you." "To Be Continued," I thought as I left.

I have often thought about my Sun Dream over the years, making numerous associations to it, never forgetting the powerful feeling of warmth that it communicated, and knowing that the dream, as we interpreted it then, allowed me my first admission of the need I had for my analyst's cherishment, and a step into receptivity—to use the terms I use now. My analyst was the right "match" for me, but there were some bitter struggles ahead, and lots of journeying into the cold and the "ice" as we began to think of it. However, it was not until I read the dream four years later, after talking about Betsy and the concept "lack of receptivity to cherishment," that I interpreted the dream down to childhood. My analyst was my grandmother. The references were crystal clear. My analyst has white hair and glasses, as she did. The dream was set in her city apartment on the second floor, which was almost unknown to me because she always came to us for visits. Also, Katherine was there as the lovely black woman who was married to my analyst/grandmother. As Nana and Katherine were my cherishing parents in my infancy—my central caregivers—so they were in the dream.

The Sun Dream had its Oedipal level, of course: Faith's analyst was married to Faith's rival, there was a jealous husband off-stage. But she herself had responded to it with the remark that it was "not sexual but psychical." I asked her what she had meant by this word, "psychical," and she told me, associating: "Warmth. It was like warm breath—like how 'psyche' means breath." And, I know now, it means closeness, relatedness. I associate "psychical" to the *I Ching*'s image of The Gently Penetrating Wind, in the hexagram "Dispersion," which goes: " . . . when a man's vital energy is dammed up within him, gentleness serves to break up and dissolve the blockage . . . When the warm breezes of Spring come, the rigidity is dissolved, and the elements that have been dispersed in ice flocs are reunited. It is the same with the minds of the people. Through hardness and selfishness, the heart grows rigid, and this rigidity leads to separation from all others. . . ."

Faith then went on to reflect that the action of therapy has a great deal to do with creating a climate in the therapy relationship—a cherishment climate, she called it. And she suggested that the climate metaphor can help a therapist assess where the therapy is in any given moment. "What is our weather now? What is the patients' internal weather now? Stormy? Icy? Warm—melting?" In dreams, too, the climate of the dream so often presents the emotional tone, the nature of the affectionate bonds, around the characters, the action. Telling the dream in therapy and interpreting it can make the climate of it change. Relationships are resymbolized.

TRANSFERENCE AS
THE STORY OF BEING STUCK

Betsy brought her expectation to be cherished and her conflict-
ing lack of receptivity right into her therapy, immediately, undis-
guised. Faith works in and through her dreams and her *I Ching*
symbol system. But the struggle between expectation of cherishment and lack of receptivity is usually, we find, much more clam-
orous, stormy; much more mingled with sexual and, especially,
aggressive strands. And so it was with one of my patients, who
showed us the lack of receptivity in its most elemental form—
anxiety about having been born at all or about being born. This is
a version of what Freud and his younger colleague Otto Rank
knew as "birth trauma."

On a Wednesday, this thrice-a-week psychotherapy patient, a
middle-aged woman, very intelligent and very obsessional, whom
I'll call Sarah, came in and, to my surprise, went over to the
couch and lay down. I had told her weeks before that if she ever
wanted to use the couch, if she ever felt that it would help her relax, she should do so; but she had told me that it would be intol-
erable for her not to see my face, read my reactions to her, for
without the visual check she would always be feeling that I was
rejecting her. On that Wednesday, however, she was desperate
for something different to happen in therapy. She had been feeling for weeks that I was not taking care of her, that I was too
harsh, too critical, that I never said anything positive about her
but only pointed to her problems, making her feel like an unlovable mess. Again and again, she complained, pounding on me,
telling me how cold and unfeeling I was being. Sometimes she
tried to act as my therapist and cure me of my callousness, but
more often she just raged: "You make me feel bad! You make me
feel closed down, and then I get so angry and I want to go away!"

Sarah had also refused to consider taking antidepressants,

96

even though she had many suicidal thoughts and spent day after day in her apartment just stirring around aimlessly, weeping, miserable. We were stuck in a tug of war. I was holding to my conviction that it would not help her if I simply praised her and stroked her as she wanted me to, mirroring her and holding her in her need to have everyone mirror her; and she was holding fast to her feeling of being accused and abused. She would not allow any reflection on our stalemate. Nor would she reflect on what had happened (in her understanding) with her previous therapist, who did stroke her and praise her. Sarah had ended up, she had told me, taking care of that therapist, to the point where she felt like the therapist's mother. She had not been able to distinguish herself from the therapist; she had to *be* the therapist. And then she finally fled that therapist.

On the couch, she told me that she had had a conversation with her brother—her only family now that both her parents are dead—and had told him that she was very depressed and lonely. He had replied that they might have dinner together except that he wasn't well. She heard this as a clear statement that he did not want to be with her. I heard it as one of the interactions that are her life pattern: she shows people that she is depressed and they try to help, but when they see her huge need they become frightened. She becomes more clinging and demanding, they take a further step back; and then she becomes hurt and furiously angry. After she told me what her brother had said and how she had reacted, she paused for a long time, then said: "Sometimes I wish— it seems like an infantile wish—that I was the only one in the world." She was silent again after this harshly delivered statement. But I felt a shift in my mind, like a rock wall breaking open, a space appearing. I felt myself shift into *amae* consciousness: Oh, so this is the kind of baby she is.

And I found myself saying to her: "I am having a thought about what you said. If you were all alone, there would be no one to reject you. Not even your mother. No bad images inside you. You would be lying in the arms of your solitude, feeding on it. Your depression—your aloneness—is a kind of power. In it, you cannot be hurt by rejection; it protects you. Why would you want to give it up? Why would you want an antidepressant? It is miserable to be alone, but it is also powerful. Your depression is like a burrow in a bad world." There was a long pause. "I am feeling relief," she said, finally. Lying with her arms crossed on her chest, hugging herself, her chin tucked into her hands, she told me in a quiet, childlike voice: "Being with people is too hard for me."

Sarah consented to try antidepressants, and she relented with me for a few days. Maybe I had understood her, she conceded, tentatively; and I took to saying to her whenever I made an interpretation "I am going to hold you *in my mind*." I was announcing the terms for my cherishment. But then she got angry again. And in her next angry phase she brought a violent dream. The central scene had an unknown, ominous man coming toward her, crossing through the dining room in her parents' house. He reached out and sliced her cheek with an open paper clip. Then he was crawling toward her on the floor with a wad of these paper clips in his hand. The wad reminded her of an intrauterine device she had seen in a TV documentary about women who had suffered damage from IUDs. He was threatening her genitals with this wad of paper clips, and threatening to force the wad into her. She felt trapped and did not know how to get away from him.

To this violent dream scene, she had all kinds of violent associations during that session and the next. She bounced from one association to another not wanting to linger anywhere, resisting analysis of the dream by talking nonstop. Finally, she leapt to a recent TV show focused on a woman with multiple-personality disorder who had been abused by her father, and stopped. Did I think, she asked, that she had been abused? She was sitting up that day, so I could see that she was terrorized at the thought, her face rigid and eyes bulging. I said very slowly and as gently as I could that the dream suggested that she felt threatened, endangered, and that her genitals were the dream's site for this anxiety. "We can find out what the anxiety is about if we follow it little by little, in tiny steps," I said. She unclenched her jaw, relaxed back into her chair and told me what she had been told about her birth—information that it had never occurred to her to tell me in more than a year of work, during which we had talked again and again about her lonely early childhood, about her mother's "postpartum depression" and her own bewilderment at her mother's moods. With this information, we went down below the Oedipal level, where she imagined sexual abuse and sexual damage, to an infant level, where she felt an elemental anxiety between her legs.

My patient had spent the first six months of her life in a "split cast" because she had been born, after a difficult delivery, with a dislocated hip. Not the (bad) doctors and not her (bad) mother, but her (good) baby nurse had discovered the problem. Her legs were pulled apart by the cast, she said, making a big V gesture with her arms that looked like she was opening them to me, for me to come and be embraced. The cast had to be changed several times. She also told me that she had refused to nurse, and then she speculated that it might have been painful for her mother to pick her up.

"Painful for you or her?"

"I don't know."

And there we were, right at the center of her *amae* state. She is damaged, and her mother is damaged. She is both desperately alone and completely unable to distinguish herself from her mother; she is alone, wrapped in her mother's depression. She really has not, cannot, get separated from her mother at all.

It gave her some comfort to tell me about her infancy, and then, the next day, she had a comforting time with a man she was in love with—a man who was quite unavailable to her and had no idea that she had constructed a great edifice of fantasy around him. In her increased sense of safety and being cared for, she had a complex dream:

> I was in a big house, maybe a compound of the various houses we had here and at our summer resort, and there were a lot of young people around, between the ages of 10 or 11 and 20, which is what I was in the dream. We were all going to play a game, somewhat like "Beckon, Beckon" or "Capture the Flag," the games I used to play with my cousins. My brother was explaining the rules, talking so fast that I knew I would never be able to remember them. The person who was "It" was supposed to identify the others, who were standing around near a big stained glass window. "This is so-and-so who is touching the oblong part or touching the red part." I didn't know the names of the parts, and it was all going much too fast. And then the scene shifted to our house here, and I was going up to the attic to hide. But I didn't get all the way there. I got to the second or third floor and went into a room, which then opened onto another room, and there was a door and other rooms behind it. There were lights on in the front rooms, so that I would be found. I went farther back, to a space that was more attic-like. But I couldn't get in because I got stuck in the door—my shoulders were too wide, too big to go through. And then I woke up.

What impressed her about this dream was "the stuckness," and she associated this to the stuckness of her life now, to her inability to finish a piece of work she was doing, to her stuckness in therapy. We talked about how she had gotten stuck in adolescence, when she experienced herself as big and gangly, but then she rejected my questions about her adolescence and returned to the dream's last image. "Really," she said intensely, "it was more like I was too wide to get born." She had autosymbolized herself again as the baby in the cast.

In this patient's therapy, the Homeric rhythm was palpable: she stormed, and then she relented a little, and then she stormed again, coldly, bitterly. Over time, her hardness will wear away— penetrating wind over water, water over stone. But she will have a very difficult time of it because she did not, like Betsy, have a protective love in her past; she did not have cherishment to mourn. "It's like clothes—they cling to you." Nor did she have consistent substitute mothers as Faith had; so she felt in the transference not distrust and apprehension, as Faith did, but raging disappointment. When she goes looking for love, she cannot do it on any terms but her own, and that means that she cannot have real relationships, but only fantasy ones where the other does not contribute any terms, any conditions, any reality, and where the other will not reject her. She loves only her image of the perfect, mirroring need-satisfier; everyone real is a disappointment, so she cannot yet resymbolize. She gets stuck.

TORTURE: THE CHILD WITH A KNIFE

Our thought about transference containing a history of development and an ego instinctual wish for development stood by unattended through a hectic period of work. Then, a week or so before the August vacation was to start, I met Faith for a Greek dinner at Dimitri's to continue the discussion. But we had to make a detour through my state of mind before we got to it.

She told me straightaway that I looked exhausted and that I

had been a real fool in agreeing to a deadline for a preface to a little book called *What Freud Really Said* at the same time that I was trying to handle a wave of anxiety from my patients about The Vacation. "You can't write well while you are under siege," she noted, "and besides, you shouldn't withstand the siege by writing—you can't write your way out of every tight spot! You ought to analyze your way out of this one. *Do* what Freud really said."

She knows me uncomfortably well. I do manage myself by literary means; I do find it easier to write than to reflect on myself or let myself be analyzed. And I do respond to being under siege with formulations. Faith calls this "packaging." I get things wrapped up, theorized and organized, finding it painful just to exist in a state of uncertainty, to be patient while a scene unfolds. In my countertransference reactions, I am always turning up some little admonition to myself: Work harder! This therapy will turn out fine—appearances at the moment notwithstanding—if you just give it more effort. Particularly when I am tired, I have to check impulses to impose my solutions on problems, to issue instructions, give advice.

So it was particularly challenging to me to have one of my analytic patients—I'll call her Mary—coming in day after day as The Vacation approached and shouting: "Why the hell can't you tell me what to do? Why do you sit there saying nothing while I suffer?" She shook with anger as she protested my departure: "No doctor would just leave a cancer patient for three weeks. Just say, well, too bad you're so sick, too bad you had to go under the knife, I'll see you later!" Searching obsessionally—she is quite obsessional—for some explanation of my horrible behavior, she went on a rampage: "I know why you're leaving for so long. It's because you don't know what to do. You're incompetent and you won't admit it. Or you're scared to tell me that I'm too sick, I'm beyond psychoanalysis. That's the reason! You are in love with psychoanalysis, and you won't admit that it isn't going to work. I'm just an experimental animal for you. They just use a knife with an animal. Too bad if I die, there will be others. Too bad if I kill myself. Why shouldn't I kill myself? I have no life, nothing. I am nothing. And this makes exactly no difference to you. You think you are so wonderful, you think you should be the head of the hospital. You wouldn't even have patients, then, you would just be away all the time being interviewed on TV. You would be way beyond other people, you would think you were so great. You would be God, a God who just said 'Die! Die! you little shit.'"

When these barrages of pain reached an edge and started to sail off into psychosis, I pulled her back. "Mary, can you hear yourself getting farther and farther away from me, from me as you know me to be sitting here in my chair listening to you?" Thankfully, she would slow down. But she did not relent. And the morning of the day I met Faith for dinner, Mary had flabbergasted me with a new tack, one that had literally made me shiver and catch my breath in its icy climate. With a terrible intensity, she hissed at me: "I know you won't do it—you won't do anything, you don't do a goddamn thing for me!—but I am going to tell you what I want you to do. I want you to help me commit suicide. You owe me that. I can't do it by myself."

"So, what did you feel about that?" Faith asked me.

I had no words to tell her how it made me feel. Such words just do not come to me, although I shivered again recalling my patient shaking with rage. It certainly does no good to say to yourself: "Well, this is a Borderline Personality Disorder—they do rage and threaten like that." But it did help me to tell Faith what I thought Mary was doing. "You see, what she has been telling me for weeks is that I feel like her mother to her as I am going away. I am leaving her to die, exposing her to the elements, the harsh world. She feels she was the runt of her litter, a baby who was barely alive, and she feels her mother pushed her away, gave her hateful tits to the younger pups. By leaving her, I am killing her. I am a monster, a murderous bitch. She would like to kill me. It's all fear of being killed and fear of killing, almost indistinguishable. Knives everywhere. The feeling is so wild and overwhelming because about a month ago she was in a patch of trouble at her job—she felt, characteristically, that she had been judged incompetent and rejected—and I helped her understand what had really happened, kept her from going over into her paranoia. Kept pointing out how she was turning the world all bad. She had let herself be helped by me, and she had loved me. I was all-good. The transference was on this long-buried, newly surfacing, slender channel of loving. She had relaxed her hatred just a little and let me say things like 'You wanted them to love you, and then you decided they didn't.' 'You thought the boss was being friendly and then you decided she was being hateful—a terrible disappointment.' Simple things. But, to her, a warm wrap of cherishment. I had listened to her and stayed out of her paranoia by suggesting that she had made decisions in the situation. 'You were hurt, but you also brought a history of hurt to the encounters.' Now I am leaving her."

I did not know whether this patient was going to keep up her fierce protest right until the moment of my departure—so that I would have to be as punished as possible with worrying about whether she would kill herself. How much did she need me to suffer as she had suffered? As it turned out, she relented just a little. With two sessions to go, I could feel her shifting into a reflective mode about the weekend—a shorter separation—that had just passed. She said, "I don't know what it was that came over me on the weekend. Something made it impossible for me to sleep, night after night. I grew weaker, and angrier. I was consumed with anger. I took . . . I am embarrassed to tell you this. . . . I took a pillow from the couch and I punched it, beat it, cried at it. For hours. It was my mother, and I was telling her that she ruined my life."

The pillow from that couch and the analyst—me, behind the analytic couch—both got punched by this patient for the same reasons, out of the same feelings. Her metaphor, her auto-symbolism, helped me understand my role: the pillow, the punching pillow. And I worked in my own analysis on how I am and am not prepared for this role. Through the days before The Vacation, my reactions to this patient's fusillades got woven through my reports to my analyst on other things happening in my life, the writing, and the meaning of my own analyst's upcoming vacation to me. "I will be very busy while you are gone" is my protest mode, as it has been since I was a child who dealt with all disappointments by being capable and considerate. This works very well much of the time, but there are people and situations and challenges that get me to the limit of the defense's usefulness, where real anger lies. My analyst once put the problem area in terrifying simplicity: "There is such a thing as killing with kindness."

My conversation with Faith that evening at Dimitri's tracked through my self-questioning onto the more general question of how the patient's developmental story, when it is turned into the transference, makes demands, like the baby's demands, on the therapist's cherishment. We were seeing transference as the story of the patient's development written onto the analyst, but also countertransference as the story of the analyst's development given to the patient. With a difficult patient like Mary, one of the sort that Ferenczi specialized in, who seldom come into *amae* moments—and she continued battling away with me for nearly two years more before her hatred relented with any consistency—the central problem for the therapist becomes how to survive until peace comes. Empathy is in the service of surviving. To feel a Betsy's loneliness or a Sarah's stuckness, to deal with halting development or developmental halt, is quite a different matter than to be held down in a trench day after day after day.

Even in our Greek restaurant, with all her recent Homeric cultivation, Faith's first association on this topic of surviving the analysis went to the East: "Really, what you have been talking about—the story of Mary's analysis—is your own capacity to absorb her aggression without becoming aggressive. Being cherished may lay the foundation for becoming cherishing, as my Sun Dream showed, but there must be more to becoming able to cherish when you are being attacked. So I think we need to talk about what in the Taoist tradition is called *wu wei*."

ON NOT DOING

Literally, Faith explained to me, *wu wei* means "not doing." It is the ideal of the sage Lao-tse, who recommended it as the best way to deal with aggression—one's own, that of nearby others, and that manifest in all worldy affairs, from domestic arguments to wars. Warning me that I might find this ideal strange, maybe ridiculous, Faith suggested that I prepare myself by listening to one of the poems of the *Tao Tê Ching* (again, in Stephen Mitchell's translation):

> *The Master doesn't try to be powerful;*
> *thus he is truly powerful.*
> *The ordinary man keeps reaching for power;*
> *thus he never has enough.*
>
> *The Master does nothing,*
> *yet he leaves nothing undone.*
> *The ordinary man is always doing things,*
> *yet many more are left to be done.*
>
> *The kind man does something,*
> *yet something remains undone.*
> *The just man does something,*

and leaves many things to be done.
The moral man does something,
and when no one responds
he rolls up his sleeves and uses force.

When Tao is lost, there is goodness.
When goodness is lost, there is morality.
When morality is lost, there is ritual.
Ritual is the husk of true faith,
the beginning of chaos.
Therefore the Master concerns himself
with the depths and not the surface,
with the fruit and not the flower.
He has no will of his own.
He dwells in reality,
and lets all illusions go.

(38)

Two of the thoughts in this poem made perfect sense to me immediately. Most activity—most doing something—does just generate something more to do. Doing things, people often get to the point where they reveal motivations quite other than those they thought they had, particularly if they are given to paying themselves compliments over their conscious motivations. Moral people all too often *enforce* their morality, showing that they were really interested in power, not goodness. And morality, as a kind of codification, is a degeneration of goodness, which is not a code but an attribute of good people. People do long for codes when they have lost their way and are living in some form of wilderness, and they do make rituals out of the codes when they have become even further confused, a situation usually marked by much debating and schisming over the meaning of the codes. The Ten Commandments, with their history of coming in lightning to an uprooted and confused people and then becoming a lightning rod for institutional faction, are a dramatic religious example. In the secular realm, psychoanalysis has certainly had its rule-boundedness and its schismatics.

But what is it to do nothing and yet leave nothing undone? It is much easier to grasp what a sage says no to than what she says yes to.

"I don't think 'not doing' means doing *nothing*," Faith said one afternoon while we were taking a walk near a still, shining lake. "I think it means not doing with force; it means doing without force. What Lao-tse's poems show again and again is that force begets force; forceful actions bring about forceful reactions, and pretty soon all fall down. That's what happened in *The Iliad*. But Lao-tse was not recommending a turn-the-other-cheek approach. And he wasn't recommending sitting on a mountaintop detached from the world. *Wu wei* is not passivity. He was talking about leading people, about getting them to want what you want, not by force but by example, by being who you are. The model is the person who doesn't go along with force, who cannot be forced."

Faith told me as we walked that when she was a student at Bryn Mawr she had written a paper about *wu wei* that showed how the science fiction writer Ursula K. Le Guin created a Taoist sageling character in her *The Left Hand of Darkness*. A few days later, I read the novel—which is brilliant, stunning—and met in it Genly Ai, an interplanetary traveler who becomes a sage as he learns to understand and trust a character named Estraven. Like all the people on his planet, Estraven is both male and female, creative and receptive. He holds to a religion without institution, priests, codes or creeds; he practices "nusuth," which Le Guin wittily calls "no matter" (rather than "not doing").

Genly Ai is very advanced in his political thinking—he is the Envoy for the Ekumen, an organization for uniting all the peoples of all the planets—and he is capable of Mindspeak, a cherishment language that goes directly from unconscious to unconscious, heart to heart, telepathically, without words. But Genly Ai does not know how to receive Estraven's commitment to the Ekumen or his friendship; he is threatened by Estraven's man-woman sexuality and his passion. Genly Ai and Estraven have to make a journey together across a treacherous glacier, a climate without warm wind; they have to make sacrifices for each other and spend many hours sitting close to each other inside a warm tent, conversing, before Genly Ai is able to come into receptivity and to accept a female part of himself—to know himself as psychologically man-and-woman, encompassing. Then he grows stronger in the face of the fear and hatred directed at his ideal, the Ekumen, the universal democracy. When he has become more receptive, his ice floes dissolve, he is serene.

Entering into the world that Ursula Le Guin imagined helped me imagine *wu wei*—the ideal got less fictional, realer. And it made me sense something aggressive that I couldn't quite grasp in myself, which was making this "not doing" ideal strange to me. "I love the ideal," I told Faith, "but I am also haunted by photos—assassinated advocates of nonviolence lying in pools of blood. Defenseless vicitms. The not-doer seems so vulnerable to attack. And Estraven does, after all, have to get killed for his political convictions. He does not survive."

"Lao-tse's poems do not say "never use force" or "never respond to force with force." There is no moral code. He talks about generals in war, for example, who use force because they make the judgment that, in a given circumstance, it is necessary; but then, he says, they stop, never glorying in what they have done and never going one step further than they have judged necessary. To abuse Hektor's body would be unthinkable for a Taoist sage. There is a beautiful line about the proper attitude for a person who must use force:

He enters a battle gravely,
with sorrow and great compassion,
as if he were attending a funeral.

(31)

A person who has this attitude toward aggression can absorb other people's aggression. That is the only way to prevent other people from acting aggressively toward you or to keep from getting caught up in spirals of aggression meeting aggression."

"So, you're suggesting that therapists practice *wu wei*, too. Absorb aggression in order to cure aggression? Be receptive in order to make receptivity possible for the patient."

"Yes," Faith said, "but it isn't only aggression that you need to absorb, it's all kinds of agitation, fear, anxiety, and all the sexual desire that is entangled with these. With Betsy, it was more fear of abandonment that I had to absorb than aggression; with your Mary, there was more aggression, maybe a kind of fear of being killed or ceasing to be—a fear of almost psychotic proportions."

I suddenly felt hesitant. "We are going to have to face up to the fact that we know there are different sorts of patients and different pathologies, different kinds of unreceptivity. It's so entrancing to have a general cause, 'lack of receptivity.' We wouldn't be the first people to think we held a key to the mysteries. A General Psychological Theory."

"But while you're being cautious, don't lose the path. We were following the implications of Freud's idea about transference as a manifestation of the ego instinct, weren't we? A repetition but also a developmental story." Then Faith added: "You do not get an analytic patient to change by chiseling away noisily, iron upon rock; you get her to change by having been analyzed yourself. Then you are the warm and gentle wind, the water that wears away stone."

Faith then heard me out on my anxiety about what makes it

possible to be a punching pillow, to practice *wu wei*, without getting fatigued or hardened, without being aggressive back. "Well, look what you do," she replied. "You get your analyst to help you. Then you get me to listen to you. And there are other ways—getting supervision and consultation, going to groups, presenting at case conferences. And you'll go turn it somehow into writing, which will sustain you, too, when there are readers. While you cherish your patients, you have to get cherished."

She was certainly right. There is a basic rule: the cherisher must be cherished. But I told her that I also think there must be a particular ego interest—a self-preservative interest or growth interest in the broad sense we had been considering—in being receptive. Being receptive to a patient's world, the world as it comes through the patient, has to feel in my interest. I was thinking that there must be, paradoxically, something protective or preservative about receiving aggression in this *wu wei* way. It is part of receiving *all*—good and bad, joyful and sorrowful, pleasurable and painful. It's as though you say: "I want you to grow, and I want to grow, so I will receive, absorb, your growth inhibition and turn it to good use, for both of us." Absorption leads to expansion. That's what we were calling resymbolization.

Psychoanalysis has a concept, projective identification, that seems to us to refer to the defensive process this absorption interrupts. People throw their aggression—project it—onto others, but then, when they feel that aggression bouncing back at them, they cannot recognize it as their own. They think that other people hate them, not that they have provoked the hatred or caused other people to become agitated as the recipients of their hatred. But if an analyst can cherishingly absorb the projected aggression, hold it, *wu wei*, the patient can eventually come to recognize it as her own, resymbolize it. What comes from the patient filters through your own cherishment core so that it can be dissolved, melted, loosened, and eventually turned into something expansive, growth producing. This idea seems to be expressed in one of the Lao-tse poems where he stresses that the world-animating Tao is the female, receptive principle.

The Tao is called the Great Mother:
empty yet inexhaustible,
it gives birth to infinite worlds.
It is always present within you.
You can use it any way you want.

(6)

The poem put me in a reflective frame of mind, and I told Faith how striking it seems to me that in all the great Axial Age texts that we found ourselves drawn to for thinking about cherishment, there are symbols of "the whole world" or all worlds visible and invisible. Intricate catalogues, encyclopedias, compendia, cosmogonies, genealogies. The *I Ching* itself is a cosmography, and a catalogue of all possible human situations. When Thetis cherishes Akhilleus in *The Iliad*, she gives him armor and a shield that has crafted on it an image of the whole world: a cosmographic rim around a multidimensional icon of domestic and agricultural scenes and battle scenes, weddings and funerals. Pages of poetry interrupt the flow of the narrative to present this symbol of everything, everybody, everywhere. The shield, like the other kinds of holistic symbols, is a protection, a talisman, a mandala, and a model of The Receptive, the earth, as the carrier of all things, good and evil. The more you are able to be receptive to all things, the less any one thing or one assault has a way to get a hook into you, disturb you, by standing out. And it is as though the poets have a cultural function to create for communities what individuals have created in themselves: images or ego ideals or autosymbolisms of their receptivities. These are the nourishment that prevent people from developing lack of receptivity; the containers of the communal growth principle.

The night after this exchange, I had a dream, an autosymbolism, that told me how far I had really come on this part of our journey. In this dream of development and obstacle, the *wu wei* conversation mingled with a piece of my history that I had told Faith over lunch. When I was thirty-four and had just finished a five-year project of writing a biography of my teacher, Hannah Arendt, her friend and literary executor, Mary McCarthy, created a big storm for me. Mary McCarthy had the right to refuse me permission to quote from Hannah Arendt's papers—in effect, to doom the project—if she disapproved of my manuscript, which she did. My writing, she said, was amateurish and awkward. To fire off a letter of protest had been my first impulse, an impulse I had followed in many other challenging situations. But then I waited, wrote back calmly, enlisted others to talk to her, waited further, and she finally came around, relented. I think a flare of competitive craziness had lit up in her—she didn't want someone other than herself to be able to tell Hannah Arendt's story; but then the flare fizzled out and she settled down into the generous friend she usually was. In my dream, Mary McCarthy, using my analytic patient Mary's favorite fantasy weapon, a knife, set upon some defenseless innocents:

> **A group of young women dressed in the way my students favor at the moment—huge black leather Army boots, bare legs, tiny cut-off jeans, halters letting show silver belly button decorations and tattoos, just like the young woman who served Faith and me our lunch today—were being attacked by Mary McCarthy. She was holding a knife up over her head; and she was on a monumental scale, like that Delacroix painting of Liberty Leading the People. But she was against the people. I came up behind**

her and adroitly took the knife out of her hand. I had a
deeply satisfied feeling about how I had disarmed her, and
I expected someone to praise me, too. I don't know who.
J [my analyst]? But when I woke up I was quite anxious
about having dreamt a need for praise.

Faith teased me a good deal about this dream. "You haven't at
all gotten over your anxiety about needing praise. Still expecting
rejection. You're not a tranquil sage. But you're making progress
through your analysis on disarming aggressive people—maybe
including yourself—by being who you are. *Wu wei.*"

Chapter 4

When Cherishment Is Missing

For [an] explanation of the origin of infantile anxiety I have to thank a three year old boy whom I once heard calling out in a dark room: "Auntie! Speak to me because it is so dark." His aunt answered him: "What good would that do? You can't see me." "That doesn't matter," replied the child, "if anyone speaks it gets light." Thus what he was afraid of was not the dark but the absence of someone he loved; and he could feel sure of being soothed as soon as he had evidence of that person's presence.

—FREUD, *THREE ESSAYS ON THE THEORY OF SEXUALITY*

*A*s we thought more about *wu wei*, and practiced it more in our therapeutic work, Faith and I began to think of "not doing" as the adult version of fulfilled childhood *amae*. Without effort, overcoming, or winning, the child whose expectation of love is fulfilled has a certain power, and when poets express nostalgia for a powerful beauty and innocence of childhood, this seems to be what they mean. Like Lao-tse:

> *He who is in harmony with the Tao*
> *Is like a newborn child.*

We found this idea brilliantly developed in an essay that the great Sinologist Richard Wilhelm, the *I Ching*'s German translator, wrote on "The Art of Living." The essay ends with an explication of the hexagram "Inner Truth" where, Wilhelm was convinced, the *I Ching* speaks like a child the secret of "the art of action," or right conduct, which is not a triumphing but a capacity to disarm those who are bigger, potentially harmful, overbearing. The child is helpless and dependent, but also powerful. As Wilhelm puts it, the child's "joy of the heart, internal joy, is preserved intact, and inner trust is offered to one and all."

> The human being is the weakest of all creatures, for nature gave him neither laniary teeth, nor horns; neither claws nor armor plating. Helplessly and defenselessly he is born into a world of monsters, helplessly he lies there . . . No other creature except man is that unfit, is that dependent on the world; on external kindness . . . The smiling eyes of a child are more powerful than any malice, any anger. Such eyes disarm even the most depraved, and the tiger does not bite the man who knows how to

approach him in this way. This then is the art of action. It pre-supposes being childlike in its highest sense, it presupposes that the joy of the heart, internal joy, is preserved intact, and inner trust is offered to one and all. Such trust is accompanied by dig-nity . . . [This] is reminiscent of the boy in [Goethe's] Novelle, who tames the lion with joy and therefore represents a person confronted by cosmic energies. And this constitutes the secret of proper conduct, conduct as the art of living.

As Richard Wilhelm's allusion to Goethe's *Novelle* indicates, he did not think of this vision of the dignified "not doing" and thus right-acting child as Eastern. Not long after we read Wil-helm's essay, we found the idea articulated quite clearly by William Blake. In his *Songs of Innocence and Experience: Shewing the Two Contrary States of the Human Soul,* Blake shows joy of the heart as "Infant Joy," a delicate two-stanza duet between a new-born and a cherisher (who is depicted as the mother in the hand-colored engravings with which Blake enwrapped the poem):

> *I have no name*
> *I am but two days old.* —
> *What shall I call thee?*
> *I happy am*
> *Joy is my name,* —
> *Sweet joy befalls thee!*

> *Pretty joy!*
> *Sweet joy but two days old.*
> *Sweet joy I call thee:*
> *Thou dost smile.*
> *I sing the while*
> *Sweet joy befall thee.*

"Infant Joy"—the serene condition of being able to banish any-thing but joy by saying "Joy is my name"—is paired with the poem from *Songs of Experience* called "Infant Sorrow," in which only a lonely, angry infant speaks. With the poem of cherishment and conversation, Blake paired the poem of isolation and unreceptivity:

> *My mother groand! my father wept,*
> *Into the dangerous world I leapt:*
> *Helpless, naked, piping loud:*
> *Like a fiend hid in a cloud.*

> *Struggling in my father's hands:*
> *Striving against my swaddling bands:*
> *Bound and weary I thought best*
> *To sulk upon my mother's breast.*

Why did the mother groan? the father weep? Why did this newborn struggle and strive? Blake insists that the world is dangerous; being born is a leap out of the womb's safety for the baby and a leap into pain for the mother. From the beginning there is frustration to be overcome, contained. But the frustration of this baby is specific—he *thinks* and *decides* to sulk, which means to turn in on himself, because he is not the other baby: he did not spontaneously name himself Joy and immediately hear back "Sweet joy befalls thee!" The uncherished, experienced baby puts up a first ego defense of unreceptivity: "Here there is danger and loss, and I must protect myself, close off."

We began to wonder if our conversations about our patients and about how therapy works implied that there are but "two contrary states of the human soul"—joy and sorrow epitomizing them. Innocence and Experience, or No Fear and Fear. Being undefendedly, receptively dependent and being anxiously, unreceptively dependent. Had we arrived by a very long route at Blake's simple poetic credo?

We were certainly on the territory of Takeo Doi's theoretical credo. Looking again at *The Anatomy of Dependence*, we realized that in his bare, unevocative language, Takeo Doi did posit but two contrary states of the human soul. He named the sorrowful, experienced state as it appears in adults *shinkeishitsu*, which is an amalgam of anxiety neurosis, a good deal of obsessionality, and a hypochondriacal self-preoccupation serving as a cry for help and care. Throughout the century, *shinkeishitsu* has been considered the basic and most common form of neurosis in Japan. Of such patients, Doi says: "Their primary wish to be loved had suffered critical frustration . . . This, however, did not necessarily lead to the repression of the wish to be loved. Instead, it seemed that the anger or direct hostility due to the frustration was usually repressed in the service of keeping the original wish to be loved alive. Yet the early frustration led to manifold distortions of the wish and to a continuing fear of further frustration. The symptoms of various kinds could be interpreted as the intrapsychic working-over of early traumatic experience."

The simplest kinds of intrapsychic workings-over that Doi studied can be seen in young children. *Suneru* is to pout or be petulant—to sulk upon the mother's breast. A more smoldering sense of injury and desire for revenge characterizes a frustrated child whose state is *uramu*, to harbor a grudge or to be resentful. An even more angry child gets defiant in actions or speech, uncooperative: *futekusareru* is to assert a defiant independence when a dependency desire has been thwarted or when the child does not permit himself or herself to express the desire—a self-thwarting. To act in a perversely negative and suspicious way, becoming obstinate and sometimes peculiar from repeatedly unsuccessful attempts to *amaeru*, is *hinekureru*. Doi saw these basic reactive states as the foundations for later, more characterological and more complex states. The little pouty sulkers, the grudge holders, the defiant ones, and the stubborn, self-absorbed no-sayers all go off in different developmental directions from the same start in frustration of *amae*.

FREUD'S PSYCHOPATHOLOGY
AND DOI'S

In *The Anatomy of Dependence*, Takeo Doi constructed a schema of illnesses in the form of a tree: there is the root condition, frustration of the ego-instinctual expectation to be loved; then manifold derivatives that result from manifold intrapsychic workings-over of that root condition. So the forms of illness he took for granted certainly look different than those in the Freudian psychopathology, which is a psychopathology of the sexual instincts. But as we thought about them, these seemed to us complementary modes of thinking and assessing, one aimed primarily at the sexual story, one at the cherishment story, which we see as intertwined. We found ourselves asking again, as we had over Freud's and Doi's visions of The Baby, Why not both?

Takeo Doi's tree-like schema of illness types is wonderfully simple, and Freud's terribly complex. When the libido theory dominated psychoanalytic thinking, Freud's well-known oral, anal, and phallic-genital stages were each imagined as station stops at which the train of development could either get halted or get backed up. To use the technical terms: diseases represented fixations at stages, or regressions to earlier stages or combinations of both fixations and regressions on these lines. Obsessional neurosis, for example, was understood as a regression from a phallic-genital stage that had been uncertainly reached back toward the anal stage, where a child had developed some degree of fixation. An obsessional neurotic could not then fully move along to the genital stage again or move into mature sexuality. Later, Freud also talked about stages in the differentiation of ego and superego from the id. In this theory, the obsessional neurotic was somebody who was "anal," but who was also dominated by his superego. In a third way of describing illnesses, Freud emphasized conflicts over love objects, which tend to concentrate into different forms at the different stages—the pre-Oedipal period, the Oedipus complex, the dissolution of the Oedipus complex.

Weaving together these types of theory, Freud described his three basic categories of illness—hysteria, obsessional neurosis, and narcissistic neurosis—and three corresponding character types. The hysterics, like Dora, were, Freud thought, dominated by their sexual instinctual lives, their ids, and characterized by physical symptoms—from fainting to nervous coughs to compulsive masturbation to paralysis of their limbs—that virtually substituted for their sexual lives. Obsessional neurotics, on the other hand, with their rituals and fixed behaviors and repetitive thoughts, are so superego dominated that their self-chastisements take over their sexual lives, banishing their feelings, giving them a robotic quality, a peculiar insensitivity along with their usually very striking intelligence.

About his third type of illness, "narcissistic neurosis," Freud was less clear, more puzzled, because he found it difficult to assess the different forms that a faulty connection with reality can take, and where to draw the line between a neurotic disturbance of connection and a psychotic break with reality. As psychoanalysis has developed since Freud, and as analysts have treated more psychotics and near-psychotics (the so-called Borderlines, like my Mary), it has become apparent that there are different sorts of narcissistic disturbances, and study of these has become key to both theory and practice. In the neuroses, love objects are assumed to be relatively constant, and the ever-fluctuating drives and conflicts over objects are the sources of trouble. But in the psychoses and borderline conditions, the objects themselves and the ego's ability to connect to them are understood as the patient's problem.

It is particularly for these more disturbed, ego-fragmented people who have trouble establishing object relations in the first place, or holding objects in mind and heart with any constancy, that Doi's reflections on the effects of lack of cherishment make such immediate sense. Sometimes love objects do not exist for them at all, and they live quite incapable of loving, bunkered inside themselves, terrorized, cut off—in our terms, completely unreceptive to cherishing, as they were quite uncherished as children. Fear of self-fragmentation rises up constantly. They say they aren't human, or real; they feel they don't exist or will soon cease to be.

Psychotic patients make their thwarted expectation to be loved vividly apparent, but they cannot tell its story, much less voice their disappointment. It is walled off in them, repressed, or locked into the preverbal level at which it began. A transference can form in therapy, but only with enormous work can a therapist uncover the buried expectation to be loved and help the psychotic speak about it. The danger of repeated loss is too great. By contrast, the experience of infant sorrow in people who are neurotic is not so complete, so traumatic. You can hear on their infant sorrow *amae* channel the imploring: "Care for me! Make me feel warm and safe! Nourish me! Grow me—help me develop, help me over my helplessness!" And you can hear, intertwined with this, messages on the sexual-instinctual channel that Freud was so alert to and that his psychopathology maps: "Give me pleasure! Excite me, and let me excite you! Make me feel good and special and first in your attention! Send me right out of myself—let me be ecstatic—over my limits, or back to my original narcissism, when there seemed to be no limits."

The same objects, the same people, can, of course be the objects of these different drives or needs and wishes, and the drives are not so simply distinguishable as these expressions of their demands imply. But we were compelled by this way of thinking, listening, and we decided to pursue it by constructing some portraits—like short clips—of our patients, using the complex Freudian schemes but looking into them in *amae* terms, with the simpler "two contrary states of the human soul" in mind. We experimented with trying to construct Cherishment Diagnostics, looking for the underlying cherishment stories, especially in dreams and fantasies, that typically go with the Freudian neurotic types of illness and character. To hear the full range of human expressions of drives and thwarting of drives, we felt, our listening channels had to be as intertwined as the drives themselves are. Then we realized, too, that another way of describing what it means to be *wu wei* is to say that in "not doing" you are receptive to the full range of intertwined drives in yourself, so that you can meet people in their full complexity, denying them nothing of their complexity, disarming them with your own openness.

SHORT CLIPS AND COMPARISONS

We started by revisiting Sarah and Mary, who were both quite obsessional, although Sarah is more of a sulky pouter and Mary, much more narcissistically injured, is vengeful. Both Sarah, who got stuck coming into the world and then kept getting stuck in her childhood and adolescence, and Mary, who raged at me for leaving her to go on my vacation as she had raged at her mother for leaving her as a child, obscured and controlled their cherishment desires with icy, harsh regulations and character rigidities. They pounded themselves into submission, held themselves tightly in, stripped their lives down into ascetic modes—as Faith's self-critical Betsy did in her simpler way. Both allowed themselves only the most limited sexual gratifications, which had a masturbatory quality to them, marked by fear of any submission to another, any relaxation. Mary always chose alcoholic, abusive men whom she pushed away when they failed her—or even before they got a chance to try not to fail themselves. The harshnesses both Sarah and Mary practiced were designed to keep them from dependency and involvement with other people, and yet they were driven by their dependency needs, their expectations to be loved.

Each has an image in which she keeps her *amae* embalmed. Mary's is a game that she used to play as a child. She calls it "My Perfect Life." Originally, this was a "pretend" in which she fantasized that her mother took her dirty pajamas, put them in the washing machine, and then presented them to Mary, who, when she put them on, expected to be suddenly very happy, all clean and warm. Later, it became a game in which she made a little plastic figure, a spaceman, sail his spaceship down to this planet, landing among a crowd of little plastic figures, Mary's tribe, where he made everybody happy. Later still, in high school, Mary herself would sit making a list of all the beautiful things she would like to have in her beautiful, clean house, her House Beautiful; she expected that the items would suddenly materialize in House Beautiful, and she would be happy, with a perfect family around her.

This kind of magical thinking or fantasizing, with all its emphasis on cleanliness and perfect order, is different than that typical of more narcissistic people, whose efforts to get cherishment so often turn into efforts to get other people to serve them. I have a patient, a man now sixty-five years old and beset with various debilitating medical problems, who is completely dedicated to satisfying his own desires, especially his desires for women who will serve him. He uses people—uses them up—so forcefully and with so little awareness of them or of his tactics that when he found himself alone, all his slaves having fled his tyranny to the best of their abilities, he was stunned, mystified, frightened. His sadism is unknown to him, he emphasizes again and again his good character, his uprightness and superiority, which he wants me to ratify. But this hard, driving, and driven man also revealed to me one day that he finds himself—it seems so odd to him—haunted by a scene from his early adolescence. He is lying on a chaise longue in the garden at his parents' house, quietly reading a book—in his memory, it is Hugo's *Les Misérables*. In the kitchen, his mother and a maid are preparing dinner, his cherishment meal, chatting quietly, delicately moving to and fro, and he feels that he is connected to them, he is with them, there is no miserableness "and all is right in the world." In this fantasy his mother is inside him, he has assimilated her and has her being just as he wants her to be, quiet and busily preparing his meal in the next room. This is exactly what she was not. In reality, she was frantically attentive to him: she intruded on him constantly, crowded in on him, expecting excellent behavior of him at every moment, narcissistically invested in him, her perfect son, expecting him to go to Harvard and bring glory to her.

Faith and I compared this man with another of my patients, also a very narcissistic character, but much less exploitative and manipulative than the chaise longue fantasizer. This performing artist had tried as a child to please his mother, to win her love—and especially to win it away from an older brother, her favored son—by performing. He wanted her to be proud of him. In his adolescence, he got a big break in his business—he was commissioned for a solo performance in a very prestigious place, a storied hall. He invited his mother, but at the last moment she had something else that she had to do. Just before he was to go onstage, he received a telegram from her. Then, during the performance, he suddenly lost his place—a whole section of his script disappeared from his memory and from the performance. He was humiliated, shamed, and the entire direction of his work changed afterwards; he reoriented his creativity, scaled back his ambitions, and began to drink heavily, laying down a track into later alcoholism. But he also developed a fantasy. He is a rescuer of women who are split, whose performances in life are interrupted by outbreaks of mental illness, women who are dissociative. By healing women, he imagines, he will heal himself, get over the wound to his narcissism that his mother's nonappearance at the performance represented or summarized. But he is never quite able to carry out his project, and never quite able to succeed in his art, either. He never really receives any cherishment from his women. They are too dangerous, and he will not let me touch the symptom that represents his isolation. He, too, dissociates, disappears, does not show up.

Then there is a woman who is locked in self-regard. Her life is, she advertises, perfect; she has accomplished everything she wanted to do in her career and now organizes her day around cultivating her body and spirit. The patient cannot walk by a mirror without checking her body; she cannot greet me at my office door without checking herself in the glass that covers the prints in the hall. It is as though she is ceaselessly saying "Mirror, Mirror, on the wall, who is the fairest—and the bestest—of them all?" But when she asks the people in her life to render confirmation of her fitness and they get sarcastic, she is devastated. This is her big problem. She is really in therapy to cure others of their lack of appreciation, or to break off with them if they cannot be cured. So impossible is it for her to acknowledge that her life might have any blemish that she cannot hear her boyfriend's efforts to *amaeru* her, to get her attention and sympathy when he feels unsatisfied. As a child she had won her mother's love, but she was never secure in it. She might at any moment be bested, and she might at any moment be punished.

Considering these patients and others, we tried to make a formulation in terms that combine the cherishment lexicon and the Freudian one. As a type, the narcissist, we said, is someone who cannot recognize an "other," who acknowledges no one as "not-me." Originally, the narcissist responded to his or her chief caregiver—usually the mother—by assimilating her mentally, by swallowing her up and having her inside, where she is not separate, not independently existing, where she can be just as the narcissist wishes her to be. Freudians speak of the narcissist's omnipotence. Such a person then becomes almost completely unreceptive because he or she is filled up, a complete little world, a self-sufficient unit. The basic attitude toward other people is "You must do things my way" or "You must be as I wish." When the wish is unsatisfied, the narcissist takes a crash in self-esteem.

What we see in our narcissistic patients' histories is usually a mother who was very narcissistically involved with her child, never able to let him develop freely, no matter whether she was physically present or operating from offstage while she physically neglected him. She was an overwhelming mother, imposing to her baby, agitated in her handling of her baby. The mother also tended to expect the baby's love and sacrifice of self, to expect fealty. She assumed her baby could love like a little adult, she promoted precocity, and then was disappointed when the baby loved like a baby—that is, when the baby expected to be indulgently loved. The baby feels the need to get away from this intrusive, boundary-less mother, and does so not by flight but by assimilation, by taking her in, containing her. However, the budding narcissist also disidentifies strenuously with the mother-within, or from those features of her that were frightening. In effect, then, the narcissist rejects part of himself, the mother-within part. Faith has a patient who forcefully proclaims "I just don't want to get sucked in" over any situation that seems to her messy, slovenly, depressed or depressing; she refuses to be touched by anyone else's pain and stands in great self-righteousness before "the weak," like a philanthropist who would like to be praised for generosity without ever coming out from behind her checkbook. And this "the weak" is her mother-within, whom she will not touch and tries all the time to devalue and eject.

Things feel different to the baby who will become obsessional. Although sometimes a baby of this sort will be reacting to chaotic, overstimulating caregivers, more often he or she had a caregiver who caused a great deal of stress with cold, perfectionist, mechanical, even mechanistic handling. The caretaker overmanaged or micromanaged every detail of the baby's existence or neglectfully presumed the baby's ability to act as an independent agent, taking care of itself. In one way or another, obsessional caretakers dust and polish their babies rather than cherishing them. Particularly in the anal stage, as the Freudians have long noted, the future obsessional is made to feel very internally agitated over cleanliness, order, regularity—and this agitation may live on in rather hysterical physical symptoms, particularly of the bowel. There is to be no indulgence, but rather a kind of spare, cold discipline. Unable to control the internal agitation such a regime creates, the child turns to external regulations, either those generated by the caregiver or others suited to the obsessional's circumstances. Rigid and repetitive behaviors or thoughts become normal. The obsessional hears a voice inside his head (in Freudian language, a superego) that reads off these regulations: you should do this, and this, and this, and this other thing! Immediately! But often the voice goes on so dunningly, so insistently, that the agitation it was meant to still is stirred up all over again.

A kind of psychic engineering keeps the obsessional controlled. But each day seems to bring a bombardment of unsettling events. New or stronger defenses are always needed. At the extreme, the person becomes paranoid and imagines that a host of enemies is creating his agitation, infiltrating him, polluting him, just as they are haunting his government, his church, his workplace, his club. The rules and regulations make receptivity impossible, and even the idea of being receptive—sometimes even the idea of being touched—fills him with panic. Fears of being found out, being discovered to be bad, ruinous, clamor in the obsessional, who then hovers over all the people in his or her life, discovering any little fault they may have, pestering, dusting and polishing them. The person cannot imagine that routines of order and cleanliness are not the norm for everybody: "My wife told me," such a man said in horror, "that she did not put toilet paper down on the toilet seat at the hotel where we were staying, and I thought my heart would stop." Very commonly, he just says of others in disbelief, "I cannot imagine how anyone could behave that way" (which is not his way).

In therapy, the key task with a narcissistic patient is to get him or her to hear—to listen genuinely and receptively to the people around, first and foremost the therapist. Therapeutic *wu wei* with such a patient is not being erased or retaliating with erasure; not letting yourself be available for the narcissistic patient's gobbling up of anyone and everyone and not defending yourself with gobbling—or with running away from enslavement. Faith was disconcerted and educated in the difficulties of getting to the first step in this project by a very bright, attractive, but taut, almost gaunt young businesswoman, who was quite talkative, eager for help with her relationships, which always—like her mother's—turned out badly. The patient looked right at Faith as she talked, but then, after half a dozen sessions spent revealing archives of detail about the men she had been involved with, suddenly said, "I can't remember, what is your name?" Faith was a blank to her. She was, she said, very worried about turning into her mother, a tough, abrasive woman—but she clearly already had this woman within. She had taken her in during the years when the mother, who was divorced, frightened, lonely, brought a troop of boyfriends through the house, one after another. The young daughter cowered behind the couch as these nameless strangers came and went and her mother got more and more despairing. The patient was struggling against her self in the therapy—which was this desperate, lonely mother-within.

Cherishment

We find that the initial project in therapy with an obsessional person has to be to promote the discovery of the feelings that have been layered over with ritualistic and repetitious actions and thoughts. Slowly, the project becomes to help the patient realize that the actions and thoughts are defenses against feelings of being dirty, poisonous, horrible, ruinous, culpable; and to understand that these defenses are ultimately—in *amae* terms—against being in relationships with people. Reconstruction of the way the defenses came into existence is necessary, but the obsessional is ahistorical; the past is just past, over, not at play in the present, unremembered. All that matters is the present, and whatever episode the patient is talking about at the time. There is no big picture; no forest, only trees. People, including the therapist, are very flat and without inner lives, so the therapy has to encourage another look, a receptivity to the complexities and nuances—as opposed to the surface details—of life. An obsessional who has not come to therapy with some ability to own up to weaknesses and some ability to grasp that people back off from being dusted and polished and criticized all the time, is almost impossible to treat. Mary, who attacked me so forcefully before my vacation, has no feeling for her own rage, or for how I would experience it. My therapeutic *wu wei* has to be for not getting angry back, not letting the anger she tries to put in me make me angry, and for keeping my hope for her future focused on the capacity for love and empathy that she does have, which she can summon for the children she works with, little versions of herself. Mary can say angrily, "I am a very sick person and you made me so," while at the same time being incredulous that I can think she contributes anything to the problems that inevitably spring up in her adult relationships. My *wu wei* says: I know you have feelings—here are the angry ones!—and I await the loving ones as calmly as I can.

Faith had the fascinating experience of working with a super-smart eight-year-old latency child, a child at just the age when obsessional thoughts and actions generally make their first appearance, as they did with Mary. She could see Amy building up all kinds of fantasy places and rules and regulations to keep in check a towering rage she felt toward her mother—a very remote, severely disturbed woman—and her little brother, who got all the attention the mother could muster because he was ill. In her fantasy world, Amy was in charge of both of these disappointing people as well as of her Teddy Bear and a whole gallery of pretty starfish and butterflies, while in the world of her home and school she was painfully uncommanding: shy, unrelated, frail, and now and again explosive, she could not tool around eagerly, curiously, as latency children typically do. The main sign that the therapy was helping came when—after months of letting the rage out in Faith's office, and talking, talking, talking, as she could not at home—Amy began to report excitedly that she was making friends at school. "Allison is just my *second*-best friend," she announced a little haughtily about the first most popular girl in the whole third grade.

In both obsessionals and narcissists (and the two groups are very overlapped, there are many obsessional-narcissistic mixes) the lack of receptivity to cherishment is like a stone wall, and it easily drives all the people around such people into states of agitation and distress. Neither do these types respond to others' needs for cherishment, although they may be—especially narcissists—very charming and socially adept, or—especially obsessionals—very earnest and considerate in a rule-obeying, etiquette-oriented way. They are *pro forma*. Narcissists make their loved ones, the ones who do not sacrifice themselves completely to serving the narcissist, lose control and become enraged because they cannot get a hearing. Obsessionals make their loved ones rebel into acts of sabotage directed against the obsessional's rules. But hysterics are different.

Hysterics are hyperreceptive in some ways and unreceptive in others. Somatically, most hysterics seem to be permeable; they respond strongly to changes in their worlds of everything from light to temperature to scents. Their bodily receptivity is, then, reflected in their proclivity toward bodily symptoms; their bodies are hypersensitive to their own emotional states. They are also very susceptible to other people's emotional states and unconscious communications, so they seem to be "psychic," paranormally attuned, and they gravitate toward all kinds of esoteric lores and mysteries. Therapy is a mystery rite. But they are also very fearful, given to phobias, and expectant of disaster. Their anxiety levels are constantly high, and they cannot relax. Actually or symbolically, they duck and cringe. When hysterics receive an unconscious communication from another person, they frequently assume that it means—no matter what its content—that they have done something wrong. They feel implicated in everything that goes on around them. If a group on the other side of a room from a hysteric is having a conversation, she assumes she must be somehow the subject of it. The hysteric's world is as full of intrigue as the obsessional's is of conspiracies and the narcissist's is of mirrors.

Chrissy, for example, an attractive African-American thirty-year-old, was the fourth of eight children, born close together, who completely overwhelmed their depressed, alcoholic mother and their strangely morbid, obsessional, theologically preoccupied father. She was taken care of haphazardly, as much by her siblings—most of whom became alcoholics like the mother—and by neighbors as by the parents. Her brothers, as love starved as she, fondled and harassed her through her adolescence, and she threw herself early into feelingless promiscuity in search of attention, sexual definition, direction. In therapy, she found it excruciating to talk about her sexual history. Months passed while she gave me, piece by little piece, the story of how she was raped at age sixteen. She was consumed with shame and thought herself totally worthless. Whenever she felt her dependency on me strongly, she would rush into an erotic triangle or make her relationship with a professionally preoccupied, obsessional married man many years her senior explosively complex. Her Oedipus complex was everywhere to be seen as she sexualized her world, but the missing infant cherishment was the most persistent theme in the transference, where she consistently fantasized that she would take care of me. Dependency was her great desire, and her dread.

A hysterical person is usually, we think, the child of a depressed caretaker who was inconsistent or of a situation in which there were two caretaker figures, one remote and the other not. The baby who will be a hysteric was sometimes cherished and, more often, treated with a kind of oblivion—perhaps warm, but unconnected, from behind a veil of depression. The inconsistency was baffling. We also notice—and this is a common observation in the psychoanalytic literature—how frequently hysterics have had in childhood some kind of physical trauma or illness or abuse, and how this is the "bad" contrast in their world-view to a "good" of healing, health, genuine care. The hysteric is always seeking the warmth of the warm moments, and feeling chilled by the change, the loss, so she baffles the people she pursues with her stop-and-start manner, which seems like teasing. But hysterics also, not being able to read very well the difference between attention and abuse, tend to pursue people who are hurters, who are abusive. In diverse ways, the hysteric will try to communicate her expectation to be loved bodily: by being sexually seductive, by being physically ill or eating disordered, by imitating the loved one's body, by costuming. But all of these bodily forms are also means of armoring against disappointment; they are the efforts of a thin-skinned or permeable person to add a skin of protection. "It's like clothes—they cling on you."

Working with a hysteric, a therapist must resist the seductiveness, the endless drawing of everyone into entanglements, crises, upsets, uproars, temper tantrums. The therapeutic *wu wei* is "not doing" the hysteric's scene, not taking a role in the drama. But, at the same time, the therapist must be able to cherish the hungry and hurt baby. The hysteric needs to be helped to understand that she is not a bad person who has been rejected because of her badness; or that she is not at fault or faulty by nature, by curse, or by some kind of bodily legacy or karma. If the hysteric plays the role in his or her family, as is common, of the scapegoat, the one who takes on all the family illness and trouble, the one everybody else finds inadequate or difficult, the therapist needs to help show how this is a "family systems" problem. There has to be an address to the hysteric's depression, which the hysterical patient I called Chrissy put in a nutshell by sighing, "My family is wacko, I am wacko, what more is there to say about it?" The therapist must not get drawn into this kind of despair or be in any way an abuser—a successor to previous abusers, including longed-for abusers.

Faith compared the hysteric to a ballet dancer who is equipped with exactly the hyperextension of the limbs that ballet requires aesthetically, but, by virtue of that unusual capacity—that receptivity to the possibilities of ballet—is very prone to injury. Her greatest gift is her greatest liability. The therapist can help the hysteric cultivate her receptivity so she becomes more discriminating; help her keep from channeling what she receives directly into her damaged sense of self, her idea that she is unworthy and deserves rejection.

When we had reviewed a range of our patients, Faith and I looked once more at Takeo Doi's psychopathology. We made a map out of Takeo Doi's catalogue of psychological conversions of *amaeru* and set it beside the three Freudian types, which was easy enough because Doi's pouting sulkers, grudge holders, defiant ones, and stubborn, self-absorbed no-sayers branch out into three basic sorts of people, although he does not have the complex Freudian developmental lines to show how the branchings come about. A first kind resort to *sumanai*, expression of apology, regret or remorse; they disguise their desire for cherishment with self-abnegation or self-reproach. These are Freud's hysterics. And when they are severely hysterical, they are in a mode Doi describes as *yakekuso ni naru*, to lose control and make histrionic or masochistic demands for pity, favor, or recognition.

Doi's hysterical type, like Freud's, is hypersensitive, and in this is very different from the obsessional type, whom Doi described as *toraware*, caught up, preoccupied. This obsessional person converts his fear of rejection into repetitive thoughts, excessive attention to his body and cleanliness, and vigilance in social situations—a kind of conspiracy mentality. Some obsessional types, Doi says, are recognizable as *kodawaru*, which is to be finicky, difficult, rigidly fixed on details, impossible to engage or get close to.

Doi's narcissists are *wagamama*, which means selfish or egocentric. They have grown up continuing to demand the indulgent love all babies wish for, expecting attention and entitlement, currying favor and special regard. Theirs is the general Japanese *amae* gone out of bounds and unrestrained, never either outgrown or transformed into a capacity to give cherishment.

Not surprisingly, the Doi type that is most different psychodynamically from the Freudian counterpart is the narcissist. Doi understood the *wagamama* person as a spoiled person, somebody who was inordinately indulged or indulged past the developmental point of no return. He is a man who never outgrows his tie with his cherishing mother—and in the Japanese context, this would also literally mean that he never leaves his mother behind but takes her into his family or (if he is the eldest son) brings his wife into her house. A Freudian narcissist might be a spoiled child, too; but he would be as much or more likely to be dangerously emotionally neglected and abused, even if the object of a great outward show of attention. But the key ingredient from Freud's viewpoint, since he believed in primary narcissism and Doi did not, is the narcissistic withdrawal of love from the world of objects into the self. Freud's narcissist has his mother within as a fantasy, Doi's is still at his mother's breast.

"MY FISH HAVE SUCH COMPLEX PROBLEMS"

No scheme for understanding and treating people should be used mechanically, and no scheme really can—if you are honest—be simply applied. People are too complicated, mixed. So, as we talked along and felt the ways in which combinations of "cherishment diagnostics" and Freudian character studies can be helpful diagnostically and in treatment, we found ourselves halting before an example of everything at once. We were pulled toward a patient of Faith's whom we'll call Roger.

Roger is hysterical, a fine example of histrionic and masochistic demandingness (*yakekuso ni naru*, in Doi's terms), but he also carries in him an encyclopedia of problems and traits. He has most of the neurotic features Freudian diagnostics can portray, while being, on that map, over toward the psychotic range, where object relations do not form or stabilize, where distinctions between self and other are blurry, shifty. There are people who wear their expectation to be loved not just on their hysterical sleeves but over their entire bodies, and he is one of these. His existence is like a long, drawn-out scream: "Take care of me!"

Faith had the startling experience of having Roger as her very first patient, and she came to observe him, to know him, and to care very deeply for him, all in wide-eyed amazement. As we talked about him, she wanted to write about him, and this is her rendering of his therapy story, and of how she heard and interpreted a vivid *amae* moment that came at the end of their work together.

Roger had a file at the community mental health center that was three quarters of an inch thick. But fortunately for both of us, the file was lost the day he and I arrived at my cramped, dingy little office: I was neither overwhelmed nor prejudiced by his documented history or the various diagnoses he carried. I just met him head-on.

And he went immediately into my unconscious. My first patient was the first of my patients to appear in my dream life—and I remember him now just as vividly in his dream incarnation as in reality. In my dream, he showed up deeply asleep, fetally curled up, on the couch in my den. My therapy gave him peace.

At my clinic, on the other hand, Roger had first appeared, thirty-five years old, tall, good-looking, fair skinned, and brightly blue-eyed, with his wife. I was faced immediately with a challenge, and had to decide what to do about the wife. From the way that Roger looked to his wife for every move he made, I decided it would be just as well to invite her, at least for the moment, to sit down.

Roger's wife was the tether that kept him in and of the world. He had to have her there, to help him, protect him, cherish him. But the wife was immediately pushed aside as he allowed himself to look at me and, with a convert's fervor, to attach himself to me. His story came pouring out, couched in his expectation that I was going to fix everything, take over his life.

Talking at a terrific pace, not very coherently, Roger presented the recent events that organize his attitude toward everything and everybody. The story had two parts, which somehow went together in his mind. In the first, quick and violent, he was walking down the street. A group of men came up to his friend Steve, who was walking ahead of him. They shot Steve dead. Close range. A Mob killing, Roger said. In the second part, he was at his job, and another group of guys got onto a low roof where he was working and then shoved him off. They hadn't actually touched him, he admitted. He was not directly injured, but his body was never the same again. Now he is always in pain, what he calls "total body pain," although he admits that no medical workup has ever found a problem and the episode was officially termed an accident. He should be a weatherman, he told me, because his body is so sensitive that he can feel rain coming all over it.

Having gotten very agitated telling me these events, Roger veered off into his big conspiracy idea. He had been complaining to the guys on the roof several days before the accident that Kenny, one of their number, had been harassing him. Kenny is a "queer," and he wanted Roger to do things to him—too gross to tell about said Roger, disgusted. But these guys, somehow, when they heard Roger's complaints, turned into Kenny's agents. It was Kenny who arranged to have Roger shoved off the roof.

For most of the first session, Roger went on about both the murder and his injury and how the medical and mental health systems have failed to help him. His wife sat quietly; he ignored her. But when he left, he told me how good he felt because I would, of course, take care of everything. I watched him as he left, his legs shuffling and dragging slowly down the hallway.

When the missing file turned up, I learned that I was not the first person to be baffled by Roger. A varsity of male therapists had seen him, as had teams of prescribers in the medications clinic. At various times in his mental health system career, he had carried diagnoses from most regions of the *Diagnostic and Statistical Manual,* including Dependent Personality Disorder, Post-Traumatic Stress Disorder, Manic Depression, and Paranoid Schizophrenia. He had been on almost every drug available to match these conditions. No one would give him Benzos because he had a history of addiction to Percocet, which he bought on the street. His drug of choice after Percocet was marijuana, which he has smoked every day since age 13. He had constantly importuned the clinic's doctors for drugs, and some of them considered him a malingerer.

At the beginning of his therapy, Roger loved to come—and he never brought his wife again. He regaled me with the details of his daily life, which consisted of dealing with all the medical and mental health and disability and welfare agencies. Whenever the agencies denied him satisfaction of his needs, he flipped into wild harangues about the people who were out to get him and the system that screwed him over and the insensitivity of the doctors to his pain. God and others should take care of him. "I took a lot of shit from institutions, and I just ate it." He also talked about family, or the lack of it. His world consisted of his wife, two children, divorced parents he had barely seen in recent years, and his friend Tom, an unemployed drug abuser and alcoholic. "Tom and I are like twins," Roger said. "We even dream the same dreams." Telling me about Tom, he immediately associated to how he had always had a "rough time," that he never felt loved, that he was never parented, and that he feels that he raised himself.

Taking care and being taken care of were Roger's great themes. He told me that he liked to help people the way I did, but also that he needed help. "I want to exercise, I know I have to for my back and legs, but I want the doctor to be right at my side in case the pain comes up. I might not be able to handle the pain, it will be too frightening.

But none of these medical bastards will do it my way." This was a long pattern. He had wanted to take care of his mother after she was divorced, he revealed, but a stepfather had come on the scene very quickly, and he "got bumped." Now he feels himself to be part of a world of women. Once when I asked him how his interview with the man who had investigated his accident had gone, he said simply, "Oh, you know, it was like what would have happened to any other woman who was sexually harassed."

At the beginning of the therapy, Roger's fear of homosexuality and his paranoia fitted neatly into standard Freudian terms: he was hating what he loved, rejecting what he wanted, making his target into his enemy; often, he was identified with his mother. In his associations, he got younger and younger. Remembering that Kenny had come looking for him again a couple of years after the accident, Roger raged about how he would like to have killed him—murdered him—shot him on the street. "I thought Eddie Savitch had a twin," he said, alluding to a famous Philadelphia pedophile who had recently been arrested as he picked up a young boy, and alluding to his own twinship with Tom. Kenny "wanted to put his mouth on me, he wanted my underwear, and my shit and stuff."

But as the therapy went on, this material, which I listened to on the sexual-instinctual channel, began to give way. Things floated into Roger's head out of the blue. He saw a woman on a daytime TV show who suffered from total body pain, but no one believed her, her pain was not acceptable to the doctors. He ranted on. Then, suddenly, he tilted his head back, stared into space and said, "There's no place like home." I asked him what "home" meant to him, and he went into a long disquisition on home as the place that the government wants to invade to take it away and to leave you abandoned on the street.

He became more and more critical of his wife. She was

fat, she was masculine, she could have grown a beard. But then, he was himself fat and ugly, like his wife, because he can't exercise due to his total body pain; perhaps he is unlovable. There was trouble at home, they were fighting all the time. I became the saintly, feminine one who could do no wrong and who loved him. He wanted to bring his guitar in and play it for me. Then he didn't come in for four weeks.

When he came back after his long resistance to therapy, he was angry. He lambasted me for making him walk up the stairs. He criticized me every time I spoke. And this went on for weeks, continuing through the time when I had to remind him that my internship was going to end in several months and he would have to be turned over—once again—to another therapist. He ignored this reminder. But when I delivered it again six weeks before my departure, he had a dramatic reaction.

"Well, it's not as if I am in love with you or anything," he said quietly, tensely. "If I were, I might be really angry. But it's a fucked-up system." With this, he got up from his chair and lay down on the floor. He took some dice out of his pocket and began to throw them on the rug. His father, he said, who was quite a gambler, had had a stroke a few years ago. Then he told me, considerately, that I looked tired, and he could understand that I didn't want to hear about his problems. And so he got up off the floor.

Then he started spewing anger about how no one was helping him—not the doctors, the disability, the government—and he wanted to hurt someone. Who? "Not anyone innocent. They got their fun, and now someone is going to pay"—presumably a reference, once again, to Kenny and his crew. In a quick flash of fury, Roger punched the wall with his fist and yelled, "That faggot!"

The next time he came in, Roger was fuming about the mental health center and all the terrible organizations. The Oklahoma City bombing was a good thing, he insisted, because the government is so terrible. The new social worker who was on his case was going to make house calls—unlike me. He needed Valium. He was going to get the social worker to recommend hospitalization. "Therapists should do everything for you. I need a one hundred and fifty–person army to support me," he declared grandiosely. All he could see that day was death and destruction.

One week on Thorazine (at Roger's insistence) calmed him—made him stuporous. The next to the last time he came in, Roger explained that he could not go into the hospital because he could not leave his fish at home without him. They have "such complex problems," their water's temperature, their tank's plants. No one else could take care of them adequately. Then he asked if he could lie on the floor, and he did, fetally, for five minutes, saying only that it was a good thing I wasn't wearing a skirt, because he would have to look up it.

When he got up off the floor he was joking, and I remarked on his sense of humor, something he had always valued in himself. Then I went on to note that he and his wife shared a kind of joking, humorous style. He agreed, then talked about his daughter, who is so mischievous, describing her very affectionately. I pointed out again that he is mischievous himself, and he could try to show himself some of the affectionate, cherishing appreciation he was showing his daughter. He got very emotional and begged "You can't leave me! I love you, I know you're married but I needed to say that to you. I just want to say thank you to you. I've had a great session, the best I've ever had."

What Roger did in this last session, we think, was to struggle to get born. In his *amae* moment, he imagined himself coming out from between Faith's legs as his best self, resymbolized, and he expected her to love him, which she did by suggesting that he cherish himself; then he could love her back—openly and without aggression—momentarily. If he were ever to get well, he would have to be reborn like this many times over. The birth— the *amae* moment—Faith elicited, witnessed, and responded to could have happened only after a long process in which he had taken her as his mother, told her his whole story of being unloved and unable to grow up, which he represented as being attacked and cut down and cut off and broken and cast into total pain, and then gotten furious with her because his love for her was unbearable to him. Her *wu wei* was that, while she heard his huge dependency need for total care, her "not acting" helped him in a way he did not expect. She gave him the help that allowed him to try to help himself. The moment of his birth struggle and Faith's suggestion that he cherish himself was an achieved reciprocity between Faith and him.

THE INTERPRETATION OF THE GRADUATE STUDENT'S DREAMS

While we were talking about Roger and how his therapy unfolded, the sequence of it, we startled ourselves with a thought. Freud had remarked that symptoms are a patient's sexual life; but we were finding them to be, more broadly, a patient's developmental story presented as if in allegory, as the story is in dreams. We were finding the story of an unfolding therapy to be a recapitulation of the patient's developmental story. And when we turned our attention to another of Faith's patients, whom we'll call Jessica, we began to think of recurrent fantasies—like Mary's "My Perfect Life" fantasy—and of dreams as stories of development, too.

We had had this idea in outline before, especially when we talked toward the beginning of our conversation about Faith's Sun Dream and her cherishing grandmother. But with the richness of our patient review working in us, in our receptivities, we had the idea again, full figure.

A dream, Freud believed, represents a fulfilled wish, and ultimately a childhood wish. Associating to the dream in analysis, guided by the analyst's questions and comments, the patient can, slowly, like an archeologist descending into an ancient city, a diver into a sea cave, come upon the wish. But, we felt, Freud's claim may have been too narrow. Representing childhood wishes is one key function of dreams, more obvious in some dreams than in others, as Freud himself noticed. But dreams have other functions as well. And one of these is, we came to think, to tell the story of the dreamer's development and its obstacles, and to give a sign of how the dreamer wishes to become well, to go on developing or have his or her stuck development reactivated. Some dreams—or, more often, dream sequences—are histories, or autobiographies, and prognostications. Autosymbolisms in Ferenczi's term. Particularly developmental are those dreams dreamt in the course of a therapy, for they picture the therapy as part of development, often as a return to growth after a halt. Dreams in therapy point the way out.

In the unfolding of such a developmental dream, the unfolding of the ego's interests and frustrations, defenses and aspirations, is given in images, like a pictographic narrative. We think that Freud was headed in the direction of this idea at the very end of the Dora case, where he remarked of the two dreams he had interpreted there: "Just as the first dream represented her turning away from the man she loved to her father—that is, her flight from life into disease—so the second dream announced that she was about to tear herself free from her father and had been reclaimed once more by the realities of life."

Faith's Jessica, a wonderful dreamer, brought to one of her twice-weekly sessions a long and, she knew at the time, very important dream. It contained, Jessica said, *everything*—but, of course, she had no idea and neither did Faith what this feeling of *everything* meant. Jessica and Faith worked on the dream at many different junctures in her two-year-long therapy, and Faith and I took stock of the accumulating interpretation in a long conversation we had about her. We could see her developmental story in the dream, and further, in two subsequent dreams that the big dream seems to have precipitated. We could see how her therapy was influencing her story, changing her dreaming direction, resymbolizing her.

The big dream came during the Christmas holiday, five days after Jessica had discovered that her husband was having an affair and two days after he had hurt her deeply with a very typical piece of what she called "erase me" behavior. In the wake of this episode, she focused on her husband's attitudes toward her and his general presumptuousness toward women. She could understand precisely her husband's strict obedience to the fundamental rule of blaming—he blamed her for his own faults. We could talk about how blaming prevents self-knowledge, how putting the problem on another stops growth. But she had no insight into her own pattern of accepting blame. When he erased her, he reinforced her tendency to negate herself, but also her tendency to fire off retaliatory shots of rage, followed by self-accusations about what a terrible, angry person she is. Toward the end of a session, she mentioned that she had had a dream, but that there was no time to tell it. "Don't worry, you weren't in it," she said teasingly. And then she clearly felt anxious that she had been teasing or presumptuous about my interest in being in the dream. She moved into a condition—we had been there many times before—of anticipating my disapproval. But she did tell the dream in the next session (and gave me a transcript of it).

> "*I was having a lobster dinner with A [one of her children] and H [her husband] on the wooded area at the side of our property. It was Christmas Eve. Strange to have lobster, I thought. Messy. I couldn't eat it all. "I'm not that hungry, I'll just have the claws," I said. One lobster hadn't yet been cooked for some reason, and at one point it started begging, claws snapping aggressively as it reached for food on the table, only to be pushed away like a dog. The scene had shifted here to my parent's kitchen table with my husband and A seated in Mother and Dad's places. I couldn't imagine that it would eat flesh of its own species, but at one point a piece of my lobster fell on the floor and the lobster hungrily scampered toward it. I thought to myself that we should have cooked the lobster because if it hadn't been fed for awhile it wouldn't make a very good meal—it's too starving.*
>
> "*Then, for some reason, I left to go to my music lesson with F. at his house. I got there and no one was home. I also forgot my recorder. Another student was waiting, with a recorder in her hand. Then F. and his family members came home, so I could tell him in person that I was there but forgot my recorder. Would I have to borrow his? But he was preoccupied.*
>
> "*Then I was in my car, heading home. I realized that I was undressed and disheveled. I'm in my car naked, or almost naked, and I pull into an area that looks like I could change while driving—I'd done this maneuver before. Then there were all these other women around in bathrobes or so, as if there had been some sort of tail-gate*

*sale type thing—waiting in line to pay, or something. I
was sort of trapped in this parking area but then I got out
and was thinking how I'm sure no one at home cleaned up
the dishes of the lobster dinner. Typical. I'd have to do it."*

Jessica told me right away that the dream was about
therapy. The lobster was herself, starving for affection
(even food of its own species), but asking for it in an aggressive manner. "Weird that it was my parents' kitchen,
and when I reached up to the table it was at the place between my mother and father. Also as a child, I didn't eat
much at any one sitting, but I was hungry throughout the
day. I ran hungrily towards a scrap, scarce resources,
starving. Do you think my unconscious is an astrologer?
The lobster is me—Scorpio with a Cancer rising—a lobster! Why devouring my own species? Is that what in-
censed my parents? Something sick about me? Was I
sickly? I was very aggressive with my parents because they
starved me—my husband does too!" She went on to consider the music teacher, who represented her father, but
also a therapist with other patients—other students, who
were better prepared. She was anxious about therapy as
about the lesson. "I really want to accomplish something
significant in therapy, but I am so fearful of the process—
the unknown, the loss of barriers, of you. How can anyone
know that another is truly trustworthy?" About the third
part of the dream, which was so much vaguer in her memory, she was silent. I anticipated that this was really the
center of her feelings, but it was nearly a year before she
reached it.

Several days after she told me the lobster dream, Jessica had a brief but very powerful dream:

*I went to Professor H's office and explained that I hadn't
been in because I'd had so much work over the semester.*

She said she was glad I was there, that she really trusted/liked me and I could have come sooner. She wanted help with organizing books or something about helping her to import/export books or something from/to Germany and the U.S.A. I knew it would be a lot of work and I was feeling lazy or inadequate, but I went along.

Over the weekend, when she could not continue with analyzing the Lobster Dream or tell me this second dream, Jessica indulged herself with shopping and threw herself into a whirl of social activities. All the while, she was feeling very anxious about the need she attributed to me to defend myself against her. When she returned, I emphasized how much she wanted to connect—not to be starving. I was the professor-therapist in her dream, and she was wanting to be engaged in the import and export of love business, the business of wise books. She agreed: "It's like the song 'Constant Craving.' Is that the human condition?" The next morning, she awoke with a third dream:

A group of adults, cold authority figures, were trying to get this baby to do something—to cooperate in some way— they were surrounding him. I was one of the adults. The baby remained stubborn and difficult. Then I decided to take a different tactic, so I picked the baby up very mater- nally and sweetly said, "What's wrong?" and kissed the baby (a boy). His face and lips were all scrunched and hard and he rejected the kiss, but then he softened and very sincerely, articulately and eloquently talked to me. He explained his behavior, but the only part I remember was that he said, "It's all going too fast, I can't do it that

quickly, that's why I appear so uncooperative." The impli-
cation of what was going too fast was "to be myself," "to re-
veal myself."

Jessica thought that this dream might be about expectation. Her mother and father had expected her to be a
certain way, perhaps more mature. I expect her to be a
certain way—to free associate. I noted to her that she was
"childlike" telling me these thoughts, and she took this as
criticism. She said that she did behave in a childlike manner with her husband, sometimes being flirtatious, sometimes trying to show affection, sometimes wanting to
break him out of his cold concentration. "Am I childlike
because I don't want to take responsibility for myself? Is
it a 'take care of me' kind of thing? Do I act spoiled and
demanding like a child if my needs aren't met?" As she
typically did, Jessica slid into self-criticism.

Later, we came to understand the second dream as a
corrective upon the music lesson in the Lobster Dream.
She went to her teacher's office and was received cherishingly, as she so deeply wished to be: she was a talented,
trustworthy person who would be invited to join the
teacher in her work. No envied other student got the
post. Similarly, in the third dream, she is an unhappy infant among cold authority figures, but one of the figures—herself—transforms the scene by being cherishing.
The baby is able—articulately, even eloquently, like a patient who has achieved some insight—to say what the
problem is: the therapy process is going too fast. "But you
will understand, you will pick me up, hold me." The
dream also shows Jessica beginning to identify with me,
beginning to become her own therapist.

As the second dream replaces the failed music lesson
with a scene of academic success, the third dream

replaces the third part of the Lobster Dream. Jessica slowly came to understand what her car journey from the music lesson to the women in bathrobes meant. This journey, which involved her changing clothes, being naked and fearfully exposed for a time, recalled all her fears about being bad, being scolded—by her husband as well as by her parents—but it focused on her mother, who was often depressed. The mother spent her days during much of Jessica's childhood in a bathrobe, disheveled, unable to get dressed until she rallied for the father's homecoming at dinnertime. Going to the bathrobe women meant becoming like her mother, and ending up a dishwasher, the one who has to do the cleanup from the lobster dinner. This is what happens to girls who are starving lobsters and who fail their music lessons: they are all exposed and depressed and slavish and shameful. The third dream is, again, the developmental corrective; it points the way to recovery. The scrunched up, starving baby is cherished and can explain that he is recovering, even though the process is frightening. He is what the mother is not: calm, self-aware, articulate.

Faith and Jessica came to understand this sequence of dreams as a portrait of Jessica's childhood followed by two revisions— two developmental wishes for the future, two correctives. Faith and I made a more theoretical map when we discussed the dreams and compared them to others. We saw the lobster as auotsymbolizing Jessica's infancy: she was starved and she responded by getting hardened and grasping. Sulking, like Blake's "Infant Sorrow." She was both defended in her shell and screaming in pain, so that her parents found her unlikeable. As a result, when she tried to do anything, to learn anything, to grow, she was inhibited. Her ego went into a kind of dormancy, while unconsciously, she went right on expecting love, trying to grow, to develop. Her unconscious ego was not just an astrologer, but a superb dreamer, a strong creator of an ego ideal. While she had great difficulties in the world, where her inhibitions spoke so loudly, she carried on inside herself remarkably. In her dreams, a Blake baby spoke her story with eloquence. She had had what Sandor Ferenczi once called "A Dream of the Wise Baby."

Using the terms of Freud's original libido theory, we could say that Jessica in her oral stage was, simply, emotionally starving. This was her predisposition for hysteria Then she had her ego dormancy during the period Freud knew as the anal stage and described in terms of the struggle between children and their caregivers over toilet habits, discipline, obedience. He also emphasized the sadism and masochism that manifest themselves in this struggle. What we find most noticeable is the way in which this libidinal struggle, which is obvious in most children, continues shaping the ego's sense of itself—the child's self-esteem. For Jessica, the result of that stage was summarized as "I was not prepared." She did not have her musical instrument; she felt deficient, unable to compete with other players. In therapy, an ideal of herself as a talented, capable, appreciated person formed in her, but she could not yet make it conscious, she could not follow it, actualize it —although she could dream of it being actualized with her professor. And she could allow herself to feel her therapist's appreciation for her, which was crucially bound up with her growing hope that therapy could help her.

Jessica's ego dormancy kept her, also, from what Freud knew as the genital stage. She was a girl who stayed sexually a girl. She often seemed "childlike" to Faith, and in her dream she was a boy baby. She had a sexually amorphous quality, which Freud had noticed to be typical of hysterical people. Certainly capable of sexual pleasure, and quite sensuous, she was nonetheless moved more by her intense need for, and inability to receive, cherishment than by sexual desire per se. Freud might have read her forgotten musical instrument as her missing penis—and the dream image may have an element of Freudian penis envy in it—but on a more fundamental level the forgotten instrument is her sleeping ego's desire. "Would I have to borrow his?" also meant, for her, "Is there an auxiliary ego available for me? A relationship?" Later, her professor provided the auxiliary ego and the relationship, as Faith did in the therapy.

Using the Freudian concepts diagnostically and therapeutically—while always seeking, at the same time, their cherishment meaning—lets concepts like "envy" emerge synthetically. "I'm wondering if envy," Faith noted in her clinical journal, "in all the developmental stages, is the direct result of missing cherishment. You envy what you don't have, and what you assume is being withheld or given to others. But envy focuses on those parts of the caretakers' bodies that represent relationship—with others. The penis is what Daddy relates to Mommy with; the breast is what Mommy relates to your brother or sister with; the womb is where Mommy keeps a rival, or where she keeps Daddy's penis." Envied organs represent the ego's instinctual drive for relatedness.

We knew that Faith had set us a task for later thinking with this note, but we concentrated on concluding our discussion of Jessica by saying of her: she will have to disidentify with her mother, get out of that old bathrobe. That is her therapeutic task. As we had turned her dreams and her associations this way and that, looking at them in their intricate, symbolic interlockings, we had felt her identification with her mother more and more as what it most importantly is: the way she has set her lack of receptivity in place, confirmed it, perpetuated it—and based her enviousness on it. It is as though she had unconsciously said to herself in her infancy: "I think it best to sulk over here away from my mother's breast. Perhaps someone will feed me if I do what they ask or if I appear sick? Perhaps mother will love me more, and more than others, if I am like her?" The way out of this place was to be cherished and to be cherishing.

As we talked about Jessica, we came to this sense of her and to a formulation, which we wrote in our notebook. "Helping the patient overcome the identification formed in ego dormancy with the caregiver's lack of cherishment is the therapeutic action." This, we felt, was a succinct example of how combining the Freudian scheme and *amae* psychology can guide our work.

"Well," Faith remarked, looking at our sentence, "that is rather a different way to talk than I had when I told you in New Haven how I wanted to write a dissertation on theories of therapeutic action. Back then I thought that somehow a patient who experienced the analyst's cherishment would be restored to being able to expect love—openly, freely. Would be able to receive love."

"Is that so different?" I asked her. "Isn't it the identifications with the caregiver's lack of cherishment that initially closed the patient down, inhibited her growth? The analyst, then, offers an alternative—a new identification can be formed. Development is restarted. And this time the identification is a more conscious one, a cultivated one. Allowing yourself to be receptive again is the essence of what your *I Ching* Confucians call self-cultivation."

SYNTHESIZING THOUGHTS

We have observed to ourselves several times that when we have a long clinical conversation in which we find ourselves discovering and reinventing psychoanalysis, adopting or adjusting our tradition and cherishing it, we are also—unknown to ourselves at the time—staging another level of synthesizing work. We are getting ready for a more fundamental reformulation.

One afternoon, months after we talked about Jessica, I was reading my way through Freud's *Three Essays on the Theory of Sexuality* in order to prepare for a class. I called Faith to say that I was impressed all over again with how Freud's emphasis on the oral, anal, and phallic-genital stages of libidinal development, on the unfolding of the sexual instinct, kept him from exploring the ego instincts. He would note that the baby's self-preservative drive, which he thought of as Hunger, is related to the mother's breast, the first love object. But then he would immediately look to suckling as a *sexual* pleasure—the first sexual pleasure, and in many ways the paradigmatic sexual pleasure. The breast became for him the first *sexual* object. He didn't question whether the suckling baby might feel itself not just pleasured but also preserved or safely sustained—growed, as we say—in its relatedness, by the mother's cherishing. He wasn't thinking of the baby as cherishing the mother's milk, cherishing her touch, her warmth, her singing, her affection. The breast is also the first *affectionate* object, the first cherishment object.

We started talking again about the brief period in Freud's writing when he *did* claim that normal development requires that "the affectionate current" and "the sensual current" stay harmonious and close over time, not splitting apart, going toward different objects. He wrote then about adult men who cannot get their love directed toward one person, but have an affectionate object and a sexual one—a chaste motherly one and a whorish one. Had he been more alert to female desire, he might have imagined, as we did, the heterosexual female counterpart, who has an affectionate object—usually a mother figure—and a sexual one, a male. It was a short step for us, then, to talk about why so many adult heterosexual woman split their allegiances: they are affectionately "homosexual" and sensually "heterosexual"; deeply tied affectionately to women friends while sexually involved with men. So much of the battle of the sexes, the misfitting of the sexes, has to do with the way in which both men and women split their affectional and their sexual currents. The commonest heterosexual scenario, the one Jessica and her husband lived, involves a woman who feels her man cannot give her affection—so she loses her sexual desire for him—and a man who looks for affection from his spouse and a sexual relationship elsewhere.

Faith and I mused over the telephone about these combinatories and also the ones typical of people who have same-sex sexual partners along with their maternal affectional objects, and then she went off to look at the *Three Essays* passages I had referred her to. "So I can play with all this while I go put in my half an hour on the treadmill," she said. My phone rang later and she was there, breathless from her exercise but even more from excitement. "This is bizarre, but I am full of images of Dennis the Menace. Do you remember Dennis the Menace? I want to tell you what I was thinking about latency. Mine and Dennis's—and I bet yours, too.

"Here it is. Just listen," Faith continued. "When a child is in latency, with her sexual drives somewhat quiescent, she is—as all kinds of empirical psychologists say—in a cognitive growth spurt. Like Amy, my eight-year-old patient, was. But she is also in a big cherishment period. Children then—at seven, eight, nine—are often so sweet, even sweetly indulging. They rush around forming relationships outside of the family, at school, in the neighborhood, with other kids' families, other kids' pets. I know I *lived* at my friend Penny's house. And latency kids seek affection, even from the most unlikely people. That's Dennis the Menace and Mr. Wilson. Dennis tried his best to get Mr.

Wilson—the grouch, the sulky, pouting, disappointed grouch—to be a cherisher, and sometimes he succeeded. He cherished Mr. Wilson. And he cherished himself with all kinds of self-enhancing mischief and fun, getting his parents to indulge him. He's the archetypal latency boy. Snakes, snails and puppy-dog tails. And think of Eloise in the Plaza. Latency kids love those stories of her touring the place, chatting up all the people.

"Now I was thinking," she said, "that what we have been talking about—remember back to the conversation about Jessica—is that when the sexual instincts are not really going full blast, when they are quiescent, as in latency, the ego instincts preponderate and can guide the sexual instincts. When the sexual instincts charge up, as they do going into the Oedipal period or later in puberty, the ego instincts take the back seat. And these can be the reckless times, when holding and safety and self-preservation are not what a child most obviously yearns for. These are experimental, adventurous times, limit-testing, full of rebellion against sexually desired and forbidden figures."

"You're talking not just about an intertwining but about an oscillation," I suggested. "Yes, that's it exactly. This is what Freud needed, an image of instinctual drive oscillation."

When we had gotten used to this image, talked it through, we came back to Jessica's Lobster Dream and its sequels to look again. We saw it in a different focus. In the first part of the Lobster Dream, we saw Jessica screaming out her ego instinctual self-preservative needs—hunger, holding, attention, closeness. Then the lobster moves into a triangular—an Oedipal, a libidinally dominated—relation with her mother and father at the kitchen table. She is in the ego dormancy we described, but she is there not just because of her frustration and her aggressive envy of their relation, their meal, but also because of the ascendancy in her of her sexual instincts. Her aggression gets rivalrous, possessive, grabby, devouring. Then the music lesson part of the dream shows her as a *latency* child, with her begging, beseeching sexuality quieted and her ego-instinctual needs emergent again. This is what we had missed on our first effort at interpreting her dream. She was going like a *latency* child out into the world to take music lessons, to seek assistance from another kid, to relate to a teacher, to be charming and lovable and industrious as latency children are when they seek cherishment. The child's cultivation of lovableness prepares the way for later receptivity. But she felt herself hindered. Later in the dream sequence, when she goes to see her professor, she is doing her *latency* again, much more successfully. She is doing her latency after her psychotherapy has helped her assert her self-preservative needs more successfully. She can receive.

Normal development, we found ourselves saying, is development in which the ego instincts and the sexual instincts come, after normal oscillations, to a kind of harmony. A balance, like the newborn's original balance.

> *He who is in harmony with the Tao*
> *is like newborn child . . .*

The oscillations can be very different in different people, as can the harmony. Some people are more moved by sexual desire than by *amae*, some more by *amae* than sexual desire; some continue to oscillate in adulthood, some become more fixed. The end or goal of development should not be seen only in terms of object choice—and *proper* or *normal* object choice at that, which means, in the history of psychoanalysis, heterosexual object choice. It makes much more sense to us to think of the goal as a more or less stable, or not too widely or wildly penduluming, harmony of intertwined cherishment and sexual drives. We had been thinking and writing about dreams as portraits of ego-instinctual drives and development, and about transference as a re-creation of the ego-instinctual story, but here we had come to a way of picturing how this cherishment story intertwines with, oscillates with, the sexual instinctual story. And we could think of "normality" not as normal achieving of pleasure aims or normal types of object choices, but as normal harmony, the secure inner harmony of the person who is *wu wei*. Whether the harmony goes with heterosexual partnership or homosexual or bisexual does not matter for the harmony itself.

"You know," I said to Faith after we had spent weeks working with this oscillation idea—discovering that it was really built into much of our writing but just not clearly formulated, not precipitated into an image—"there is another piece to this." I noted that we had been complaining about Freud's abandonment of the distinction between the ego instincts and the sexual instincts as he spun out his second instinct theory. But we hadn't confronted his reasons for trying to give aggression a greater role in his theorizing, as it certainly deserves. While we talked about *dealing with* aggression—about being *wu wei*, about listening to the Homeric rhythms—we postponed talking about what aggression is. "Are we thinking of three instinctual drives: ego-instinctual, sexual instinctual and aggressive, or death, instinctual? Or just the first two? I'm wondering if we could think through what it would mean clinically to talk about two forms of aggression, one arising from thwarting of the self-preservative ego instincts, and one arising from frustrations of the sexual instincts. The first would be, fundamentally, envy and destruction aimed at envied relationships, including the envied caretaker's relationships. And the second would be, fundamentally, possessiveness, aimed at the rival. Each form of destructiveness could be turned on the self. Would these two forms of aggression encompass all of what Freud was calling aggression? Would it compass masochism?"

"Well," Faith joked when we got this far on our conversational journey, "we never go a step ahead without coming upon a completely exhausting vista. We'll think about this. But we should celebrate that we seem to have made it to the end of latency. Pubertal sexuality has come on our conceptual horizon. Aggression is ahead. We are not just acknowledging sex and aggression, the great late Freudian duo—for who could not?—we are letting them into the cherishment story's theory. Growth. Development."

"Beware adolescence!"

Chapter 5

The *Amae* of Everyday Adolescent Life

The Master said, "At fifteen I set my heart on learning; at thirty, I took my stand; at forty, I came to be free from doubts; at fifty, I understood the Decree of Heaven; at sixty, my ear was attuned; at seventy, I followed my heart's desire without overstepping the line."

—THE ANALECTS OF CONFUCIUS

*J*ust as Faith and I were beginning to think about how cherishment and sexual instinctual needs can intertwine in a harmonious, mature *wu wei* adulthood, and to contrast that vision with adolescence, in which the needs typically clash and bang, wrecking havoc, a college senior came onto Faith's caseload. Charlie vividly reminded us that an adolescent's "Take care of me! Help me grow!" *amae* current almost always comes in a wrapping of acutely anxious self-consciousness and shamefulness.

Like many contemporary twentysomethings, Charlie was prolonging his adolescence, struggling with how to get an adult life started, unable to make a declaration of independence from his family. Stuck, anguished that he was without people who believed in him, this strapping soccer player had resorted to couch potatohood and depressive overeating. He was angry at his harsh, uncherishing father and bewildered by his mother's nagging, impatient style. Wearing the now obligatory cap with its brim in the back, he had come sheepishly to Faith's office, nervously reached out his hand to greet his new therapist—the first therapist he had ever seen—and then, totally embarrassed, stammering, made his first communication to her: "I'm afraid I smell like onions."

Tongue-tied, he tried to explain that he had just come from his job making sandwiches at the local deli. "It's just to make money so I can get going." Then he began to cry. So there he was, helpless in just the way Takeo Doi noted as characteristic of patients revealing their *amae* needs. But his helplessness also took a specifically adolescent form: his cherishment story was written all over him, intertwined with a sexual instinctual story of fearfulness about women, but he could not begin to understand either.

His emotional life was completely baffling to him, and he was ashamed of it and of himself. Faith found herself instantly translating his feelings into words in her own mind: "I feel about two years old. My body bothers me—do you find me repellent? Would you hold me? You're a woman. I can't be a man. I just hate it that I need your help." She set to work looking for a way to convey "We will believe in you and your growth" to him.

The awkwardness of adolescence, we agreed while we were talking about Charlie, is like learning to walk. You want to be able to stand emotionally upright, in a body you can accept as your own, more or less balanced, without the hands you have been holding—or trying to hold—and without having to return too frequently to catch a hold again. If dependency is a hard theme for people to take up over childhood—if, as Takeo Doi said, there is a deep desire in the West to eliminate dependency—it is doubly difficult to take up over adolescence. But then, almost everything that has to do with adolescence is hard for adults to think about: getting away from, or being able to look back on, the awkwardness and painfulness of the period is a big motivation for all kinds of intolerant pronouncements on adolescence and animosities toward adolescents themselves, who so often get turned into some kind of enemy, some Generation X. Many adults are so adolescent themselves that they feel compelled to distinguish themselves by being prejudiced; it is like adolescentophobia.

The same semester that Charlie came into Faith's office, a new batch of undergraduates came to a class I offered under the title "Narratives of Adolescence." I wanted to read and discuss with Faith and with my students the psychoanalytic literature on adolescence, and to compare that literature with a collection of novels and memoirs and films about and by adolescents. What we all discovered on this tour was that an effort to stay receptive on both the Freudian and the *amae* channels—the effort we were making as clinicians and as theorists, and the students were testing out on their own experiences—was steering us away from a bias that is common to most psychoanalytic therapeutic approaches. We noticed that the more stress analysts of any theoretical persuasion put on early or pre-Oedipal caretaker-infant relations, and the more they emphasize the *determining* importance of these early relations, the less attention they give to latency and adolescence. This is so no matter how, specifically, they imagine The Baby—that is, whether they accept the Freudian instinct theory and ideas about primary narcissism or not. Even among those who write about primary love, no matter whether as primary sexual object love (as Ferenczi and Michael Balint did) or primary ego-instinctual love (as Takeo Doi does), adolescence is overlooked if that primary love or its lack is held to be all-determinative. For many "Object Relations" theorists, adolescence hardly exists, all important development tracks having been laid down so early.

By contrast, there are some analysts, following leaders like Anna Freud and Peter Blos, who believe that adolescence is a developmental "second chance" during which much of what went developmentally wrong in early childhood can be repaired, either in a therapy or, given helpful circumstances, by the adolescent's own processes of resiliency. "When I was seventeen," as one of my students put it, "I finally stopped being three and murderously jealous of my baby brother." These analysts also stress that adolescence is a time of upheaval, which for them means that possibilities for psychic repair are opened because, internally and in relation to the world, so much changes for an adolescent. Growth is the name of the game. Both more danger and more possibility for growth arise.

Early childhood determinists, who underplay the possibilities for change that come about in adolescence, seem to forget that therapy itself is the most obvious example of a later influence that can reshape development. But this phenomenon speaks to the way adolescence itself appears in adult therapies. Theorists have trouble recalling with any emotional vividness the upheaval of adolescence, just as patients—including analysts when they were patients—have trouble recalling in therapy what adolescence was really like.

Patients know that they cannot remember their early childhood, and they have to discover that a childhood can be reconstructed from the way it is replayed in the transference relationship with the analyst. But, like all adults looking back on adolescence and regaling their kids with "when I was your age" anecdotes, patients think they remember it well. And they do, as a history of events, a catalogue of behavior. They can tell you about their first crushes, their growth spurts, their struggles with their parents, their escapades. However, as Anna Freud once noted, it is difficult for them to remember, or reexperience, their adolescent *emotions:* "What we [analysts] fail to recover, as a rule, is the atmosphere in which the adolescent lives, his anxieties, the height of elation or depth of despair, the quickly rising enthusiasms, the utter hopelessness, the burning—or at other times, sterile—intellectual and philosophical preoccupations, the yearning for freedom, the sense of loneliness, the feeling of oppression by the parents, the impotent rages or active hates directed against the adult world, the erotic crushes—whether homosexually or heterosexually directed—the suicidal fantasies, etc. These are elusive mood swings, difficult to revive, which, unlike the affective states of early childhood, seem disinclined to reemerge and be relived in connection with the person of the analyst."

Faith and I have certainly observed the truth of Anna Freud's reflection, but we have also noticed that sometimes the emotions missing when an adult remembers her adolescence are not repressed, offstage, but rather busily at play all over the person's life in the present tense. These emotions don't *reemerge* in the transference with the analyst because they never did disappear, they are still the major player emotions—just not given the name "adolescent." Most people have an overriding adolescent dimension that keeps right on going through their adulthood; they never stop having adolescent moods swings. And there are certainly social conditions, like the ones we live in now, that favor prolonged adolescence, or that do not favor "getting some altitude" (as my students say) on adolescence. This social phenomenon does have its benefits, too: creativity certainly draws on adolescent emotions, adolescent playfulness and enthusiasm, as much or more than on childhood qualities.

THE JAPANESE BEETLE AGAIN, IN ADOLESCENCE

When a Charlie comes into one of our consulting rooms or a student into a classroom and puts *amae* needs, adolescent emotions, right *there*, like a handshake, we, as adults, can feel the intensity. But to get more intimately into this adolescent territory, most of us need an entryway from our ongoing experience, a break in the adult day-to-day. For us, that entryway rose up in the form of a psychic adventure.

We were taking a walk and talking about *amae* in adolescence and how it relates to the *amae* of childhood when our adventure began. Suddenly, Faith remembered a poem that she had written when she was thirteen, in 1965. Even after more than thirty years, she could recall all of its messages about feeling the odd

one out, alien, uncomfortable in her body. The poem was entitled "Alone," but it could very well have been, in Blake's manner,
"Adolescent Sorrow." Two lines of its gawky iambs also came
back to her:

> *Alone, alone, nothing but sand*
> *Alone, alone in this strange land.*

Faith told me that the poem referred to a color photograph in
a book belonging to her brother. *Boy's Life,* she thought it was
called. In the photo, a blue-green Japanese beetle was walking
"alone, alone" across a great expanse of tawny desert. After she
had reflected on the poem and how powerfully the picture had
affected her, she gasped: "Oh, my God, that's the beetle—that's
Takeo Doi!" She was alluding to the dream she had told me
about in New Haven, when our *amae* conversation was launched
on Anna Freud's centenary. Faith had identified *this* beetle walking alone on the sand—a beetle from her adolescence—with the
beetle in that dream, which morphed out of an angry peacock
and represented Takeo Doi.

We were in awe at the resourcefulness of her dreaming mind
when we grasped what had happened: her "timeless unconscious," as Freud called the dreaming mind, had seized upon an
image that had struck her thirty years earlier and sent it forth to
represent Takeo Doi and "the expectation to be loved" emergent
then in Faith's transference to her analyst. Her dream took on a
new dimension: she could see that the dream was about herself in
her metamorphosizing adolescence as well as about her child self
expecting love and her adult self missing her analyst, alone in
"dreamy neediness," reflecting on *amae.*

Having opened herself again to thinking about the Japanese
amae beetle, Faith then had another burst of association. The
song "I Want to Hold Your Hand" came floating into her mind,

and with it a string of memories about herself at age thirteen, in love with Paul McCartney and spending hour after hour reading teen magazines about The Beatles. "I wanted Paul McCartney to love me," she said, "but I also wanted to *be* a Beatle, to be traveling with them in different lands, to have mobs of people loving me the way I loved Paul. In my poem I was a beetle, but in the frustrated state of being a beetle alone. And that was the sexual instinctual side of the dream—really, until this moment, the hidden current in it. I could become the object of desire, a Beatle."

We marveled, as we have many times, at the endless interpretability of dreams. Faith, feeling like her whole adolescent self was in that photograph, urgently wanted to look at it again, but she could not find the book in her mother's library. Her brother had no memory of it. Then she recalled that after she completed the poem, she had torn the photograph out of the book—overriding her conscience, under compulsion—and attached it to the poem, which she had given to her eighth grade English teacher. Trying to console her, I had suggested, unrealistically, "Be patient, it will turn up somehow."

So, several months later, taking a break during a work weekend, we went out for lunch and then strolled into an antiques and collectibles marketplace, browsed around, and drew up to a shelf of books. As though answering a handshake, Faith reached out to a tall, green-covered volume and said, haltingly, incredulous, "I think this is the beetle book." Then, reined in by the unfamiliar title, *Book of the Outdoors*, she hesitated: "Maybe it's not, but I would be so grateful if this were the beetle book. It would be like one of Homer's omens."

Tensely, Faith laid the book on a table and flipped through. No "Alone" beetle. So, page by page, methodically, she set out through the dense collection of outdoor life pictures. And suddenly there it was. Uncanny. She took a deep breath and put her hand on the page, stroked the glossy surface as though the scene might come to life, animate.

Faith's beetle was marching across a beach in the "Seacoast" section, not on a desert. And it was not a Japanese. *Calosoma scrutator*, the green caterpillar hunter, is a *Carabidae*, a ground beetle native to the American East Coast. The expert source quoted in the *Book of the Outdoors* was John Pallister, an entomologist at the Museum of Natural History, who was interviewed by the author, John O'Reilly. "When I was thirteen," Faith said, astonished at how well known to her this text was, "I was sure this Mr. Pallister was a wise man. That must be part of the reason why the beetle got associated in my unconscious memory with the sage Takeo Doi."

She had been impressed with Mr. Pallister because he was gentle and attentive, as was clear in his conversation with Mr. O'Reilly:

> "Do you find many insects on beaches?" I asked him.
>
> Mr. Pallister smiled tolerantly.
>
> "A lively place by day as well as night," he said. "There is plenty going on. The casual observer wouldn't see much. They're there, but you have to look for them."
>
> Leaning back in his swivel chair and locking his hands behind his head, Mr. Pallister proceeded to give an entomologist's version of the seashore. Sometimes it was a grim picture, featuring death struggles in the insect world. At other times it was filled with bug song. There was intrigue and there was beauty . . .
>
> "The beach," said Mr. Pallister, "is a great place."

Mr. Pallister, anything but a casual observer, missed nothing of the beach hubbub. The incessant and intricate predatory maneuvering filled him with amazement, and so did the amatory rites, the intrigue, the bug song. He could see in his chosen corner of things all of the powers, the changes, of the world. He was a Homer of the beach.

We could not stop talking about the book, about finding the book. Excited and with a sense of miraculousness, we went over and over everything that had happened during that day, up to the moment when Faith was drawn to that shelf and reached out her hand so unselfconsciously, so receptively. The morning seemed, as we reconstructed it, full of premonitions. At lunch, we had been talking about what wishes and ideals had guided us toward adulthood. On the way to the antiques mart, we had bought madelines at a bakery and joked about what further memories they might provoke in us, in the manner of Proust, *à la recherche du temps perdu*. The talk had been free associative; we had been like a walking psychoanalytic session.

Finally, we came to think that Faith had really gotten back to the emotions of her adolescence, to the feeling level her poem marked, in our talk. She was having the conversation she had lacked then and longed for when she was "alone, alone." And she was relieved by the conversation of the shame that she had felt for being "alone, alone," for feeling uncherished and not a beloved Beatle. She had come into a moment of heightened receptivity to her own unconscious and to the world, or to say the same thing another way, a moment in which there were no hard, protective boundaries between her wishes and the world. She had been in a condition of almost pure expectation to be provided for, indulgently loved—in the infancy-like core of adolescence, the state she had longed for when she wrote the poem. But this time the world did provide. The beetle book was there again. It wasn't miraculous, this provision, it was primordial—that is, we found ourselves saying that the world is like this for those in re-activated "infant joy," infant receptivity. The world provides to those who can receive; the beach is a great place for them. Faith had had a moment of deep enthusiasm, the kind of moment, we think, that underlies the most intense experiences in adolescence and in adulthood of creative play.

Experiences of receptive enthusiasm like Faith's are rare because the defenses we build up around our cherishment core, around infant joy, are so thick and complicated, and because the world is so dangerous. It is particularly dangerous in adolescence because adolescents are also dangerous then in themselves, to themselves. For both biological and psychological reasons, the sexual instinctual drives are on overdrive, and cherishment needs almost totally hidden in the storm. One of our colleagues, mother of two teenagers, expressed the matter succinctly: "My son is a testosterone bomb and my daughter is incomprehensible." The ego is preoccupied with struggles for control, for giving the self guidance. Relaxation is hard. And the ego instinctual drive for cherishment feels dangerous itself, not least because it draws an adolescent into the vicinity of adults, successors to the parents, with whom adult sexuality is possible. Even asking for help seems dangerous. Then peers with whom adult sexuality can be practiced, rehearsed, are in adolecent throes themselves and can be quite uncherishing. Making connections equals being vulnerable, and being vulnerable means being unloved.

In childhood, the world consisted only of the caretakers, a very small world; in adolescence, the world is infinite, and all the dangers multiply. One of my "Narratives of Adolescence" students wrote a paper on Freud's patient Dora—the patient who had felt herself to be a pawn in an adult game—which captured precisely the adolescent's anxiety: "My basic feeling, every day of my life, is: I'm supposed to go out there and make my place in *that* world—you forget it! And all the overachievers I live with, they feel the same way, I can assure you, even though I only discovered it last week. I thought I was the only one." This is the voice of an adolescent who is beginning to reflect on "alone, alone, in this strange land." He would rather, like Takeo Doi in America, have everyone say to him, "You will never need to help yourself, we will indulge you, darling, and the world will provide."

STOPPING AND STARTING

Faith's experience of being in a purely receptive adolescent state spurred us to a gallop of thoughts about how and why such experiences are so rare, how they are prevented by all kinds of defenses and dangers. But we could not get going on writing any of these thoughts. For weeks, we read many articles and books about adolescent development while we attended our classes, saw our patients, talked. But the conversations stimulated by the beetle book episode were too many and too diverse, like bug song on the beach, and we could not find our way.

When I was invited to give a lecture at a "Psychoanalysis and Culture" symposium arranged by the New York Psychoanalytic Society to celebrate its seventy-fifth anniversary, I suggested to Faith that we turn our attention to writing the lecture together, using the occasion to focus our thoughts. The lecture could, then, be a first draft or a trial balloon for "The *Amae* of Everyday Adolescent Life" and also for our book's last chapter, which we were imaging under the title "Cherishment Culture." "Wonderful," Faith said. "But don't think that I would even consider standing up in front of hundreds of people to present it! A nightmare! You have to do that."

Immediately, we hit more trouble. We found it difficult to write for an audience of psychoanalysts. Stereotyping them, making "them" all into tweedy graybeards, stiff and stuffy Hollywood analysts of the 1950s, rigid in their views, we expected them to respond to us in the kind of impenetrable and affectless jargon that is, actually, the norm in psychoanalytic journals. "They will not be amused if we quote the *I Ching*," Faith sulked. "They will think we are weird—or that I am weird and that I have turned you, the reliable historian of psychoanalysis, into something New Age." She worried testily about not being taken seriously, while I worried in rationalistic tones about whether I would be able to get it right and about whether rightnesss would be appreciated. Then she felt daunted and self-conscious about being a "late bloomer" or a tagalong to my reputation. "Who will believe any of these ideas are mine?" she asked angrily, with all the vehemence of a youngest child who cannot get a nod from the higher-ups, whose ambitions had been mocked many times. Envious thoughts about people who had achieved—so she imagined—happinesses unavailable to her began to well up in her. Our conversation was often about envy. Slowly, we came to the idea that envy may be the fundamental form of disappointed cherishment needs—and then we recognized this as one of the last ideas Faith had had months before while she was considering her patient Jessica's "penis envy." We were spinning in circles.

I began to have a dream, a nightmare, I had not had for nearly twenty years but used to have recurrently: I enter a huge, overflowing lecture hall, start to give my lecture, and all kinds of disturbances arise. There are hecklers, people leave, the lights dim, the microphone doesn't work. Disaster. One night, the police came into the dream scene and took off a young man who was carrying a block of Monterey Jack and two baguettes. This young man, I concluded after working it over in my analysis, was my exhibitionist part, who makes the rest of me very anxious about being perceived as aspiring to be a Big Cheese—named with the proper name of my very own analyst, Jack. And not just one baguette, but two. "I like to be well fortified," I joked to Jack, but the joke was a bit on me, as I slipped and said "well for*tri*fied." I could feel my envy of Big Cheeses, or of people who allow themselves to be Big Cheeses without guilt, behind my defenses. Faith's description of "penis envy," whether female or male, as envy of a grown man's—the Big Man's, the Daddy's—organ for relatedness seemed to have been woven into my dream, and also to have been explicated by the dream.

While I was busy dreaming lecture disasters, Faith had the stage fright. Her fear continued to focus on how our work might be judged different, odd, unconventional. "But, so what?" I kept asking. "Why not?" And there we came right to the fundamental difference in the way we had reacted to our adolescences. I assumed I would be found different and odd; I felt different and odd; and difference and oddity slowly became normal for me, my view from the margins slowly became my room with a view. All my anxiety gathered around being good at being what I was, a writer, an intellectual—that would win me love. Faith felt different and odd, too, but she eventually wanted to be relieved of the feeling. As a young adult, she made her ideal of being a sage more secret and took a visible turn into conventionality. She continued as a self-cultivator, but kept her intellectual and artistic interests largely to herself while she worked diligently at fulfilling another ideal, represented by marriage and child-rearing and a lovely home and beautiful clothes. Her fear, she understood in retrospect, was about the complex process of overcoming the split in her ideal—her own variant on the common career-versus-motherhood problematic of our feminist generation.

As the date for the New York symposium drew closer, we became aware, finally, of what our slowdown, in all its confusion and profusion, was about, and why we were having a joint regression over the lecture. We felt ridiculous and stuck in something like a mud of anxiety, but we could see that we had slowly shifted over the months since Faith found the beetle book. We had needed time to learn to speak the cherishment language we had been developing, to get used to the way of experiencing we had built up together, and to adjust our ideals for ourselves to the ideal we now called Cherishing. By going out into the world and experimenting, cherishing and paying attention to others' needs for cherishment, others' ways of cherishing, we had been doing and studying *amae* in everyday life, letting our thoughts settle, seep in. Not just with our students and our patients, but everywhere we were practicing. With our families and friends. At the grocery store, on the commuter train, at our desk in Dimitri's restaurant. And we had also begun to take into account how our conversation, our ideas, affected other people. Our ideas had been ahead of our practical actions, and then our actions had been ahead of our ideas; we had been up and down with our abilities and our ambitions, one day childlike, the next gigantic, like Alice in Wonderland eating the grow-big and the grow-small toadstools.

"You know what has happened," Faith announced summarily. "Our book is no longer a baby. *Cherishment* is an adolescent. It is having an identity crisis! *We,* for heaven's sake, are having an identity crisis. We are not thinking about adolescence, we are *being* adolescents, and so is the book. When the book was little and stayed between us most of the time—just a little green shoot—we understood it. But then we got into an adolescent enthusiasm, in love with the ideas. Now it's a show getting ready to go on the road, getting wordly, and we are in that awful 'What will people think?' molasses of shame that makes adolescence such a torture. We even have the mood swings."

Finally, looking for the way out of our turmoil, we came to the conclusion that we needed to focus our attention on how emotional and intellectual growth can be held steady—and that meant to focus our attention on what we had been informally calling "our ideals." We needed to consider the mental structure known to analysts as "the ego ideal" and how it works. "Look," I said, always the mapmaker, "we need guidance, and we need it from our own internal compasses—and that's what the ego ideal is. The concern we have been putting to the ego instincts—to insisting that there are such things as the ego instincts, including the ego instinct cherishment—implies another step. We have to ask how the ego instincts' aim, the cherishment search, becomes set up in people: that means how the ego ideal develops. Cherishment appears first in the matrix of mother or caretaker and child, but it has an adolescent development. We need to look at how it follows its growth principle, to reach outward. How does it become worldly? How does anyone get cherishment from the world, not just the caretakers? or give it to the world?"

Excited by the spurt of these questions, I resolved to go the next day to the library and order up the psychoanalytic literature on the ego ideal. "We have to stop just using this concept, the ego ideal, and see if we can say concretely, developmentally, what we mean," I announced. "And we shouldn't be afraid to let the chapter just take a form that reflects our experience of being adolescent while we think about adolescence—a chatty, multiregister, go for it, quick-change operation, full of our enthusiasms." Following this permission, Faith, doing her favorite kind of research, went off to look through her clinical journal. The next time we met, she gave me a sketch she had made of a patient whom we had often discussed, a child of today's Japan, the Japan in which the communal ideals and family roles that Takeo Doi had studied in *The Anatomy of Dependence* are shifting.

Michiko came to therapy because of increasing depression and bulimia, but she started right in with a statement of her *amae* needs. "When I first came to America on a high school exchange, my host family showed me love. That is what I wanted." Her *amae* needs do not baffle her, as they do most American adolescents, who lack the Japanese vocabulary. Michiko is, however, simply incredu-

lous that her needs have never been met. The promise of Japan was not fulfilled for her. Of all my patients, it is this one—the Japanese one—who makes me repeat to myself like a mantra: "Incredulity is the core of depression."

Her parents in Tokyo are both professional people who put in long, long hours at work. When she was only a year old, eighteen years ago, as Japan's postwar economic revival went into high gear, they made the decision to put her in what she called a "boarding school," because her mother had to finish her doctorate. Later, when Michiko was in elementary school, she lived at home again but was often left alone or put in charge of her little sister. "My friends went home, and their moms were waiting with a snack. I got no reaction or affection. In second grade, I missed my mother so much that I went to her school to wait for her, and one time I went to her room there and said, 'Mom, I miss you.' I was crying and she was crying, too, because she thought she was missing a lot, I think."

Michiko's little sister is bulimic, and Michiko herself shows her need for love in her eating, which is disordered in complex ways. Being left to eat alone as a child had made her hate food. She developed the habit of vomiting after she had eaten by herself. And then, while she was in America on the high school exchange, she ate happily for the first and only time in her life, and gained weight. When she went home, her parents told her she was fat, and she started dieting. More generally, she reverted to her submissive behavior with them, trying to shield herself from their constant criticism. Since childhood, to win her parents' love and approval, she had worked to be a top student, qualifying for a prestigious private school. But her parents had never praised her, and they had punished her physically—a startling practice in Japan—for small infractions of their rules or academic shortcomings. Once she set on fire a report from school of her perfect performance on a test, which her parents had shown no interest in. "My hair was burnt. I was trying to hurt myself with fire, but I wasn't really connected to what I was doing." Now she is sometimes haunted by an image of herself lying in a bathtub cutting her wrists. "I didn't think that was scary. I thought I could even try it." She talks about harming herself in a distant, mechanical tone; and in a voice full of shame, she—a very beautiful young woman— talks about getting plastic surgery to make her face beautiful and "to make it so I like myself."

Her ego ideal reflects her experience in America. Unlike Takeo Doi, she discovered in America the *amae* she missed at home; and she had dedicated herself, solitary and driven, to winning a scholarship so that she could return to America for college. "In Japan, my dictionary was my friend, and I was working so hard all the time to learn English; here, I only wanted to be with people, I needed this 'twenty-four-seven,' that is how the radio people say it." She told me that in Japan it is considered very impolite to eat and talk at the same time, so she becomes conflicted when she is eating in the company of her college friends: she talks at the table and then eats later, by herself, which makes her vomit. She contrasts this dilemma to a powerful experience she had had earlier with her American host mother: "When I was in the kitchen with my host mother, I would stand near her, as near as possible, while she made dinner. I was not her child, but she loved me. She talked and ate when she made the dinner and she talked at table when we ate the dinner, but with her this never bothered me. It was stronger than habit."

While Michiko was at home on a college vacation last year, she resolved to try out with her parents her Americanized feelings and capacity to speak of *amae*. She told her parents that she loved them. "Japanese don't say 'I love you,' but I wanted to tell them how I feel and think about myself. They were uncomfortable, but they listened. And I told them that I thought we should all go for family therapy." Her internal struggle to follow the ideal by which she wants to reform them, and herself, continues as she continues to struggle with the parents.

We could see in Michiko's story how she had formed in adolescence, not in childhood, her image of a nurturing, cherishing internal mother, able to reshape, repair, absolve shame, and it was clear that she was trying to reactivate this ego ideal development in her therapy with Faith, her newest American host mother. But we could also see that the ego ideal had been unable to keep her depression from overpowering her. While we were considering why, another immigrant came onto Faith's caseload—this one with no *amae* vocabulary at all.

Stella is Irish, in her mid-twenties, the single mother of a three-year-old child and herself one of a dozen rambunctious, hardy, but also hardened County Cork farm children. Right away, she told Faith her adolescent cherishment story, without having any idea of the need she was conveying. As a lonely thirteen-year-old, she had climbed under one of the big beds in which this crew of siblings slept. There she curled up like a little child and went to sleep. No one missed her. But when night came and she didn't show up for dinner, there was concern. A search. Finally, real alarm. Late in the evening, she woke up and put in an appearance. A moment of relief, and then the show went right on as though nothing had happened. As she told her story, Stella became aware that she had been making a bid for attention, and she was able to note that the bid had consisted of doing nothing, of disappearing. This was her pattern.

While Faith was listening to Stella, she could feel with her how much trouble she had getting herself to do anything, giving herself anything to grow for, move toward. But she could also hear that there was hope in Stella—hope that had made her seek for attention and affection, even if so passively. When Faith noted this to Stella, she flushed and said, startled: "I never thought of myself as wanting *affection.*"

They went on. Stella talked about a time when her older sister came home from a period of working in America and slept with her in that same bed, holding her tightly through the night. The bed seemed to represent for Stella the moments of childhood cherishment, it was the furniture of her ideal of herself as a good mother to her own daughter, a good sister to herself. Faith could feel a kind of hypothesis take form in herself: It is Stella's never having thought consciously about wanting affection that has restricted her growth and her ego ideal, and it is the unconcious images of affection from childhood that have kept the ego ideal alive, even if dormant. She has greater resources in these unconscious images than Michiko has. The sister Stella lives with now has recently proposed to her that they give up on living in America and return to Ireland. Stella had said to her: "There's something in me that wants to go forward here." That is her ego ideal.

THE LITTLE SAGE AND THE EGO IDEAL

We had been talking a good deal about how the growth principle is manifest in adolescents' ego ideals when the world provided new food for thought. Faith started another of her reading groups, like the one in which she had read Homer. She took Confucius as her topic, so he joined our conversation as well. And we found in Confucius one of the great philosophers of the ego ideal. His concern was, again and again, with self-cultivation, with becoming your true self, fulfilling your nature, and he had a very deep sense for how self-cultivation grows into cherishing of others and cherishing of others grows into worldly life, concern for the world.

> Only those who are their absolute true selves in the world can fulfill their own nature; only those who fulfill their own nature can fulfill the nature of others; only those who fulfill the nature of others can fulfill the nature of things; those who fulfill the nature of things are worthy to help Mother Nature in growing and sustaining life; and those who are worthy to help Mother Nature in growing and sustaining life are the equals of heaven and earth.

There in Confucius was the basic Homeric metaphor of *trepho:* fulfilling as growing and sustaining life. But exactly *how* does this "absolute true self" become guiding? That was our question.

Another book episode provided part of the answer. While Faith was assembling texts about Confucius, comparing various translations of *The Analects* and *The Mean in Action,* she had another memory of herself as a reader—quite a different reader than she was in her beetle book memory. She saw herself in her early thirties sitting in the office of her daughter's pediatrician reading Jennifer a children's book about Confucius, *The Value of Honesty,* part of a biography series. In this book Faith had recognized her own ego ideal as it had been in her adolescence, when she had turned to the *I Ching* for guidance.

Without any delay or frustration, Faith found *The Value of Honesty* waiting for her at the free library in Bryn Mawr. There was the child Confucius with his mother, talking about his father, who had died. The father had told little Confucius: "I believe that when you grow up, you will become a very wise person, and you will help many people with your wisdom." Remembering, little Confucius sadly says to his mother, "I miss father, and I wonder why he thought I would grow up to be a wise person." "Perhaps he said that because he loved you," his mother says. "And perhaps

he thought that if you believed it, you would make it come true."
The book's illustrator conveyed the meaning of this conversation
brilliantly: a gray-bearded Chinese gentleman in white robes,
tiny, but looking just like Confucius would look as a grown man,
appeared in a puff! and settled at the middle of the page. "You may
call me Sage," he bowed. And then the tiny sage appeared on each
page while the boy Confucius was growing into manhood, sometimes at Confucius' feet or perched on his shoulder, sometimes at
a distance. "I can help you to teach yourself," the little teacher explained. Then by the end of the story, Confucius and the tiny sage
have merged. The man has become his ideal.

When she read the biography, Faith recalled—as she had in the pediatrician's office—the conviction that she had come to as an adolescent and had marked then by placing next to her photograph in her high school yearbook a text about Confucius' model sage, King Wen. Even while under arrest in the court of a Shang tyrant, King Wen, author of the oldest layer of the *I Ching*, had been able to maintain his integrity, his creativity, to refine slowly, step by step by little step, the outward aspect of his nature. The example of King Wen allowed Faith to believe that *her* life had begun—he was her little sage and he was her belief in herself as a little bit sage.

In her adolescent struggle, Faith had been more under the guidance of an ego ideal than the patient I took into analysis that winter, whom I'll call Lynn, an energetic, smart woman in her thirties, whose adolescence was, she told me, "like yesterday" in her mind. Lynn gave us a sense of what life is like if you cannot articulate in yourself an ego ideal or find in yourself a true self, to use Confucius' philosophical terms. She had labored futilely, instead, to resist an external ideal that she felt was imposed on her by her mother. Lynn had no alternative mother to identify with or to shape an ideal around—no American host mother like Michiko's, no one like Stella's sister, and no imagined figure like Faith's King Wen.

In analysis, Lynn's route to remembering her adolescence began with a reflection on how hectic her long day at the office had been. At the end of her marathon, Lynn had gone out for a drink with a new friend, "a girly-girly kind of thing, like with thirteen-year-olds, you know." Pretty quickly, their conversation had turned to men and sex, eventually to very explicit talk about orgasms.

And I'm thinking to myself, why? Why am I doing this? Why am I once again in a situation where I feel uncomfortable, showing too much, and feeling I should have stopped somewhere well short of this. I don't cut off when

I should. I was humiliated. But she was even more revealing, if you can believe it. The bottom line is I dread boredom, lack of some kind of excitement. Very little penetrates the surface. I don't interface enough with things, connect. I just do all these things, and walk away feeling disappointed. It's like when I was a kid and had the feeling "you're never going to be the one." So much so that when I was older and someone paid attention to me, I would go into shock. Now, attention is like a drug. I have a huge fear of being lost in the shuffle. And if I get noticed, I have this feeling like "I cannot let this go, it is too good to be true, it may never come again." I hold on for dear life.

A few days later, more about her girl-girl kind of friendship came forth:

I was thinking as I was driving over here about Yvonne, who was my friend when I was twelve. I was a good girl, absolutely afraid to do anything bad, getting all A's in school and never exploring anything. No dancing, no gymnastics, nothing physical. I took no risks, and I could not find any natural talents. What was I meant to do? That was my question—that is still my question. I did that twelve-year-old stuff when my parents came this weekend, like I was trying to find out from them if they thought I was somebody; did they know? But, anyway, when I was twelve, Yvonne came into my life. She was the shortest girl in the school, and I was the tallest. She was very cute, but she had acne, and she was a little chunky and she had a big nose. She also had plenty of trouble academically. But she had learned to manipulate, to lie, so she got by. My mother thought she was malicious, conniving. She certainly was! I was her doormat. This tall zombie who could be dictated to. She did get me to do normal teenage things—cigarettes and sneaking around with boys, alcohol, pot. She needed to be in complete control. When I was a senior and finally had a few other friends, I cut her off, I got apathetic about her.

Having other friends allowed Lynn to release herself from the girl who had helped her detach a little from her mother's image of perfection, but she knew that this reconfiguration had left her, still, without a path. Later in the same session:

> It's like Yvonne and my mother were engaged in a power struggle. I was the medium through which their power struggle was played out. I removed myself from the scene. That's what I do. When there is conflict, I leave. Or I give up. Give in. When there is something painful, I go away before the pain gets to me. This all sounds so disturbed, it scares me. I either let people in too much, so they are going right through my fucking veins, or I cut them off. It's that way with my friends now. They are so important to me, but sometimes I don't care if I ever see them again. It's not really depression, it's like being cut off. It's like every time I assert myself, I am being mean. I don't know the difference between asserting myself and being mean, being a bitch and selfish. My mother never put herself out for people, she does not go out of her way. But me, I go so far in the other direction! If I can do it, I will. But right now I feel just terrible saying bad things about my mother! She was, though, really kind of selfish. I could very seldom do or be what she wanted, so I got my needs met on a kind of provisions level. It was all about not being seen. I've been wandering all over the place today, can you follow it?

Lynn gave us one clear image of adolescent turmoil: no ideal of her own had grown in her. She remained tangled in her mother's ideal for her, which she failed again and again, especially as she felt her body and her sexuality to be unacceptable. If she asserted herself, tried to fulfill herself, she would be exposed as unacceptable—and this meant mean and bitchy, as well as bodily and sexually damaged. So she remained boundary-less, unde-fined, all over the place. She doubted "Are they going to love me?" constantly; and that doubt always became envy, "They all have something I don't have."

While we were comparing Lynn's colonized ego ideal to Michiko's and Stella's ego ideals lacking power to move them, Faith's Charlie, the "I'm afraid I smell like onions" soccer player, gave us a demonstration of an ego ideal forming in therapy. After she had worked with Charlie for six months, Faith could watch him identifying with her, reorienting himself, and then he fal-tered again. In a surge of adolescent love—a spurt—he lost his way, as Faith noted in her clinical journal:

> The first part of Charlie's therapy was weeks of talk about how stuck he felt. He told me that he kept getting enthu-siastically interested in a school subject or a career direc-tion, trying out a few possibilities with part-time work, and then suddenly deflated, not interested in anything. Living at home was unsatisfying too, and he berated him-self for not having the independence to be on his own. Charlie spent many sessions telling me that he was sur-rounded at home by critical adults, particularly his father, but he felt constrained to remain there to protect his younger brother. "I can't leave him. He's only fourteen, and I see him starting to get from Dad exactly what I did. All those comments that made me feel that I wasn't good enough, just secondrate." Charlie was angry, and he some-times feared that if he let loose he "might really hurt someone." It was safer to descend into watching TV and overeating—behaviors that revealed his regressive desires

to be indulged and cherished. But his severe self-chastise-
ment over these behaviors made his anger at his father
seem mild in comparison. Charlie knew he was stuck, he
hated what he knew, and crying in those early months of
therapy seemed the only way to get comforting relief.

As Charlie became more attached to me and my non-
judgmental responses to him, he made a very common
adolescent move: an identification. Excitedly he came to
his appointment one day and announced that he knew
clearly what he wanted to do. "I know I want to help kids.
I'm thinking of teaching high school, of combining
coaching with being a counselor—you know, a kind of
coach for your mind." Over the months of crying, and
feeling safe doing so, Charlie had molted and, taking off,
he wanted to share his therapeutic goods. His next step
was also not surprising: he fell in love with a girl who was
studying to be a counselor and who happened to be, he
told me, "sort of tall, like you." His feelings startled him.
Previously, he had pursued girls, but only for short-term
sexual "hook-ups," never enough to take him out of his
guy network. But this girl, "well, she was . . . different."
He couldn't approach her. He spent an evening watching
her across the crowded school dining hall, animatedly
talking with her girlfriends. He tried to position himself
to be able to say hello as she left, he composed notes to
her in his mind, he worshipped her from afar. Floating in
to one session starry-eyed, he told me: "I found out her
name is Grace, and that's so perfect because she is like,
well, you know, like graceful." But suddenly his mood
changed as he said, "But when I'm around her, it's like I'm
an asshole, totally clutched."

Charlie was a fellow who hadn't permitted himself a
tender feeling since his early adolescence, when he had
lavished sweet, indulgent love on his dog, Pat. And Pat
never disappointed. Pat was the perfect baby to baby and

the perfect adult to get babied by. Charlie developed an adolescent style of being athletic and manly, but cool manly, not a swaggerer or a bully. Behind his masculine show, however, he was anxious about his masculinity. With the precision of a sadist, his father had zeroed in on his insecurity with frequent critiques of him for losing a game or for coming in second. Charlie's response was to mount more defense, and this meant further hiding of his own cherishment needs and his capacity for tenderness, as it had meant moving emotionally away from his mother, who represented fearsome femininity. On my Freudian channel I could hear that Charlie needed to exorcise any femininity in himself by putting it in a girlfriend, by idealizing her femininity and making their coupledom into an ideal girl-boy contrast. When he finally got around to dating her, Charlie had a surge of masculine pride when he was with Grace. But on the *amae* channel, what I observed was that as he drew closer to Grace, Charlie's *amae* came into its adolescent form—with Grace, and in relation to me. "You won't believe it, but I wrote her a poem! I'm sure it stinks. But, hey, I tried. I wanted to be able to show her that I think of her the way guys who can write poetry do. Can I read it to you?"

That Charlie was also feeling—unbeknownst to himself—that he still stank like onions was apparent when he was compelled, after he had gotten quite attached to Grace, to go to his local bar and be picked up by a woman who was older, tough, belligerent, tyranical, and as crudely sexual as any of the soccer team buddies, who accompanied him and cheered him on. "You wouldn't believe the way she talks, she had me doing stuff I never imagined. How could I have been with this woman? Why do I want to be with her again? You've got to tell me why would I have betrayed Grace in this way?"

Charlie had an ideal for himself that this incident

sabatoged. He ended up in the realm of dominance and submission, his father's territory, the place where his masculinity is in question. What we could learn from it was that identification and love are not enough to heal either a problem of sexual identity or a thwarted expectation to be loved. We had a further distance to go, and we are going it now as he feels that I must have failed him by not preventing him from experiencing this split in himself between his love of Grace and his submission to The Lady of the Bar. He has to replay the history of the thwarting, too—the *amae* story—with me. During the therapy, he has become a counselor, a mind coach, for himself and others, and he has envisioned himself a man of sensibility—a poet, after his own fashion—who treats people respectfully, even tenderly at times, a man who is the opposite of the man who persecuted him at home. But he is going to have to weave this ego ideal into his character by letting himself find me unsatisfactory in the old, all too familiar way and then cherishing me—not just cherishing idealized figures like Grace or his brother, whom he is constructing as he needs them to be for himself right now. But cherishing the deidealized me.

Confucius and our patients got us started in thinking about the ego ideal, but then we had to stop to turn our attention to the New York Psychoanalytic Society event, the worldly test of our convictions and our own adolescent *amae*. So, to tide us over, I made a definitional note, a promissory note, and gave it to Faith, saying we would come back to our task when we had made our debut, taken our *Cherishment* show on the road.

Affectively, the ego ideal is our declaration of how we expect to be loved and how we expect to love, an expectation that begins in the intimate circle of our infant caretakers and expands out, on, as we grow and go out into the world. Generally, the ego ideal is the representation we form over our lifetimes of a hoped-for I-world relation; it is our intricately patterned fantasy of how we wish to be in the world, which becomes woven into our psychic life to the point of being structural, like a figure in the carpet, although it is never fixed or finished, as our ability to live up to it is never sufficient. Philosophically, it is our basic sense of why we are in the world, as individuals and as members of our species, as creatures among other creatures. In it are captured our questions about the meaning of life—questions that encompass our questions about the meaning of our lives, like a circle around the center, a mandala. The ego ideal makes us larger than ourselves, which in adulthood is our way of satisfying our elementary childhood wish to expand our boundary, to be bigger, like the big ones.

THE ADOLESCENT SHOW GOES ON THE ROAD: WHAT THE WORLD PROVIDES

I rehearsed for the New York debut by delivering our "Cherishment Culture" lecture to Faith in my college's largest auditorium—to the amusement of the evening janitor—until we were sure that it could be taken in by ear, that it wasn't just a piece for the page, for reading. This was a composition mode I had learned as an undergraduate from the poet Muriel Rukeyser, who always said that poetry had to be written for speaking, not for reading. Poets practice "the theatre of the poetry," she had said, the words sounding, being voiced, being heard, while mere versifiers think in terms of print. In Muriel Rukeyser's poetry writing classes—

where my sense of myself as a late adolescent was crucially influenced—you did not make texts, you made performances.

We wanted our audience to *experience* "Cherishment Culture," feel cherished by both the manner and the message of it. We hoped to enwrap them with the idea that the present moment in history, in the history of the world, is one in which, after the catastrophic events of the mid-twentieth century—the era of world war and totalitarianisms—there is everywhere a great longing for the world to become a cherishing place. Despite the obvious fact that horrendous violence continues in multitudes of post-totalitarian forms, the world is being laced with new awareness of how these modern social and political forms thwart human needs by breaking down boundaries between war zones and civilian places, public and private realms, and, ultimately by attacking childhood, destroying the conditions that make cherishing child-rearing possible. In the new awareness of danger, there is revived expectation for sweet, indulgent love—Takeo Doi's *amae*. Not just in children, or in individuals, especially individuals coming to new life in therapy, but in a shared social consciousness, we argued, *amae* is protesting. Since the days of "Make Love, Not War" and "The Age of Aquarius," this consciousness has been growing in and through social-political movements like feminism and environmentalism that are life-preservative, that call for growing and sustaining life. We wove together the *I Ching*'s two principles, The Creative and The Receptive, with the two early Freudian instinctual drives, the sexual and the ego instinctual, in order to suggest East-West vision of self-cultivation and societal cultivation for cherishment. It was a Manifesto for Affectionate Therapeutic Living, our lecture.

And the world did provide what we were talking about, because I was, that lecture day, in an open and receptive state, like the one that Faith had been in when the beetle book was provided. I learned a lesson, too, about coming into such a state: it required going through an ordeal. Not a grand or dramatic trial, but one of those little tests that seem to be designed by the Homeric gods, those great jokesters, for keeping a human being on her odyssey. Ultracautiously, I had made two copies of the lecture, fastening them into booklets so that they would be proof against any sudden lecture hall draft. But as I read the lecture from one of the booklets, I discovered that my office copy machine, a notorious deck stacker, had collated the pages 1, 2, 3, 6, 4, 5, 8, 10, 9 . . . Without losing my composure, I had to keep darting around looking for the right next page, praying that the right one was actually going to be somewhere in the booklet, hopefully not too far off. My recurrent lecture-disaster dream was my waking reality—it kept teasing the Big Cheese. But I also somehow felt this reality to be just a joke, just the surface.

Finally reaching the last page without having to recite the text from memory or invent a new one, I was euphoric, but I also realized that along the way I had come into a calm conviction that no matter how I got to the end, the audience would be with me, the cherishment idea would reach them, reach into them, because the very phrase "the expectation to be sweetly and indulgently loved" would open all those people to what it translated, to *amae*. Underneath the strain of coping with the script, keeping cool, I felt no fear, no need of defenses. *Wu wei*.

My relief and enthusiasm so compelled me that at first I didn't realize how "Cherishment Culture's" audience was buzzing. There was a swell of excited talk in the hall when the moderator, Albert Solnit from the Child Study Center at Yale, who was already dear to us as our host for the Anna Freud Centenary, asked me to take questions from the floor. As people came to the aisle microphones, one after another, eager and interesting, most of them speaking very personally, touchingly—this at a "scientific session"!—I could show them my receptivity mode spontaneously, unscripted. Even those few in the audience who questioned antagonistically, wondering if we weren't being sentimental or naive about the state of the world, did not feel dangerous. I felt *intimately* at ease. There was reciprocity, exchange of sweet and indulgent love. With six hundred people!

Both Faith and I were particularly taken with a passionate young man, all aglow, who wanted to know if "cherishment" had not already been described by the Danish philosopher Soren Kierkegaard as "the power of love." I told him it probably had, for something so elemental has surely been described by many people. As Takeo Doi had acknowledged, *amae* is universal, although the Japanese may be richer in *amae* words than others. But cherishment language has to be created again and again because cherishment is originally preverbal, manifest in an affective state, easily eclipsed in a dangerous world; it is manifest in exactly the state that that young man was in, and many others around him. We could feel what we had invoked in the lecture: *amae* as a mode of protest against a dangerous world. A woman came up to us in the foyer after the session, gave us her business card—she is a therapist in Connecticut—and told me "that was like a warm bath on a cold day, thank you." Perfect.

THE EGO IDEAL'S
DEVELOPMENTAL LINE

For our work, the most important results of the New York debut were that "Cherishment Culture" had gotten, in many ways, a real hearing and that we had learned that the cherishment concept has what the *I Ching* calls "influence." After the lecture, Faith consulted her old friend and wrote out into our notebook several lines from the hexagram to which she was directed, "Dispersion." The lines felt to us beyond our reach, too big for us, and also somehow not, somehow simply modest.

> In times of general dispersion and separation, a great idea provides a focal point for the organization of recovery. Just as an illness reaches its crisis in a dissolving sweat, so a great and stimulating idea is a true salvation in times of general deadlock. It gives the people a rallying point.

People had been moved. And after they went home, some sent letters, requests for copies of the lecture. Others sent invitations. We accepted invitations to give the lecture in other places, then to teach a course at the Graduate Faculty of the New School for Social Research, where there is a program in psychoanalytic studies. "Elisabeth," Faith said to me while we were reorganizing our schedules to accommodate this opportunity, "I have suddenly gotten the feeling that we should send our lecture to Takeo Doi and let him know that his writings have gotten this new echo, this influence."

I became corresponding secretary for our project because we had agreed that after the lecture, Faith would have to stop giving *Cherishment* her weekend attention. She had her four-day-long doctoral qualifying examination to study for, which meant that she had to review the content of the thirty courses she had taken to date, covering the whole field of psychology. Thick folders of class notes mushroomed all over her den while her *Cherishment* files traveled by cardboard box to my office. But before her retreat officially began, I asked one thing of her.

On a business trip several weeks after the New York lecture, I slipped into a dreamy kind of state as the train I was on went streaking over the Schuylkill River bridge. Below, a fleet of four-person University of Pennsylvania racing sculls flicked across the river, and I found myself wanting to write a sprinting little essay, like a school exercise: "My Ego Ideal." I wanted to reconnect to our vein of talk about the ego ideal, and to do so while I was still under the influence of the lecture experience. As it turned out, I was more under the influence of the racing sculls:

> My ideal is balance. It has two dimensions, which are as single as the two oars of a racing scull, as single as the two-part word *kaloskaiagathos*, beautiful-and-good. The Greek ideal was good actions which are beautiful, beautiful achievements which are good. Aesthetics and Morality coupled. Balance is keeping position while in motion: do not seek either to transcend the world or to be a world unto yourself; do not live only in the future or only in the past; do not set yourself above any other or below; find the whole in each detail and treat each detail of your life as the whole. Do not do what you would not have others do—and not just unto you. All your words and deeds should flow from you smooth as a stroke. Do to and for yourself in order to be able to reach out lovingly, responsibly; otherwise, you will lose your common sense for your needs and others' needs, lose your balance.

I called Faith from New York, told her how interesting it had been for me to write this, and asked her to take a study break and play this game. "Just write whatever comes into your mind," I teased in shrinktalk. My essay had startled me by being so full of *do this* and *don't do that* instructions; it set me wondering about the relationship that must exist between my ego ideal and my superego, that psychic agency so famous for its admonishing tone. Faith's statement, when she presented it to me, startled me by being such a catalogue of clear *I wants*, without instructions.

> I want to be at ease with myself and with the world. I want to possess an inner joyousness that comes to expression in my life's work and in my relationships. Ideally, I see myself as a teacher, whether in psychotherapeutic relationships, actual

classroom teaching, or in my interactions in the world. I want to be a teacher of self understanding and self acceptance and of understanding and acceptance of others. Green-shooting those in my life directly and those who come in contact with me indirectly through my ideas. I need to cultivate beauty in and around me. Inner beauty: of emotional calm and tranquillity, of liveliness and vitality in my mind, of truthfulness—and more humor!—in speech, and of health in my body. Beauty in outward expression: ease in my body, my movements and gestures, my speech and laughter. My clothes, house, garden, vacation places, too, will be beautiful. I want to cultivate the expression of my nature as a beautiful art form, very refined in proportion, and very warm and accessible. Beauty is the form of the "affection" principle, cherishment, the content. I want my intimate relationships to be the domain in which I grow and practice my nature. I want Jennifer to find happiness, contentment.

While Faith went off to study for her exams, I went through all our notes about the ego ideal and started sketching a lifeline for it, thinking about our statements and about our patients, but thinking also about cultural values and images. When Faith was at last successfully through the exams, we celebrated with a dinner at Dimitri's and I gave her my working draft for "Reflections on the Ego Ideal." "Pretty amazing." She laughed. "I slave away at the exams and am rewarded with an essay I coauthored at the same time." "Pretty amazing to me," I told her, "that when I needed help I consulted either your voice in my mind or your friend the *I Ching!*" We joked about how we have both become able to carry on our conversation when we are not together, each having taken in the other's thinking style, set up the other internally. When we talked about this mutual inhabiting, we realized that we should describe it at the end of the developmental line in our essay because it is an example of how ego ideals meet, a way to define friendship in terms of the ego ideal. To mark the thought, we composed a little paragraph on one of Dimitri's paper napkins:

> Your friend is the person who knows when you are close to your ego ideal. Your friend has perceived the threads of your ego ideal as they have shown up in the wishes you express, the people you choose to be with, the projects undertaken, values articulated, forms of presentation chosen, jokes told, memories treasured, frustrations endured. She understands your ego ideal as you do, but more consciously. Your shortcomings, although acknowledged, are not felt or judged as failures. The love in friendship is idealization along the lines of the idealized one's ego ideal. This is growth-promoting, and the very opposite of narcissistic idealization or expecting others to be as you wish and need them to be for yourself.

We put this thought at the end of our coauthored essay, which begins with an historical introduction focused on how the concept of the ego ideal evolved in Freudian psychoanalysis. There has always been trouble and controversy among the Freudians over whether and how the ego ideal and the superego are separate, which we address by thinking of the self-promoting yea-saying ego ideal as a product of the ego instincts, and the admonishing, nay-saying superego as a product of the sexual instincts. Secondly, there has always been a tendency to define the ego ideal as a transformation of primary narcissism, to see it as narcissism continued by other means. But this is an unnecessary assumption if you think, as we do, that primary narcissism belongs to the sexual instincts. We prefer to think of the ego ideal as the drive for cherishment transforming over time, and being, at the same time, woven into the unfolding of the sexual instinctual drive and the emergence of the superego. The ego ideal can mature into the agency that creates harmony between itself and the superego. Put in the negative: being frustrated in the quest for cherishment, and not finding cherishers to take in and identify with, makes the ego prone to fissures and faults; and a faulty ego ideal lacks power to pull forward, guide development, create harmony between itself and the superego.

Considering ego-ideal formation over time, and working with our combination of Freudian theory and *amae* psychology, we began at the beginning. The groundwork for the ego ideal is the infant's sense of being boundaried, which, concretely, means having a skin, being defined by being touched and touching, coming to know an outside and an inside. The first ego ideal is a body ego ideal. "This is the way I want to *feel* cherished and the way I want cherishing *feelings* on my body," a child thinks. The ideal is (to resort to words, again, for what is preverbal) "I want to be with Mommy (or Daddy, or another caretaker) like this." One of our friends has a little boy who showed this level of the ego ideal making its way into language when he said to his mother one day, while snuggling on her lap and stroking her arms, "Mommy, I like your skin better than mine."

We think of this first body ego ideal as like a "vibratory skin," experienced as giving a shape, but also as being pleasurably receptive, welcoming to cherishment. In iconographies around the world, vibratory skin appears as a halo, a nimbus, an aura or an aureole—some form of powerful holding or enclosure, a swaddling representing destiny, that connects a divinized child or childlike adult with the cosmos and its power, usually associated with solar warmth and light's growing power. In the divine child iconographies, the haloed child has a blissful, smiling expression, an expression of contentment or serenity. Similarly, in the earliest freestanding sculptures of the Axial Age, the so-called "archaic smile" seems to represent the infant's ideal state of being touched, as that ideal is carried into later life.

Children play out or play outward this first body ego ideal

with the first possessions they cherish, the things that the child analyst D. W. Winnicott called "transitional objects." A piece of blanket, a pillow, a teddy, a mitten, maybe a place, perhaps part of a person or a person, becomes the medium through which children relate to the world, adventuring out of the two-in-one relation they need with their caretakers, as at first with their mother's breast or bottle. The transitional object is the prototype of all future forms of the ego ideal, the touchable version of an ideal based upon touch. The two-year-old child who is learning to be able to separate from her mother, or practicing (to use Margaret Mahler's term), can do unto the transitional object as the child has had done unto it, and it can also say through the symbolic object, in effect, "This teddy is me, as I want to be, exploring, growing big, moving on my own two feet into the world."

The products of a child's body, particularly its feces, are also versions of itself in this way, so children relish giving their feces as gifts, smearing them or depositing them with special people. During the toddler period that Margaret Mahler and her colleagues called the "rapprochement sub-phase," children keep rushing back to the parents they are separating from, often bringing toys and objects as offerings, connectors, signs from themselves and from the world—transitional objects in reverse, as it were. They are by this time fully capable of keeping their love objects in mind and memory, and they cherish their constant objects with things, as they register their frustrations with tantrums. "This is me as I want to be: giving to you, cherishing you." "This is me as I want to be: in your reliable lap." Aggression, traditionally in theory so associated with the anal stage, is enormous under conditions in which cherishment is not available or bodily gifts like feces are despised, held to be dirty and disgusting.

It is toward the end of this stage—in libido theory terms, the anal stage—when shame begins to be felt as the affect that arises with failures in efforts to get love and also with failures to establish good-feeling separateness and boundaries. This was Charlie's trouble period. He was deeply ashamed of himself—of his smell, metaphorically—and that shame surfaced when he tried to love Grace cherishingly and be cherished by her. He took the aggression that came with his frustration into his sexual affair with the bar woman. She felt compellingly necessary to him as a place to put his shame.

This is also the stage where *amae* becomes so culturally important and culturally influenced. Takeo Doi emphasized how parents and children in Japan usually develop together a clear sense of "you will not be loved if you do that, or if you are that way," and shame is avoided by obeying such instructions. Michiko's parents went pathologically far with their shaming behavior, but under more normal conditions, too, shame is the first level of reaction to thwarted expectation to be loved. Guilt comes with further frustration and the feeling "I must be responsible."

A child who feels shamed, shy or bashful, unsure in its skin and frustrated in her efforts to give and take, come and go, with the parents, will, if her expectation to be loved is continually frustrated, become not just shy but fearful—her shyness turned on herself, isolatingly. Guilt, then, is the affect that comes with efforts to reestablish lost cherishment unions by overcoming a boundary, transgressing, committing the child equivalent of crimes of passion. In psychoanalytic terms, these are crimes against the rival parent or against siblings who seem to be getting the love. Crimes of envy. A child who is guilty has trouble building an ego ideal that says "You can be like this," because the child—like Lynn—is always feeling "You will be punished, you ought to be punished, you are responsible."

As children become more visually oriented and conceptual, their ego ideals take on visual characteristics in addition to the earlier tactile ones. The process is cumulative. They move into the domain of body comparison as they move into the Oedipal period, or, in libido theory terms, into the phallic phase of rivalry and guilt. Their bodies are so small in comparison to their parents'; their genitals are male or female in comparison with the opposite sex. The ego ideal then reflects the child's effort to reconcile his or her own sense of present size and future growth—so the little sage imagined by the boy Confucius in *The Value of Honesty* is both little and grown-up, like so many of the ideal images adored by children of this stage. Dwarves, elves and gnomes are the child's size but also grown-up, able to defend against an evil figure—like the Witch in *Snow White*—who proffers deceptive appearances, like poisonous apples. In cultures where totemic animals are adopted by individuals and groups, the totemic animal can function for the child as an ego ideal representative, much as an assigned name does in other cultures.

Early Oedipal children's visual ego ideals have a reparative or augmenting or aggrandizing quality: they counsel, "You will grow bigger, you will have the sexual characteristics of both sexes." Suffering by comparison is the shame of this period, and much ambition gets directed at fighting this shame. More generally, the ego instinct for love gets directed at mastering situations, learning to do things, being able to speak—and eventually to reading, writing and arithmetic. All this, sometimes called "the instinct for mastery," is directed by an ego ideal of competence, cleverness, capability.

The first two versions of the ego ideal—the two-body ego ideal versions of "having a skin-boundary" and "being bigger"—provide the foundation for this third one, "being competent," which grows on top of them, sometimes obscuring them quite thoroughly, sometimes not. The Oedipal child is operating as an imitator of specific persons—"I want to be like Mommy, like Daddy"—but other figures meld into the ideal, as do their activities. "I want to be a cowboy." When people (more than bodily or affective states) inform the ego ideal, it is sometimes called "the wished-for self-image," a phrase originated by the analyst Edith Jacobson.

Cherishment

The wished-for self-image is very bound up with the surge in the ego instinct of mastery, and with the child's fascination with activities, competences, including the specific sexual activities of men and women, which are imitated in sexual games and games with sexual content. Curiosity grows strong. In this stage, the ego ideal has not a tactile or visual emphasis, but an internal voice: like the little engine that could, it says "I think I can! I think I can!" The superego, as it begins to take on its mature form in the Oedipal period, is made up, as Freud said, of identifications with not so much the parental figures as their superegos. The harshness of the parental superegos is summoned to control the sexual instincts. Admonishments from the Oedipal superego, guilt, are in the domain of the auditory, and they come to intermix at this time with the ego ideal's encouragements and shame. Together they make up the "voice of conscience." For sins of the domain of conscience, the sinner is struck dumb or somehow ostracized from the community of the parents and their society.

In latency, between ages six and ten, the ego ideal, like the ego generally, stabilizes. A normal Dennis the Menace latency could be described as one in which the ego ideal is neither too exacting, and thus unfulfillable, nor too amorphous, and thus unguiding. It says neither "You must!" (as opposed to the "You ought to!" of the superego) nor "Don't bother!" Ego ideal stability in latency augurs well for a youngster's ability to weather preadolescence, when the cherishment ego ideal of early childhood, never abandoned, has a resurgence. In a growth spurt comparable to that of infancy in its intensity, the preadolescent needs again the protective surround, the protective skin, of the mother or caretaker.

In terms of the sexual instincts, early childhood sexuality—oral desires, anal desires—has a resurgence with the onset of pubertal drives, and it is mightily defended against. So the youngster who is drawn to the mother is also guiltily running away from her as a sexual and sexualized being. Thus ego instincts and sexual instincts push and pull in different directions; the ego-instinctual nostalgia is indulged as a twelve-year-old nestles up to his or her parents, while the sexual nostalgia for the mother is felt as forbidden and rejected.

Like a latency child, the preadolescent idealizes states of undifferentiation or self-sufficiency or, in the nostalgic mode, states of ideal relatedness prior to sexual differentiation. But the preadolescent's ego ideal is also laced with the regressive fantasies typical of the period. While the body is changing so rapidly, these fantasies are very clearly expressed as concern with skin and with body image generally. Both boys and girls experience their bodies as sites of attack and criticism; the slightest of body-focused slights are monumental. Almost every adult has a memory of being found too tall, too short, too much like the opposite sex, too light, too dark—too *something*—that sits in them like an incurable wound. One of my patients felt that she was stamped for life in middle school by a teacher who teased her about her red hair by saying "Better Dead than Red." It is among the ten- to twelve-year-olds that racial and ethnic slurs—particularly about looks—etch in so deeply and painfully.

A preadolescent's "Do not touch me!" is proportionate in its vehemence to the complexity and contradictoriness of his or her desire to be cherishingly, affectionately touched and to be sexually touched. Both boys and girls imagine themselves lost in the undifferentiatedness of couples or groups. They imagine that it would be wonderful to run away from home and be everywhere and nowhere. Girls, particularly, worship androgynes—sometimes in the person of an older woman who is free, active, beautiful—and are often conscious of their desire to be both sexes. Meanwhile, boys are in awe or envy of female reproductive power, although they usually have this feeling under great repression and express it only indirectly in their creative projects.

Cherishment

As early adolescence is reached, parents are usually deidealized. A process of disillusionment is also usually spurred by particular episodes in which the parents are less than magnificent, and the adolescent's disappointment demands a new ego ideal to replace the one that grew with and in the Oedipus complex. Friends begin to fall heir to the parental idealizations or to fill the adolescent's need to reverse the parental idealizations; *somehow* the resurgent Oedipus complex must be exited. This is where my patient Lynn got stuck. She looked to her girlfriend to help her escape her mother's expectations, but the liberation never came; she felt herself to be too unacceptable to generate her own standard. Now, after two years of hard work, she can appreciate herself.

Friends—or sometimes the friends' ego ideals—become the main sources of a teenager's ego ideal ingredients or wished-for self-images, and the ego ideal begins to function in the process of separating from the parents, individuating, consolidating "me" as an independent person. Parents are often distressed that their children choose companions who seem so unlikely, so different, weird, inappropriate, bad. But this is just the point. The companion is supposed to supply everything the adolescent cannot find inside or in the parents. The companion—or later a group of companions, even a secret society—is the challenge, the "as I want to be" and the "who I want to be with." The friend is the adolescent's transitional object for adventuring into adulthood, for trying on identity possibilities, for doing "Let's pretend we're . . ." And if no friend quite fills the bill, a book or movie or music hero or heroine is called upon, as Faith called upon The Beatles. An early adolescent will often look to the present culture, or sometimes the romantic or idealized cultural past, for idols to replace the parental idealizations and supplement what friends can supply as well. Sometimes a teacher or coach can be half parent, half friend. Diaries can be the friend as well as being the place where a friend is eulogized. When Michiko said "My dictionary was my friend," she meant she was learning English as other kids make friends, in order to become the person who could speak up and have her needs met, to become a person in emotional America.

It is usually only in late adolescence that the ego ideal becomes a matter of values, maxims, philosophical propositions, world-views, religious or spiritual beliefs. The body ego ideal layers and person-centered Oedipal layers are not left behind, but they get woven into what might be called a character-and-culture ideal, an ideal way of being. This is an ideal of relating to others—eventually of relating to "the world," all others. Late adolescents are idealists, their ideals presenting them as artists of themselves or promoters of their own evolution or cleansers of their own obstructions. In various ways, they imagine themselves turning themselves into what they value.

It was at this point in our essay that we came back to our Dimitri's thought about friendship and how friends appreciate each other's efforts to turn themselves into what they value. We knew we had come into a long debate within the European tradition. The captain of one debate team was Aristotle, the philosopher who most clearly extolled friendship as a union of like-minded souls, a union of similars, "kindred spirits." His was the vision that held sway until the Renaissance, when essayists of the opposing team celebrated the differences or complementarities friendship could embrace. Ego ideals were thought of as bonds, and then as bridges. And moderns have lined up behind one concept or the other, agreeing only that friendships between men and women are peculiarly difficult, whether bonded or bridged.

We find this to be one of those either/ors that urge people to underestimate and misrepresent complexity. Friends are both similar and dissimilar. Their challenge is to be both, and to respect in their adult lives the bridging typical of adolescence and the bonding typical of late adolescence. As we had noted in our essay, among adolescents it is very common for the best friend to be the incarnation of the ego ideal: my friend is who I am not but wish to be, and being with my friend helps grow me into my wished-for self—even if a bit of envy ferments us. But as it deepens, this complementarity turns into bonded equilibrium. The friendship is like a gyroscope; it runs along its wire, leaning left, leaning right, threatening to capsize with misunderstandings, but going on. Forgiveness is always needed. Careful attention to the knots is always required, and playfulness prevents as well as heals the scrapes and knocks. There is *wu wei* in the balance between friends as there is an internal *wu wei* harmony.

We wrote up this last part of "Reflections on the Ego Ideal" while we prepared to take an August vacation together in Greece, to write our last chapter on *amae* in adult life. After thinking about adolescence, *being* adolescent, and experiencing the adolescence of our work making its way in the world, we were ready for a post-adolescent adventure in the place Faith called "Homerland."

"It's been a year since we found the beetle book," Faith reflected while we were standing at Kennedy Airport with the hundreds of other people who were going to board our 747 headed for Athens. "That was a waking experience that had the quality of a dream—all condensed and full of meaning, portentous. When I look back on it now, it makes me realize how much of that feeling I had—left over from adolescence—of being alone, alone, in a strange land, has disappeared this year. I don't feel like a stranger in the world, so the world is not so strange. And I want to be a traveler, going to other lands. With all these people! Odd, isn't it, how these internal shifts, growings, go on so microscopically, through such inchlike daily events, and then suddenly you notice you are not the same?"

Chapter 6

Cherishment Culture

It is in playing and only in playing that the individual child or
adult is able to be creative and to use the whole personality, and
it is only in being creative that the individual discovers the self.

—D.W. WINNICOTT

Getting here, to the island of Aegina, thirty miles off the Pireaus port from Athens, where we are writing this last chapter of our book, was not easy. The flight from New York ferried many Greek Americans to their ancestral homes for the big August celebration of the Virgin Mary's birthday, and then carried a hundred or so Israelis, including many young children, on to Tel Aviv. Everyone but us traveled with huge suitcases, duffels, and many rope-tied cardboard boxes full of gifts and goods for their people at home. The airport services groaned audibly under the weight of this informal family import-export business, while the telecommunications services labored to supply the vast needs of these travelers' cellular phones, little portable TVs, beepers, the multitude of devices by which people stay fastened electronically right in place even as they voyage around the world. The atmosphere was convivial, full of excited conversation, but also charged with xenophobia, fear of flying, visions of terrorism, and religious fervor. Among these pilgrims, we felt the mixture of chatty courtesy and nervous contestation that is typical when contemporary strangers spend twelve hours pressed into each other's lives, squeezed and squirming like fish in a barrel.

Our companion for the flight was Theodore Zeldin's *An Intimate History of Humanity*, which we took turns reading. We had selected this elegantly erudite Oxford historian's beautiful book for company because we had been dipping into it for months— we had cited it in our "Cherishment Culture" lecture—but had not had the time to really share it with each other, talk it through. Somewhere over Italy, we came to the paragraph that had made me buy the book after browsing it in a Philadelphia bookstore:

The age of discovery has hardly begun. So far individuals have spent more time trying to understand themselves than discovering others. But now curiosity is expanding as never before. Even those who have never set foot outside the land of their birth are, in their minds, perpetual migrants. To know someone in every country in the world, and someone in every walk of life, may soon be a minimum demand of people who want to experience fully what it means to be alive . . . The rise of Christianity and other religious movements in the Roman Empire is an example of a new gossamer spreading over a rotting civilization; though outwardly emperors and armies continued to give orders as though nothing had changed, individuals, feeling that official institutions were ceasing to be relevant to their needs, sought their consolations from each other. Today, a similar switch in attention is happening: the earth is in the early stages of being criss-crossed afresh by invisible threads uniting individuals who differ by all conventional criteria, but who are finding that they have aspirations in common. When nations were formed, all the threads were designed to meet in a central point; now there is no center anymore; people are free to meet whomever they wish.

We imagined that we were going to feel the planetary gossamer that Zeldin was describing, and practice in it what he called "the art of encounter." His book shows him as an adept at striking up conversations, truly recognizing persons as persons, enjoining them to talk intimately and honestly about their lives, their loves, their hopes. In a Zeldinesque world—something like the opposite of a Kafkaesque world—people talk directly, on the level, with each other. His ideal, his ego ideal and his cultural ideal, is a vast version of what Faith and I have been exploring together: "Conversation is one of the most important ways of establishing equality."

Cherishment

"You know," Faith said to me as we waited hour upon hour for our bags in the Athens airport, sweat-drenched bustle, fatigue and short-temperedness lapping round us, "I feel so different in my vocabulary. When I traveled abroad before, I simply didn't look about me in this way. My perception has changed, and now I am looking at cherishment stories. I see cherishers, and I see people in whom cherishment is missing. I watch the people missing cherishment clutch up or grate or crash when they meet, and I am trying to keep from getting drawn into the fray. Not to be aloof, but to transmit around me a steadying, cherishing energy."

Looking about with different eyes, from a stance for which *wu wei* is the ideal, is the result of having adopted—to use one of our favorite quotations—"self-cultivation as the method of conducting study." We had encountered this description of the essence of Chinese philosophical practice in Fung Yu Lan's *History of Chinese Philosophy* and used it often to remind ourselves that we are not in pursuit of Truth or true statements about Human Psychology; we are cultivating ourselves in and for relatedness, which generates the words and concepts that we then use to work further. Our conversation keeps our conversation going, and us growing in it. The people we encounter look different to us now, after so much talking, not because we have found access to the "right" or "true" way of seeing them, but because we are aware of our way of looking and engaging, as it is evolving, as we are evolving. That is the *I Ching*'s central advice to adults: that in continuing to develop your character you must take care " . . . not to become hardened in obstinacy but to remain receptive to impressions by help of strict and continuous self-examination."

Our fresh impressions of global travel in the late twentieth century and of ourselves as travelers settled as we moved into and got accustomed to our whitewashed bungalow, rented from Greek friends, and our front terrace view of Aegina's Sanctuary of Apollo—the view I had enjoyed nearly fifteen years ago, as I sat on this terrace reading *The Interpretation of Dreams.* The remains of the fifth century B.C.E. temple are down the hill from us: a partially reconstructed floor, and one single standing fluted column, dusty yellow with the morning sun and reddish purple in the evenings. Behind the temple, the sea stretches out toward the Peloponnese, usually serene, glistening azure, but now and again turning gray and angry, whipped up by Poseidon's trident. We are surrounded by a few gnarly olive trees and a large grove of pistachio trees on which the clumps of nuts grow daily rosier. The harvest will take place in September. But for now there is a deep quiet of ripening in our grove, and it has fostered a reverie that we fell into on our first morning here. We remarked to each other—we cannot remember which of us launched this reverie— that the orchard must be like the one in which Laertes received his son, the great traveler Odysseus, who had come home after twenty years of war and wandering to find his house occupied by men who coveted his wife and his goods, abusing fundamentally the rules of hospitality so central to that culture.

The orchard reunion scene in Book 24 of *The Odyssey* shows so poignantly how Odysseus has become a man who has to go in disguise and to check himself, stopping at every moment to assess, to strategize, because the world he moves in is simply too dangerous and perverse, too uncherishing, for spontaneity, for expressing cherishment needs directly—or even for being a hero in the mode of *The Iliad.* He had received perfect hospitality from the Phaiakians, who delivered him home, but most of his journey had been a study in abuses of hospitality, preparing him for what he finds in his own house. Then, Penelope, to be absolutely sure that the bedraggled and blood-splattered avenger who has just rid her hall of her enemies is Odysseus, tests him. She, too, has become a person wrapped in caution, stiffened, over twenty years of threat to her household and her integrity. After the couple finish their testing of each other's identities and loyalties and—finally—spend a night of lovemaking and storytelling, Odysseus goes off to the orchard to find his father:

> *The son paused by a tall pear tree and wept,*
> *then inwardly debated: should he run*
> *forward and kiss his father, and pour out*
> *his tale of war, adventure, and return,*
> *or should he first interrogate him, test him?*

Of course, Odysseus must test the old man—and then Laertes tests *him*, requiring him to show proof that he is indeed Odysseus. Reassured, Laertes nearly faints in his joy. Odysseus cradles his father in his arms like a baby, cherishes him, and tries to calm his fear—quite justified—that now they will have to face a civil war on Ithaca as the families of the men Odysseus has slain come seeking revenge.

The last two books of *The Odyssey* are a dense, rich group portrait of a family struggling to reunite, to be open to each other, in a time of social and political chaos, a spiral of retributions. There is nothing in this situation that augurs well for the future; there is no moment like the one described in the hexagram "Dispersion" that the *I Ching* gave us after our lecture in New York as a sign of how the world needs a cherishing idea:

> In times of general dispersion and separation, a great idea provides a focal point for the organization of recovery. Just as an illness reaches its crisis in a dissolving sweat, so a great and stimulating idea is a true salvation in times of general deadlock.

Neither Odysseus himself nor any idea offered by him were a rallying point. He had simply, and cleverly, slaughtered every one of the island men who had abused his hospitality. But these were his own subjects, relatives of the men who had sailed away with him to Troy! After the brutal paroxysm, the poem does end with the tender scenes of reunion, but there is no vision of how the cherishing of which Odysseus is so capable will ever translate into peace in his kingdom. His cannot be a household like that of the Phaiakian royalty, who had received him so graciously and listened so sympathetically to his wanderer's story.

Through our first days in Greece, we kept coming back to Odysseus' experience, and to the topics it focused for us: how does a person who wants cherishing and wants to be cherishing live in a dangerous world? How can cherishing ideas and actions have influence in a dangerous world? *The Iliad* tells a grand story of forgiveness and reconciliation as Akhilleus stills his rage and extends his hospitality to Priam, but *The Odyssey*—this poem of adventure and fantasy, often light-hearted and funny—is, finally, a tragedy.

On the other hand, the *I Ching*, a book in which there is no tragedy, only changes—ups and downs, waxings and wanings, season upon season—does specifically tell in "Dispersion" what it is that a person can do to "overcome the egotism that divides men," to address the condition of "mutual distrust" that produces personal and social and political standstill and stagnation. The image of overcoming is very beautiful and very far from the Odyssean way: "When a man's vital energy is dammed up within him . . . gentleness serves to break up and dissolve the blockage." Public ceremonies that bring hearts into unison, awakening "a consciousness of the common origin of all creatures," are important, as is "cooperation in great general undertakings that set a high goal for the will of the people." People who are "free of all selfish ulterior consideration" must appear. They are enjoined to "forgo what is near" in order to win what is afar—that is, to set aside partisan goals and narrow group perspectives: "One must have a wide view of the interrelationships of life." The *I Ching* sounds like Zeldin as he says: "However, the originality of our time is that attention is turning away from conflict..." People are challenging "the tradition that conquest is the supreme goal of existence; more attention is being given to understanding other people's emotions than to making and unmaking institutions."

Talking about the stark contrast in *The Odyssey* between the final brutal battle scene and the tender reconciliation scenes, we have been making notes about the standstill, the stagnation, and the dispersion in the world that are corollary to the chapters we have already drafted about people's individual stories and their therapy stories—including our own individual and therapy stories. The stopped growth, the states of missing cherishment, the unrelatedness, the stuckness, the adolescent confusion and vulnerability that we have written about have effects in the world, both creating and reflecting cultural situations. How does a culture embody and convey cherishment, or fail to? How can a culture in standstill be revitalized, reanimated, reawakened, and the people overcome their divisive egotism in and through it? Zeldin clearly had these questions in mind when he noted that people start drawing close to each other in conversation when skeptical intellectuals—like the early Greek philosophers, heirs to Homer—have helped them realize that exchanging opinions is more helpful to them than bowing before some image of The Truth, for "everything is constantly changing, and multiple, and very complicated." "The invention of democracy, too, required that people should say what they thought and express themselves in public assemblies."

We think there is a growth principle in cultures that is manifest in this kind of gathering, assembling, this talkativeness. And we have been thinking about culture as all the means by which people, meeting and talking, can translate their sense of cherishment from elemental caretaker and child relations into public and political relations. This translation process that *is* a culture becomes the foundation, then, of translations between cultures.

One culture meets another culture, is open to another culture, on this foundation of child-cherishing turned into public cherishing. And, inversely, any culture that attacks child-rearing or makes child-cherishing impossible, or that cuts off the reciprocities that are founded in such child-rearing, is imploding, strangling itself. "One must have a wide view of the interrelationships of life."

THE VOYAGE TO HYDRA

We began our work-vacation conversation focusing our attention on these large themes. But we wanted to proceed in the way that we have learned: to pay attention to what comes up directly out of our day to challenge us. We grow only if we are receptive to what the world provides and devoted to exploring it—and ourselves in it. So we decided to travel, taking a day trip from Aegina Port to the island of Hydra, an hour to the south on the hydrofoil *The Flying Dolphin.*

The weather was, as usual, brilliantly clear, the sea green-blue as it lapped against the white cliffs of the coastlines, and our fellow travelers were quietly, happily, on lookout while they chatted among themselves in half a dozen or so different languages. To everyone's delight, a school of small dolphins raced up to the boat and then raced off, playfully. Faith exclaimed: "Oh! They make me want to tell you a pure cherishment story—about a dolphin—that I read in one of Ram Das's books called *How Can I Help?* Maybe we should be looking for cherishment culture underneath the sea!" She told me that Ram Das had described a man who went scuba diving and got caught way offshore with a severe stomach cramp. He managed to struggle to the surface, but he could not take off his tank and he was too cramped to swim in. Just as he thought he was going to slip under, as he was about to give up, a dolphin appeared and snuggled up to him, inviting him to hold onto its fin. The dolphin swam him to shore and dropped him off! Then went out to cavort around happily with his friends after this service.

We were marveling at this story when *The Flying Dolphin* made a stop at the port on Poros to pick up another small group. Among these tourists, there was a French family who had excursion tickets for Hydra, like everyone else, except that theirs, prepared in advance by a travel agent, had reserved seat numbers. The rest of us, with unreserved tickets, had simply picked seats according to our preferences—in the bow, in the stern, in the center, by the windows or not. The boat was only half full. But, nonetheless, the French paterfamilias felt that he and his wife and their teenage daughter should have precisely the seats to which they had been assigned, despite the fact that three portly Greeks, overflowing with shopping bags, sacks, straw hats, and newspapers were occupying the chairs.

The Frenchman began to explain in rapid, annoyed French that the seats were his. Immediately, tension rose all over the boat. The Greek man to whom the Frenchman addressed himself had no idea what the problem was, and when the tickets with their reserve numbers were waved angrily in front of him, he was obviously still perplexed. But graciously, the Greek made an effort to figure out the situation with his traveling companions, two elderly women. The Frenchman could not tolerate the slowness of their response and, intensely agitated, he began to berate them.

The Greek threesome looked at each other and began to laugh. The Greek man then rose, picked up his cane, twirled it, and put on his white straw hat jauntily, like Maurice Chevalier. The three all laughed heartily at this. Gathering up their possessions carefully, they moved with great dignity and good humor into a nearby row of seats. We could see that the Frenchman was impressed, but it was more important for him to be livid, to sustain his rage. So he herded his wife into her seat, unrolled his French newspaper and sat down sullenly. There he stayed, fuming and tied up in his righteousness and his newspaper, isolated, until his daughter, who had gone to the café, came back to claim her seat.

While the daughter had been at the café, a heavyset woman whose nationality we couldn't guess had lowered herself into the seat next to the daughter's and hoisted her shopping bags onto the daughter's seat. Both the daughter and the father, now roused up again, told the woman in French that she would have to move her things. She didn't understand. They told her again, louder, faster, gesturing. Finally, she more or less understood the situation and decided to move. To her husband, who arrived from the portico, where he had been smoking, she offered an enraged rendition in Russian of what had happened. Her face, which had been depressed, got gray, hard. As she gesticulated and pointed accusingly at the French family, she swelled; in gulps, she pumped up the indignation in her chest like an inner tube. Again, everyone around the scene was disturbed, agitated. We could feel once more the basic quality of emotions—they are contagious, infectious, as irresistible as yawns. It seemed to us that everyone on the boat felt suddenly as we did, isolated, sorrowful, uncherished. We were in a war zone.

Half an hour later, all the passengers, still cloudy in their agitations, descended upon the quay at Hydra and dispersed into the crowded waterfront cafés, the shops selling souvenirs and suntan lotion, "Saronic Gulf gold" jewelry, lace, cheap ceramics, Turkish carpets. Those who had luggage hired the local taxis—donkeys and mules with wooden racks on their backs—to go to the hotels higher up in the town. The streets of Hydra are too narrow for cars, and immediately, all newcomers have to adjust to the peace of being in a town without traffic.

We were only too glad to escape into this peace. We hiked all over the town and then up the narrow streets into the hills behind it, so that we could look down on the port. After lunch we went for coffee at the western end of the port, which is a magnet for young people. Below the cafés that are for them—where U2 and Sting blast on the CD systems while card games and flirtations go on in Euro-English—the young lie like lizards on the cement docks nestled down among the coastal rocks. A feeling of conviviality radiates along the young people's Café Row, right on over to the sign that points THIS WAY TO HEAVEN, which is a disco perched on the highest cliff above the town.

Faith and I enjoyed the Euroyouth culture, the post–Berlin Wall culture of national borders growing more permeable—so boisterously, chatteringly harmonious, so Zeldinesque. But our own conversation kept returning to the morning upheaval, which had the feel of Europe at the mid-century, Cold War. "Monsieur is the type," I reflected, "who is maximally susceptible to joining a group dedicated to brutality, organized for blaming others. That commitment to his own righteousness! He was so accustomed to hiding his *amae* need that he could open only a tiny crack for the Greeks' cherishment, could feel for no more than an instant their cherishing attitude."

Soon after we seated ourselves in the bow of *The Flying Dolphin* for the return trip, the French family reappeared. Monsieur walked right up to us and announced that our seats were reserved for them! Uncanny! We were incredulous. The same scene was obviously going to play out again, and we were not going to be mere spectators. Monsieur shook his ticket threateningly and began to speak, faster and faster, accusing us of trying to pull something over on him. We could not tell if he was shocked at being obstructed again or if he had anticipated this moment and was perversely thrilled. But either way, his elementary frustrations were on display: there was a conspiracy to make things go against his expectations, and his language was not operating as an immediate instrument of correction, so he was being actively attacked. In Takeo Doi's psychopathology, we were looking at *hinekureru:* this man was "acting in a negative and suspicious way, obstinate, peculiar," a child whose attempts to *amaeru* have been repeatedly thwarted.

Sharply, I asked the Frenchman to back off while we got up and settled into other seats, where we could hear him continuing on to his wife and daughter about the ridiculous Greek transport system and the imperialistic American women who had stolen his seats. Everyone on the boat again tensed, some turning inward for protection, some glaring and holding themselves back from attacking. There was shock and anger everywhere, as though the Frenchman had committed a crime before our eyes and ears.

Neither Faith nor I said anything while the boat set off for Aegina in the awaited gorgeous sunset. But then I admitted to Faith that I had been sitting composing in my best schoolgirl French what seemed to me the right riposte. She laughed and admitted that she, too, had been composing a reply, but that she had gotten stumped by being unable in her anger to remember the word for "rude." This was a psychological block, for she speaks French well, while I just substitute English words for French ones. She had wanted to zing him. I had wanted to triumph over him rationally.

We laughed at how consistent we are in our differences, how predictable. But the next morning we had a more serious conversation about the French family and about our reactions. Since we first talked about *wu wei,* we have each learned a great deal about how to practice "non action" in therapy, how to absorb and help dissolve our patients' characteristic habits of hiding their cherishment needs. But without the familiar therapy context, where your non action can work over time, water on stone, we were taken by surprise and felt compelled to act, or react. We had not become depressed and then angry like the Russian woman, but on the other hand, we lacked the radiating calm of the elderly Greeks. I had had to command the Frenchman to step back. And neither Faith nor I had been able to let the incident go—to dissolve it by ignoring it, to influence him by our non action.

What we experienced, we came to think, was how the political or the public aspect of being *wu wei* can founder on incredulity—on an old feeling, a feeling from childhood, of not being cherished. "Oh, no, it can't be that this is going to happen—again! They could not be doing this—again! People are not like this, are they?" Being incredulous, you become intent upon making what is before your eyes not be so, on making it different. A contest gets launched over who is going to be in charge of reality. You become incapable of that pause that the *I Ching* recognizes as step one in dealing with any challenging situation: "To see the danger and know how to stand still, that is wisdom." In such a pause, as we understand this counsel, you should cherish yourself. This means, first, seeing to it that you are well taken care of, protected, in caring company—you pause to gather your "right assistants"; and second, working to interpret the situation rightly, stopping to think.

This pause is a very personal achievement, but it is also the essence of the political and legal practice that redeems standstill and stagnation, that provides for redemption in "Dispersion." Our need to cultivate this pause in ourselves and, further, to find how it can be a political principle set us to thinking about the *I Ching*'s reflection that in ancient China the whole administration of justice was guided by the principle that a self-cultivated person, "when obliged to judge the mistakes of men, tries to penetrate their minds with understanding." As Richard Wilhelm's translation of the "Inner Truth" hexagram continues: "A deep understanding that knows how to pardon was considered the highest form of justice. This system was not without success, for its aim was to make so strong a moral impression that there was no reason to fear abuse of such mildness. For it sprang not from weakness but from a superior clarity."

"Of course," Faith said while I put out the breakfast peaches and tea, six days into the vacation, "we, being therapists, would like Monsieur to be in therapy. And then we also imagine him out in the world being cured by being pardoned—as though the superior clarity of the three Greeks would seep into him, like a balm, a relaxing bath. So that he could realize that they had, in effect, said to him: 'We understand that you are a very unhappy man. Here, laugh with us, take the seats—let us indulge you.' And as though their serenity would, then, go on out through the world. But we also need, I think, to recognize him as a challenge to us. He is a kind of teacher for us. Those incidents on the boat are our launch for continuing with the 'Cherishment Culture' theme. We need to ask ourselves to imagine the *culture* that would understand and pardon him, help him not be the way he is, not have allowed him to get the way he is in the first place. And he really is like an allegorical figure, a representative man, modern Uncherishing Everyman. An emotional imperialist. The one who attacks the need for cherishment in others, and in himself."

That night I had a dream that evoked a therapeutic culture. The dream grew up around the words "good humored," which we had been using all day, like a Homeric epithet, to describe the three exemplary Greek pardoners on *The Flying Dolphin*. But the dream also featured Hippocrates, known as "the father of Greek medicine" and one of the great exponents in antiquity of the idea that the human body-and-psyche is composed of four humors, each of which predominates in one of the four human character types or temperaments: sanguine, choleric, melancholic and phlegmatic. In this system, "good humored" means "of well-balanced character."

> **Hippocrates was sitting on a bench in our pistachio orchard and playing with the cat who comes over the wall in the mornings to lick the yogurt dishes. I was in this dream as a child, sitting on another bench nearby, reading. Perfect peace reigned, and I, as the dreamer, commented "good humor."**

I had made the Greek man on the *The Flying Dolphin* into Hippocrates, and I had the feeling, too, that I had made them both into the father of me—a completely idealized father, wise and playful, part of my own ego ideal of being balanced. But I also felt that the dream was directing us to explore the Hippocratic culture, to do a kind of reading of it, to consider it as an exemplary culture while we were thinking about "Cherishment Culture." So I suggested to Faith that we go visit the Sanctuary of Askleipios, the semidivine father of Greek medicine, the teacher-father of the Hippocratic physicians. His sanctuary was only another boat ride away, in Epidauros.

REDISCOVERING THE WORDS TO SAY *AMAE*

We made a plan to go to Epidauros on *The Flying Dolphin* two days later. But before we set off, to our surprise, our thoughts went in another direction. We found ourselves back at the very beginning of our effort to try to understand Takeo Doi's *amae* concept, realizing that we had overlooked something elementary.

This realization started to form while we were sitting in a café in Aegina Harbor reading a letter that had been forwarded from Philadelphia—a letter from Takeo Doi. With his greetings and good wishes, he had responded to us by appreciating the "Cherishment Culture" lecture we had sent and sending us a brief article on *amae* and ambivalence that he had written in English for a Japanese program on Swiss radio. There we found two sentences that captured in a nutshell what we sensed in the Frenchman: "Thus *amae* is vulnerable, as it totally hinges upon another person for its satisfaction. Hence, it may turn into its opposite at a moment's notice in case of frustration, thus producing a state of ambivalence." Dependency entails ambivalence. And the negative, hating side of ambivalence can virtually shut out, cover over, disguise, the positive, the love. Our Frenchman's paranoia—his sense that he was being attacked—was his strongest defense against recognizing that his love had been thwarted.

This much was familiar territory for us. But that evening something began to shift. On the west side of Aegina, where you can see in the far distance over the wine-dark sea the lights of Athens, we had dinner in a lovely taverna with our friends Fay Zikas and Dimitris Dilleos, and Dimitri's brother Kostos—a philosophy professor, a psychiatrist, and a political analyst. The talk turned to Takeo Doi's letter, which had caused quite a stir with the Dilleos children when they saw it on the table at our bungalow, they had found the Japanese stamps so beautiful. We were asked to explain the concept of *amae*.

While we were all talking about *amae* and reflecting on how Fay and Dimitris cherish their children, how they think about children's *amae*, I asked them to tell us about a Greek word that I had come across the summer before, during our expedition through the *trepho* lexicon in Homer's poems. The Liddell-Scott Lexicon had told me that *storgé*, meaning "affection," refers very specifically to a love relation between parents and children, and that this word did not exist in Homeric Greek, that it appeared only later. All three of them became immediately very excited to tell us about *storgé*, because, they said, all Greeks use this word often and lovingly. Even more commonly used is the adjective *storgikos*, "affectionate," which has generalized and applies to all kinds of people in all kinds of relationships. Then there is the adjective *astorgos*, "cruel" or " brutal": it also means "inhuman," which implies that being affectionate defines being human.

"The emphasis when we say 'affectionate' is on the emotion's reliability, even unconditionality," Dimitris reflected. "I will tell you a fairy tale about *storgikos*. Greeks, of course, say the story is of Greek origin, but then, you know the Greeks attribute Greek origins to *all* stories—perhaps to all civilization! A youth falls in love with an older woman who is a witch, and she tests his loyalty in a horrible way. She sends him to cut out the heart of his mother and bring it to her."

"Already, she knew about the Oedipus complex." His brother Kostos laughed.

"Yes, and he, too. For he does this act. But he is rushing back to the witch so fast that he falls to the ground and drops this bloody heart of his mother. Then the heart cries out to him, 'Oh, my darling son, I hope you have not hurt yourself!' You see, this is *storgikos*—she asks nothing for herself, not even life, but wishes everything for him. She indulges him. The best thing you can say today of a Greek parent is that she or he is *storgikos* to the child. And in my clinic, we often speak of a mentally ill person as one who has not had a parent or a family who is *storgikos*."

"While Dimitris was speaking," Kostos said, "I was asking myself why would your Japanese wise man, Takeo Doi, think that Western languages do not have words for *amae?* It certainly seems that we are all agreeing that *storgé* is modern Greek for *amae*. And I want to tell you of another word we have: *kissos*, which is the ivy plant. This is used metaphorically for the embrace the mother gives the child. And the very same Greeks who claim that the Greeks have invented everything in Western civilization—even in world civilization!—also say that this Greek word is the origin of the English word 'kiss.' The idea is that this *kissos* wrapping around the child is the paradigm of all kisses." Kostos wrapped one of his beefy hands around the other quite tenderly while Fay added wryly, "Yes, and we Greeks are a hopelessly theatrical people in love with imaginative etymology!"

They had a sweet time at dinner playing with their language and making little gifts of it to us, presenting the cherishment culture to which they are the heirs. But we all also had the sense that there was another step in this lexical play. We had all, in our excitement about the word *storgé*, gotten caught up in the idea that Dimitris's story contained: that cherishment is or can be *unconditional*. It cannot be, of course—it is a fairy tale or a fairy-tale psychology to think that caregiving can be limitless, even beyond death, death-defying. But everybody, thinking about being cherished, gets greedy for cherishment! And we felt, obscurely, that this greedy excitement we were all sharing somehow blocked something from our view. No one knew quite what. So Faith and I appointed ourselves the research team and promised to go to the town's one bookshop—the town's only library being closed for the summer—and look up all these words in a Modern Greek–English dictionary to keep our inquiry going. When we did so the next day, we learned two things—but not about *storgikos* and *kissos*. About our old friend from Homer, *trepho*.

Last summer, when I was following the verb *trepho* through all the cherishment scenes in *The Iliad* and the *The Odyssey*, it had never occurred to me to look up *trepho* in a Modern Greek dictionary. I assumed the word had fallen out of the language with the end of the ancient agricultural Axial Age civilization, which it so obviously reflected. I thought *storgé* had probably come into the language when the original cherishment vocabulary had faded and a new one was needed—at the end of the Homeric era, the time when *The Odyssey* could not present cherishment as a political possibility. But I hadn't taken into account that on a very deep level that ancient agricultural civilization never really stopped in Greece. People *trepho* the olive and pistachio trees outside our bungalow now as they did in Homer's day, just as the cicadas sing the same bug song at the beach below our wall as did their ancestors. So, there it was in the Modern Greek dictionary: *trepho*, translated as, among other possibilities, "cherish." We were filled with joy to find that our Homeric verb for *amae* activities is still a garden-variety verb for cherishing in this Greece which we are visiting. We looked forward to asking our friends for their associations to *trepho*, and to reporting about it to Takeo Doi.

But then the dictionary told us something else. In Greek you can cherish or *trepho* both positive and negative emotions and emotional states. You can foster or nourish or cherish a love for someone, a hope for something, or a desire. But you can also say with the verb *trepho* that you cherish a desire for revenge, foster a hatred, bear malice, harbor suspicions or fears. You can cherish an illusion. The same ego-instinctual drive, the same cherishing, can be directed at sustaining cherishment or at sustaining a negative state like envy, hate, fear, suspiciousness. Such a negative state is not cherishment *missing*, an absence or closing off of the drive, but cherishing misdirected, misapplied, convoluted. It is like the dark side of the moon.

All these Greek idioms do have equivalents in English, of course, but we had not linked them with the state we had been calling "when cherishment is missing" until we stood in that bookstore, gaping at the obvious. What is missing is the *love object* to love and be loved by, *not the loving*, which is diverted onto a negative state or feeling in the self—it takes a turn inward, like the secondary narcissism of frustrated libido. The Frenchman needed to sustain his anger; he cherished being angry rather than cherishing any person. We had even suspected that he might be thrilled to get angry for a second time, at us. "Nursing a grudge," Faith added, associating to another variant on this theme, "is how I am now thinking of envy. You get stuck on a feeling of being slighted, cut short while someone else is getting the good things, the relatedness, and then you put your effort to cultivating *that feeling of envy.*"

Her words sparked a kind of rush of association in me. "Nursing a negative state, for lack of a love object, for lack of relatedness—isn't that masochism? And sadism when the nursing one lashes out, attacks? And maybe that is really what Freud was trying to capture with the notion of the death instinct: he was trying to explain why people would want to be in pain, or how they could set themselves against getting cured—have a 'negative therapeutic reaction'—or how they could compulsively repeat a terrible experience. But he kept thinking of *pleasure* in pain, a sexual-instinctual matter. Nobody would deny, of course, that there is sexual masochism, pleasure in pain, and sadism, pleasure in giving pain. But what we're talking about is an ego-instinctual matter. You cuddle up to your pain, you *amaeru* it, nurse your grudge or your anger because this is what you have put in the place of a person. This kind of relationship to yourself—to your negative state—keeps you from being related to any person. You are split internally, loving your hate; that is your ambivalence. Your split state is, at least, safe, in a way. It has become familiar—you do not risk further frustration from a person. But when a person nurses a negative emotion, doesn't that also mean that he is nursing his own growth stoppage—and maybe that is also a way to describe what Freud meant by the death instinct. It's not an instinct *for* death but a self-preservative ego instinct that has gotten turned in on itself and fixed on growth stoppage."

Cherishment

When we reflected back on where our playful search for the Modern Greek words for cherishment had taken us, we realized that we had not been in this territory before because it had been too hard, too frightening. We want to associate cherishment, *amae, storgé,* beloved words, only with good and beautiful objects. And more and more good and beautiful objects! So to think of cherishing a negative state had been as hard as thinking "She loves a tyrant—the condition is at least familiar" or "He cherishes an evil man—that keeps him from the challenge of any real relationship." It is as hard as imagining a person having an ego ideal that says "Be fearful," "Be suspicious," or more extremely, "Be in murderous rage—murder!" It is harder to say "He loves to hate himself—and that is all he loves" than just "He hates himself." Once we had gotten to this perspective, we thought, further, that we had an answer to the question we had put to ourselves long before about aggression: there do seem to be two forms of aggression, which come in many degrees, and which can and do intertwine. One form stems from frustration of sexual instincts, and the other from frustration and turning inward of ego instincts; one is channeled through sexual perversions like sadism and masochism, and the other through ego perversions like loving-to-hate, loving-to-envy.

To think of people with sadomasochistic sexual perversions as only able to find sexual pleasure in some thing, some body part, some single activity, not with another person in his or her wholeness—that is familiar. But to think of what might be called an ego perversion is not familiar: being able to cherish only a painful, negative state of yourself, not another person. Perhaps, too, an ego perversion is more difficult to think about because it has repercussions beyond the limited areas where people practice sexual perversions. This is the convoluted *amae* of everyday life— it is out in the world, everywhere. We had met it on the boat when the Frenchman got excited to attack us.

TO THE SANCTUARY OF ASKLEIPIOS

It is so peculiar how you can know something and then, when you approach it in a different language, out of a different feeling, know it so differently. When Takeo Doi journeyed to America, leaving the home where he took *amae* for granted, feeling so displaced, so uncherished, he knew *amae* differently both because he had become a helpless, dependent baby in need of cherishing—like a patient regressed in a therapy—and because he could not find the words in English to say how he felt. As therapists, we have met the "cherishment is missing" states many times, and reflected carefully on how to diagnose them, work with them. We could recognize the Frenchman's problem as soon as we saw it—recognize the obsessionality, the narcissism, the *hinekureru* ("acting in a negative and suspicious way, obstinate, peculiar"). But, then, we knew him differently after searching around again for *amae* vocabulary outside of our language, and while thinking about him not as a patient but as a political man, a representative man who, going about in the world, would have an impact on others and would be susceptible to becoming part of a political group. We could see him then as cherishing his anger, nursing his grudge, so that he could not feel any longer his need to be related to anyone or to be sweetly indulged. His cherishment was in hiding, and to him it would have felt almost criminal to express his cherishment need. He accepted the pain of nursing his pain in order to avoid the pain of being hurt by anyone other than himself if he asked for his need to be met. Akhilleus in his tent, offended, cultivating his rage, had been for an agonizing time how this man was, we imagined, constantly. We remembered how Thetis had therapied him: "My child, will you forever feed on your own heart in grief and pain?"

Our reflections prompted me to translate into our terms what my teacher Hannah Arendt had meant when she went to

Jerusalem in 1961 to attend the trial of the Nazi functionary Adolf Eichmann and pronounced him "thoughtless" and "banal." She had not seen in the dock a monstrous, demonical madman who had *intended* to send millions of people to their deaths, but a "normal" man who wanted more than anything else to do what he was told, to carry out orders efficiently, to adhere to his job description. He made it perfectly clear that he would have had a bad conscience in the Hitler time only if he had not done what he had been ordered to do. On a very small nonlethal scale, this means: If you have tickets to sit in these seats, you must sit in these seats and no others, no matter what this means for other people. Eichmann had this convolution on a murderous scale, having moved from nursing pain on to nursing a behavior—rule-obeying—that kept him unrelated. He spoke in bureaucratise and could not imagine the human consequences of his actions; he thought in terms of numbers of railroad cars, logistics and traffic patterns, not people being shipped off to hideous pain and torment. Neither could he imagine himself as the source of actions that might connect to other people. In court he gave a rendition of the philosopher Immanuel Kant's Categorical Imperative—"Act so that your actions could be a law for mankind"—and then said that he was aware that he himself obeyed not this admirable imperative but Hitler's orders, his Führer's will. And that seemed right to him, even though he admitted that Hitler's orders had called for something that was a terrible crime—by rules other than Hitler's. When asked in court whether he regretted his deeds, he replied perversely: "Repentance is for little children."

A man like this is the perfect political agent, a dictator's dream, because he cannot judge anyone or anything outside himself. Cherishing rule-obeying, staying unrelated to people by this means, he will do anything that keeps his inner arrangement with himself, his rule-cherishing, intact. He envies and attacks any sign of relatedness in the world, anything felt as an impingement on his insulation. And nothing in his milieu, nothing in Hitler's Reich, offered such a man anything but confirmation for the way he was. Führer obedience was the norm, the rewarded condition. So that perverse world provided perverse cherishing—which, for a totally unrelated, totally unreceptive person would be the only kind of cherishing wanted: absolutely fake and requiring no real feeling, a cherishment for stones.

We hated using "cherishment" to talk about Eichmann or about the Nazi regime; but it makes psychological sense that only perversion of a basic need, an elemental human need and capacity for supplying that need, could lead eventually, in encouraging conditions, to behavior so inhuman, so *astorgos*—so cruel, brutal, evil. "Without affection" means: with all the need for affection turned off from relations with people, turned upon relations-refusing states and acts, and satisfied with living in a brutal world. This Eichmann type of man was not the only character type who could nurse a grudge and then get swept up into a violent political movement, a machine of destruction. But as an obsessional, he was particularly efficient in that kind of highly technologized, ruthless, obsessed atmosphere. He could be an example to many others.

We imagined people of different characters coming differently into the condition of nursing their negative states, their ways of being frustrated, and then moving around in the world differently, depending on how locked in themselves they had become and how their culture did or did not encourage them. The questions we had wanted to put to the Hippocratic culture at Epidauros shifted, thus, before we got there. And we could feel the shift very distinctly as we considered the countertype to our Frenchman or to Eichmann; as we considered a man always in search of relationships, remaining vulnerable to being frustrated, not stuck on cherishing his anger.

We met the countertype, Cherishment-Seeking Everyman,

when we began our trip to the Sanctuary of Askleipios. He immediately engaged us, charmed us, compelled our sympathy, even though his instant familiarity made us edgy. We could, thinking in our therapist categories, diagnose this man, too. He was a hysteric. Full of the self-reproach that Takeo Doi calls *sumanai*, and demanding of attention and pity. But he had none of the Frenchman's coldness. He was warm, effusive, sentimental. The Greek gods, looking after our education, sent us, as an archetype, an ordinary Odysseus, a wily traveler, a wheeler and a dealer: Basil the taxi driver.

We hired Basil at the port in Epidauros to drive us out to Mycenae, down to Nauplion, and then on to the Sanctuary of Askleipios—a daylong circuit. Negotiating the price for this tour was exhausting. He was so sorry to charge us anything at all—two such beautiful women should never have to spend money—but that is life, a man must eat and put gas in the car, and so . . . We would not be sorry, he assured us, for he would not allow us to be disappointed in him or his country, the most beautiful place in the world.

Basil was a dedicated conversationalist in what he called "my business English," a language he uses only in the summers, with tourists, which is completely made up of nouns and adjectives, some of them not English but Greek, or French, or German. He supplied all the verbs by gesturing, pantomiming, getting us to guess like charade players. Enacting "Mercedes . . . good taxi . . . money . . . bank . . . oranges . . . trade . . . hard work . . ." Basil let us know that his beautiful Mercedes taxi had cost him a fortune, "like Onassis," so he is hugely in debt at the bank; that his other business—growing oranges—has suffered with the trade policies of the emerging European Union, and that he will work until he is *kaput* without ever getting out of the red. The Europeans want to starve and humiliate the Greeks. But no matter. He adores driving his car, as he showed us by stroking the dashboard, the soft leather seats, planting little kisses with his hand on the steering wheel. And his two daughters are getting educations, they will be fine. Lawyers, perhaps. It is only his wife, from whom he has separated, who is unhappy. She suffers from "melancholia"—he uses the Greek word for depression—and is on medications. It breaks his heart, he tells us by pounding on his chest.

When Basil found out that we are psychotherapists, he was thrilled. Immediately, he took out his car phone and called his wife; then he insisted that we say hello to her on the phone. It seems he was convinced that some word from us would somehow magically make her feel better. Then he explained to us—we were exhausted by trying to receive this emotionally complex communication, which he was so determined to deliver—that he loved his wife very much. But her depression made him feel depressed, so he had to live apart from her and take occasional mistresses for his sexual needs and occasional ski vacations in Austria for *joie de vivre*, his *eudaimonia*. We invited Basil to join us for lunch at a restaurant he chose in Nauplion—a place run, of course, by cousins of his—and I asked him, speaking slowly, wrapping one hand around the other as Kostos had when he conveyed how ivy kisses, what it is that binds him to his wife. Basil pondered this question. And then he explained that he had met his wife when the military junta ruled in Greece—"very dark . . . *tyrannos* . . . prisons for socialists . . . bang, bang . . . my father *kaput*." He felt that he had to stay by the grave of his martyred father, to protect his family's home, to make a family. His wife, he said, was beautiful, but more, she understood sadness—which he pictured for us by drawing tears on his cheeks with his fingers. The very depression he later found so depressing, he then found kindred. She had cherished him in the time of the tyrants. His wife, he said, he calls Persephone after the girl who visited the underworld in the old Greek stories.

Cherishment

We relaxed after this storytelling by walking for miles along the seaside promenade connecting Nauplion's tourist district to the Palamedes Fort, named after the greatest inventor among the ancient Greeks. It was Palamedes who created the modified Phoenician alphabet that allowed Greek to transcend the Mycenaean Linear B, a script for merchant list-makers, and become a language for poetry. Becoming renowned for his ingenuity, so the legend goes, Palamedes inspired the envy of the clever Odysseus, who killed him, eliminating the competition. "That's the kind of reputation poor Odysseus acquired among the post-Homeric writers. He was caricatured as a kind of control freak, like our Frenchman."

Thinking ahead to the sanctuary, I went on, telling Faith that Askleipios, too, had been a victim of envy. After he had been sent off by his parents—one mortal and one immortal—to study medicine with the Centaur, he became so skilled that he was able to resuscitate the dead, and for that Zeus, who envied him, struck him dead with a thunderbolt. The old Greeks certainly knew that envy is the primary state of thwarted cherishment, because they, who imagined their gods as suffering from all the human failings, made being envious of each other and of the mortals the trigger of most of their divine murders stories. Tyranny is rooted in envy. As we stopped to take a swim off the rocks and then to dry in the sun before we went back to find Basil for the journey to Epidauros, Faith reflected: "When we get to the sanctuary, we should ask if those realistic Greeks could not only diagnose envy but cure it. Did their medicine, their psychiatry, their culture, have this secret?"

At Epidauros, we left Basil with his beloved Mercedes and some fellow taxi derivers to schmooze beneath an old olive tree. Strolling over to the Sanctuary of Askleipios, we tried to conjure it up out of its ruins, starting with entryway, the *abaton*, a dormitory. There, patients in need of cure came to sleep and to dream the dreams from which the priests and doctors would then deduce what specific treatments they needed to get back into physical and spiritual balance. The Interpretation of Dreams was the basis of Hippocratic diagnostics—as of Freudian. Baths were available, and massage and exercise rooms, an open-air gymnasium, and dining areas where patients learned to follow the prescribed dietary regimens calculated to adjust and balance their four bodily humors. Off to one side of the temple dedicated to Asklepios there was a stadium for chariot races and what we call track and field. A pleasant walk away, built into the north slope of Mount Kynortion, is the enormous theater designed by the most renowned of fourth-century architects from Argos, Polykleitos the Younger.

When a patient had been bathed, exercised, athletically entertained and fed, he was sent off to the theater, which seats nearly 15,000 people, to receive the ancient Greek version of the talking cure: tragedies, comedies, and satyr plays. As Aristotle explained in his *Poetics*, a drama brings about in its spectators a catharsis, a cleansing, that is the mental and emotional corollary of the body cleansing offered at the sanctuary. The approach to cure was, as we say now, holistic.

Sitting in the huge theater, we could only imagine what the performances must have been like, as there was no modern staging going on while we were there. No concert either, such as the famous one given by Maria Callas after the junta fell from power, for which opera lovers came from around the world. But our imaginations were helped along by some Greek schoolgirls who romped and danced around the circular orchestra, testing the miraculous acoustics. One excited teenager stood at the center of the stage and let loose with some rock singing and hip-grinding and giggling, all of which we, sitting fifty-five rows up, could see and hear perfectly.

Faith smiled as she watched the Greek girl's show. "I'm thinking about how spontaneously these children are putting their ancient theater to the modes of their culture—their internationalized TV culture—and their need to show off and be seen and be special. The ancient past percolates somehow through every person in this country, doesn't it? Like Basil calling his wife Persephone!"

"Yes, just as the Homeric stories percolated up into the plays of Aeschylus and Sophocles and Euripides that the Hippocratics' patients came to see here—and percolated right into their minds, medicinally. It's what your Chinese call transmission: 'releasing active forces.'

"Sophocles' Oedipus story percolated into Sigmund Freud's mind—and into his *Interpretation of Dreams*—and on from there through a whole therapeutic culture into yours and mine, medicinally, too! And then we hand it on. Before I got here, I never thought of myself as transmitting to my patients a tradition of healing so old—a psychogogia."

"We wanted to imagine a culture that could heal Uncherishing Everyman, or help prevent his kind of emotional imperialism from developing, and we see it has to be a therapeutic culture, a culture that is understood by the people who live it and make it *as therapeutic*. Not a culture where there are a few spas here and there for the wealthy, but a culture in which the approach to healing *and to living* is holistic, which assumes that dream interpretation and baths and diets and exercises and the theater—meaning dance and music, all the arts—are sanctified; everyday and sacred. But more, it would be a culture in which it is natural to make reference to the past, to history, childhood. A theater that acknowledges the full range of human desires—acknowledges that children both *amaeru* and desire their parents, and that parents play out their needs upon children; acknowledges Oedipus but also his father Laius' cruelty. A practically psychoanalytic theater that warns about the consequences of thwarted affection and frustrated desire. I mean, this is a place where you cure envy by telling stories of envy. A theater of practical emotional guidance."

"That phrase, 'practical emotional guidance,' makes me think now of Confucius," Faith said. "A disciple asked Confucius if there was one word which might serve as a practical rule for life, and Confucius replied: 'Will "reciprocity" do? What you do not want done to yourself, do not hand out to others.' This *shu*—reciprocity, consideration—was the summation of the Confucian practical emotional guidance, and it's what we are now saying the Greeks thought, too. If you don't want to be uncherished, don't be uncherishing."

She went on: "How different this Confucian thought is than the New Testament's 'Do unto others as you would have them do unto you.' In the New Testament sequence of thought, you are *alone* in the first step, not related, just instructed. It is all futureward: 'You do this . . .' And couched in terms of future rewards and punishments. But the Confucian maxim, put in the negative, suggests that you first ask yourself about your relationships. What have people done to you? What is your story? Then it suggests you *refrain* from doing to others what you have judged you do not wish done to yourself. You avoid what you have found harmful—that is, the relatedness-destroying things, the things not reciprocal. For the future, you draw on your past experience of being related. The point is not to repeat what has harmed you."

"You're saying," I added, "that if you first consider what you have found harmful and relatedness-destroying in your past, and then refrain from doing that, you cannot perpetuate nursing a negative state—like nursing a grudge, cherishing a frustration. Living by this Confucian maxim protects you from doing unto others a harm *you have come to want, a harm you cherish in yourself.* It protects you from inflicting your masochism on others, which is what being sadistic is. It keeps you from recycling the aggression you have experienced. This is how an authentic Confucian culture or a Hippocratic theater culture could help our Frenchman. It says, do not perpetuate harm done unto you. It says, look, we are all the products of the good and bad, helpful and hurtful things done to us, and of how we have remembered these, and now it is our job to filter out the harmful. A drama—a therapy—will show you what is harmful. Go to Askleipios and go to the theater to get cleansed, get back in balance, so you cannot dish that bad balance onto anyone!"

"That inner balance you need is what the *I Ching* calls steadfastness," Faith commented. "Do you remember what it says in the 'Inner Truth' hexagram about the toughest people, the ones called 'pigs and fishes'? To deal with such people you must first 'rid yourself of all prejudices'—that is the catharsis. And the hexagram even suggests that you let the tough person be your drama, be your teacher. Let a walking story of envy, for example, cure you of envy.

> In dealing with persons as intractable and as difficult to influence as a pig or a fish, the whole secret of success depends on finding the right way of approach. One must first rid oneself of all prejudices and, so to speak, let the psyche of the other person act on one without restraint. Then one will establish contact with him, understand and gain power over him. When a door has thus been opened, the force of one's personality will influence him . . . This force is not identical with simple intimacy or a secret bond. Close ties may exist also among thieves . . . All association based upon common interest holds only up to a certain point . . . Only when a bond is based on what is right, on steadfastness, will it remain so firm that it triumphs over everything.

You don't have to go to an actual theater if you can make a cathartic theater of your daily life as the *I Ching* counsels."

"Again, it's that pause," I reflected, drawing our conversation back to Confucius' maxim. "Confucius suggests you consider what you have received before you act, so you consider how to preserve reciprocity. It really is like what you learn from a therapy, which is a sustained pause. You learn 'I don't want to be related in that way—that is not where I want to be—I do not need that lesson again.' When you know, in the therapy relation, what you don't want, because you play out all your relations again in the transference, you have the freedom to discover what you do want and how you are going to be with others. That's the *tao* of psychoanalysis."

"The power of Zeldin's book is that he understood that historians can be therapeutic in the same way. They give people a pause in which to reenvision the past, history. People are governed by old ways of thinking. Remember his credo: 'Mentalities cannot be changed by decree, because they are based on memories, which are almost impossible to kill. But it is possible to expand one's memories by expanding one's horizons, and when that happens, there is less chance that one will go on playing the same old tunes forever and repeating the same mistakes.'"

On our way back to the port for the evening *Flying Dolphin*, Basil took us by the café where his wife works, so that we could say hello in person, and then to her parents' house, where his brother-in-law now lives. In the hillside behind the house—literally, in the backyard—there is a small stone theater, of later vintage than the one connected to the Sanctuary of Askleipios. Chickens roost on the seats, goats nibble the weeds that choke the aisles, the white stones of the orchestra floor are almost obscured with mud and debris, and all of the writing on the broken proscenium pillars is caked black with pollution. We were shocked. Ah, yes, it was a shame, Basil admitted, that the theater was only cleaned up when local rock groups came there wanting to use it for concerts. But, the government spends its restoration money on the big tourist attractions, which also support the local economy—including the taxi drivers. This little theater was also . . . he struggled for words "no hospital . . . no medicine." The theater, he was saying, sits alone, off by itself, not connected to a Sanctuary of Askleipios. Our guide understood that his wife had spent her youth next to an example of cultural atrophy, a theater divorced from the healing function of giving people history and a wide view of the interrelationships of life.

DELPHI:
AFTER THE THERAPEUTIC ACTION

When we got back to Aegina from Epidauros, the pistachio grove was ringing with adult talk and child laughter. Yorge, age five, and Calliope, age two, Fay and Dimitris's children, were giving a tour of their toys and their garden to my godson Jacob, age seven, and Benjamin, age four, who had arrived that afternoon with their parents, my former students Karen van Dyck and Nelson Moe, from New York. Yorge is very shy about speaking in English, which he understands very well, but he did come running over to tell us the gist of the new situation: "Kids! Kids!"

For the last five days of our vacation, we happily had a lot of conversation with these kids! kids! woven into our conversation, and this last part of our book feels to us now, as we are working on it, as though it has two perspectives: ours, thinking about cherishment in the adult world, and the kids' as they went out and about. But we also became aware quite quickly that the perspectives are almost the same. Jacob was our informant about this on the bus trip he took with us to visit the beautiful Doric-style

Temple of Aphaia, which sits on a hill high above Agia Marina, on the north side of Aegina. Equipped with his baseball cap, his plastic camera that takes real photos, and his money belt, he was ready, as he said, "to be a tourist." And to him this meant to take photos but also to observe things so that he could go home and tell his parents and his brother and the other kids what he had seen. Being a tourist was all about talking.

Jacob's big topic was the fact that the long-ago people who had made the temple, who had cut those huge stones without having any electric saws and figured out how to get the stones one on top of the other without using any cranes, had not used cement to hold the whole temple together—which is why it mostly fell down back in olden times. He wanted to be able to explain why something so amazing fell down. And he wanted to know whether the people who had built the little bungalows where we were all staying had used cement, like people do in New York. I reassured him. But I also noted that with Lincoln Logs and Legos, you don't need cement, and these big stones had

notches and grooves for fitting together. There are lots of good ways to build.

Later, at the beach, Jacob showed Yorge with a collection of stones how to make a temple. "It's okay if the water washes it away, you can rebuild, like the Romans did a lot, it's a game." We felt from Jacob's explanations that he sensed he had in Yorge a kindred spirit, a kid concerned over questions of dependability. Yorge has a big reputation on the island for having the ambition to become the harbor master at Aegina Port. That is his ego ideal. Every boat of any size or function that comes into view from Yorge's terrace, is noted and greeted. "There is *Aias!*" "*Argos* has got a new flag." "Look, *Flying Dolphin III!*" They are all known to him, old friends; he even knows them by their horns so that he can check on them without raising his head from his drawing board or leaving his truck depot over by the oldest olive tree. If a boat is late, he is disturbed. And any news report that one of them has had an accident makes him restless until the hurt boat returns to service.

We could listen to the boys—boys on the edge of latency—as little Sigmund Freud guys, emblems of average everyday castration anxiety, for they are on alert for dangers and accidents and irregularities. They are worriers. But we were also impressed by their cherishment theme. Is the world dependable? Is it safe for me to depend on the world the adults have put together? Can I have confidence in, trust in, the adults themselves? We were hearing how vulnerable they could be to becoming disappointed by the world, frightened, anxious—in need of a healing culture. Hippocratic culture was for this, for prevention and for cure of disbalance.

But as we played and toured around Aegina with the children, thinking back as we did on the Sanctuary of Askleipios and the theater there, we realized that we needed to think further about the capacities of a therapied, balanced person, one whom cherishment culture has helped to be *wu wei*, who can follow the Confucian maxim. In the *I Ching*'s terms, we have been talking for all this time about The Receptive, about cherishment as The Receptive—and about how to release blockages of receptivity, convolutions of cherishment. What, then, is possible? We needed to turn our attention to The Creative. What releases or rejuvenates energy for culture-making, building? What promotes the primary creative energy so obvious in the children as they played, percolating underneath the layer of their anxieties? What promotes building sanctuaries and theaters, writing plays? It seemed obvious to us, then, that we had to go to Delphi, the heart of Greece and, as the Greek legend has it, the center of the world, a place that has drawn travelers from all over the earth for centuries to feel and marvel in its sacred power.

Delphi, we both knew from having visited it on previous trips to Greece, is a place like no other in the world. The wonder of it is not the magnificent Sanctuary of Apollo that was built there over generations by supremely gifted architects and artists. The wonder is the place that holds, embraces, that sanctuary.

Delphi clearly was not chosen as a sacred site—as Epidauros was—because of its easy access by land and by sea, its openness on a plain to the thousands of pilgrims coming for the therapics of the sanctuary and the theater. And Delphi was not a place, like the great Acropolis in Athens, chosen because it was a natural fortress where a triumphal display of powerful buildings could be seen for many miles around. It does not, like so many wonders of the world, radiate monumental messages about imperial or divine power. The people who built up the sacred precinct at Delphi were neither using the landscape to draw people into the buildings nor dominating it with buildings.

No matter whether you approach Delphi from the south, up from the Gulf of Corinth, or from the east and the Aegean, the route Apollo was said to have taken when he first journeyed to

Delphi, you have to climb steeply through wild territory. The mountains are awesome as they rise from the coastal plains. And near Delphi the dark rock gorges become craggy, cavernous. When the site does come into view, built into, cut into, the side of Mount Rhodini, with the snow-covered Mount Parnassos in the background, even the huge Temple of Apollo seems very small, humble. The landscape lets the sanctuary rise up—it is not dominated; and the buildings do not impinge on the land.

From its earliest history, Delphi was built around a cleft in the earth from which vapors ascended that could inebriate people and enable them to prophesy. Originally, the old goddess Gaia, the Earth, guarded the place, but Apollo took it over after he defeated her son, the serpent god Python. Then Apollo's priestess, the Pythia, received the prophetic vapors, and Apollo's priests helped interpret her oracles. But even though Apollo was understood by the Greeks as the god who had triumphed over the early, primitive cults of Delphi, they always believed that the Earth spoke through the Pythia. Zeus, too, acknowledged the female principle of the place when he—so the second Delphic founding story went—wanted to know where the center of the world was. He released two of his eagles in opposite directions. Beneath the cloud where the eagles, after circling, came together was the *omphalos*, the navel, of the Earth; and this was right beside the Pythia's chasm, where Apollo had vanquished the Python. Pilgrims who came to Delphi were coming to the place where the baby is tied to the mother.

The umbilicus of the world, the center of the Delphic precinct, offered people from every corner of the world that the Greeks had touched a pause to contemplate their endeavors before embarking on them, to ask the Pythia for counsel before acting. The whole culture called for a pause. And that pause was, very consciously, connected to the place where the baby is tied to the mother.

When we arrived in Delphi, we went first—like the ancient processioners, and like the busloads of people from all over the earth who came that day—to the Kastalian Spring. There, the water rushes down a steep gorge into stone basins and troughs where the pilgrims cleansed themselves, and where we, modern tourists, could splash our hands and faces and enjoy the exclamations of delight all around us, in dozens of languages, over how refreshing is cold, clear water on hot, dusty skin. The Greek men—and only men made up the ancient processions—who went on from the Kastalian Spring up the hillside to the Sacred Way came from all the regions now united as Greece. Most of the groups had a city treasury along the Way where they were required to leave offerings. The pavements in the front of the treasuries and the treasury walls were stone accounting books carved with long histories of who had come, what their stories were, what their offerings were; the whole lower site at Delphi is covered with writing, in Palamedes' script. And this Sacred Way was the Greeks' greatest effort at getting people to think again about the history of disastrous rivalries and envies that had kept their cities from unity. "It is possible to expand one's memories by expanding one's horizons," as Zeldin said. Delphi was the place of envisioned political and spiritual unity.

Just below the Temple of Apollo, the procession came upon a conical stone that had been set there to mark the center of the world, the *omphalos*. The processioners had to pass by the whole history of the gods to get to the temple, where the Pythia heard their questions. Like a good therapist, she dispensed not advice, but counsel, challenge. She offered statements that required judgment and interpretation, which, as many who expected fortune-telling learned to their sorrow, means first and foremost *self*-interpretation. The temple itself gave warning, as it had carved on its pediments the most succinct maxims of Greek morality: "Know thyself," and "Nothing too much." The pilgrims had to be Confucians, appealing to their own judgment, or like consulters of the *I Ching*, ready to ask "What meaning do I find *in myself* for this image, in this situation?"

We climbed upward beyond the temple site to the theater, still clearly visible in the renovation given to it by the Romans in the third century B.C.E., and on, at the top of the slope, to the stadium. Remarkably, the Greeks managed to get horses and chariots for races up to this high mountain stadium—a huge labor to get the celebratory games to take place so close to heaven. And some unknown genius of the fourth century also created a sculpture to commemorate these games, now in the museum, a work in bronze known as "The Charioteer." He is a single standing figure, originally one of a group of four charioteers, who stood intently but serenely, joyously, ready to race. With his bright enameled eyes, he is staring ahead over the backs of long-gone bronze horses and into the sacred distance.

Then began the uncanny part of our Delphi visit. While we were standing on the starting gates, talking about "The Charioteer" and contemplating the mountainside stadium, a dense black cloud appeared over the treetops. Within a minute, the leaves on the olive trees were flashing silver in a wind, and rain began to sweep like a great broom across the stadium floor, turning it quickly into pools of orange-brown mud. The storm was so sudden, so out of the order of the dry summer weather, that most of the tourists were frightened by it and slid, shouting and getting drenched, down the paths into the cover of their buses or over to shelter in the museum. The rain seemed to have chased them off the mountain. We and one other cluster of people looked for protection to the cedars and pines around the stadium. The sky grew darker and darker. Blackness wrapped us like a curtain; the rain soaked us. Zeus thundered, and his lightning bolts went streaking across the valley.

Slowly, the rain slackened, the graying clouds pulled away

from the high rocks. Out of the other little tourist cluster emerged, then, a wonderful performance. Enter, stadium left: three young French sisters, perhaps eight, ten and twelve years old. Impatient with huddling under a pine tree with their mother, their father, a younger sister of about four who was frightened, and one of about sixteen who was busy being gorgeous and trying to keep her hair dry, they came galloping out onto the stadium floor and then raced off. Pretending they were horses—or charioteers of themselves—the three girls ran down to the far end of the track and then, screaming with pleasure, back, breathless, to the starting gates. Then again! Splashing in the puddles, tossing their manes, whinnying. They had caught the joy of the place, the out-of-the-gates racing joy that the sculptor of "The Charioteer" had shown him anticipating. They were released, receptive, theirs was a true enthusiasm—an *entheos*, a being filled with the divinity of the place.

As the storm rolled around the mountain and the sunlight returned, the French parents laughed delightedly at their completely mud-covered fillies, and even the I-am-grown-up adolescent sister smiled and offered her handkerchief. The girls were adored, the family was adoring; *amaeru*-ing in all directions as they regrouped, gathered up their backpacks, took each other's hands and set off down the mountainside. We were left standing alone at the stadium feeling the afterpresence of their spontaneous affection. Delphi, which had been such a Babel of visitors and then such a torrent of thunder and water, was suddenly so quiet that we were startled by a sparrow's cry. A luscious smell blended of wet pine, cedar, and olives suffused us. "Well," Faith said, "the gods are here—they have spoken. They certainly did put on their play!"

Feeling exuberant, refreshed, we walked down to the theater, its dark marble seats shining, washed clean, and imagined the gods looking down on the stage and on us as we looked out over the valley, trailing in mist. Still caught up in the French girls' romp, Faith suddenly did a little dance at center stage, *pas de chat*, and began to laugh up to the mountainside. Her laugh echoed off the rocks and out toward the valley. "Cherishment!" she shouted, and the rocks replied "Cherishment!" Then she drummed out a whole cadence of our words, "cherishment! *amae! trepho!* green shoot! *storgé*," and these went rippling and darting down toward the valley, too. I was caught up in her game and stood at the back of the granite slab orchestra, facing out toward the Temple of Apollo, declaiming: "On December 3, 1995, my friend Faith Bethelard and I were in New Haven to celebrate the centenary of Anna Freud's birth." Faith roared at this: "Yes! Yes! That is The Prologue to the play we wrote!" Then she swirled around and commanded me with a toss of her hand. "Now you recite Blake for these old Greek gods. Apollo, especially, will like Blake." So I performed the song of innocence

> *I have no name*
> *I am but two days old.—*
> *What shall I call thee?*
> *I happy am*
> *Joy is my name,—*
> *Sweet joy befall thee!*
>
> *Pretty joy!*
> *Sweet joy but two days old.*
> *Sweet joy I call thee:*
> *Thou dost smile.*
> *I sing the while*
> *Sweet joy befall thee.*

The sun emerged, and people began to wander up the paths again, talking excitedly about the rain and the strange way that Delphi had been transformed. A busload of Japanese school-children swarmed up the Sacred Way in their international gear—"I love New York" T-shirts, sneakers and backpacks—and then came to rest at the center of the world for a little historical lecture from their guide. "It's so funny that we both felt we had to play out for the gods our book about what's at the center of *their* world," Faith said to me as we walked by the Japanese children and along the temple path. "I haven't felt uninhibited and sheerly playful like that for . . . maybe not since I was a child. Adult joy. I owe it to the inspiration of those French horse-girls."

I answered her: "We were saying before we came here that we have so devoted ourselves to exploring The Receptive, to talking about cherishment as receptivity, and about how receptivity can be blocked, that we have not talked about The Creative. But we certainly got a lesson today! The gods gave us an audience. They received us in our creativity. But you do not talk about being creative, being The Creative, while you are doing it—any more than you talk about *amae* while you are in its feeling state, expectant, receptive. We did not talk about The Creative while we were in our conversation and writing, we had to come to this moment of celebration in the theater."

"And the lesson is that the burst of enthusiasm that the horse-girls had and then we had came after the storm," Faith added. "Being able to be receptive and open to the world even when it turns dangerous and threatening, not running away from it—taking that pause, remaining serene—that is the precondition for creativity, for the union of The Receptive and The Creative."

"Yes," I responded, "all of the great images of the whole world, images of the cosmos, that we have learned from while we have been talking—the shield of Akhilleus and the expanse of Homer's poems, the hexagram system of the *I Ching*, 'The Song of the Open Road,' *Songs of Innocence and of Experience*, the many volumes of Freud, the War Memorial, and now Delphi, this whole world on a mountainside—these are images in which the dangerous, the frightening, has been given its dramatic place. *Wu wei* images produced out of an inner confidence and surety. But Delphi is special among them, because it is a place where people can actually, physically gather for all kinds of performances of The Creative—political, theatrical, athletic, religious. And because it is so clearly grounded in an image of the baby connected to the mother Earth, it is a whole culture grown on the *omphalos*."

"There is a divine energy here that infuses everyone who comes and can be receptive to it," Faith reflected. "And everybody can take that energy home, too, as we will. Cherishment culture."

Suggestions for Further Reading and Acknowledgments

Cherishment is a footnote-free zone. But below we do want to guide any readers interested in our sources to them, and to give anyone interested in reading further on our topics a preliminary map. We are also preparing a series of topical essays: "Cherishment Culture" (*American Imago*, 55, 1998); "The Wise Baby as the Voice of the True Self" (*Psychoanalytic Quarterly*, forthcoming); "The Hidden History of the Ego Instincts" (*Psychoanalytic Review*, forthcoming). Other essays in progress can be read on our Website, Cherishment.com.

Takeo Doi has published two books in English: *The Anatomy of Dependence*, translated by John Bester (Tokyo: Kodansha, 1973), and *The Anatomy of Self*, translated by Mark Harbison (Tokyo: Kodansha, 1986). Many articles have also appeared in English, including these particularly interesting ones, listed by date: "Some Thoughts on Helplessness and the Desire to Be Loved," *Psychiatry* 26 (1963), 266–72; "Psychoanalytic Therapy and 'Western man': A Japanese View," *International Journal of Social Psychiatry* 1 (1964), 13–18; "Japanese Psychology, Dependency Need, and Mental Health," in William Caudill and Tsung-Yi Lin, editors, *Mental Health Research in Asia and the Pacific* (Honolulu: East-West Center Press, 1969), 335–43; "Psychotherapy as 'Hide-and-Seek,'" *Bulletin of the Menninger Clinic*, 37 (1973), 174–77; "Psychotherapy: A Cross-Cultural Perspective from Japan," in C. B. Pederson, *et al.*, editors, *Mental Health Services: The Cross-Cultural Context* (San Francisco: Sage, 1984), 267–79; "The Concept of *Amae* and Its Psychoanalytic Implications," *International Review of Psychoanalysis* 16 (1989), 349–54; "The Cultural Assumptions of Psychoanalysis," in J. W. Stigler, *et al.*, editors, *Cultural Psychology: Essays on Comparative Human Development* (Cambridge: Cambridge University Press, 1990), 446–53; "On the Concept of *Amae*," *Infant Mental Health Journal* 13 (1992), 7–11; "*Amae* and Transference Love," in E. S. Person, *et al.*, editors, *On Freud's "Observations on Transference Love"* (New Haven: Yale University Press, 1993), 165–71. The secondary literature on *amae*, particularly from anthropologists, has been surveyed by Frank Johnson in *Dependency and Japanese Socialization: Psychoanalytic and Anthropological Investigations into Amae* (New York: New York University Press, 1993). See also the article we quote in Chapter 2 by Carla Bradshaw, "A Japanese View of Dependency: What Can *Amae* Psychology Contribute to Feminist Theory and Therapy?" *Women and Therapy* 9 (1990), 67–86.

All Freud quotations are from *The Standard Edition of the Complete Psychological Works of Sigmund Freud* (London: The Hogarth Press), with volume and page noted in our text. On transference see *On Freud's "Observations on Transference-Love,"* cited above, and on the earlier history of Freudian technique see Martin Bergmann and Frank Hartmann, editors, *The Evolution of Psychoanalytic Technique* (New York: Basic Books, 1976). There are three volumes of Sandor Ferenczi's papers available in English, and several recent essay volumes give good introductions to his work: Lewis Aron and Adrienne Harris, editors, *The Legacy of Sandor Ferenczi* (Hillsdale, NJ: The Analytic Press, 1993); P. L. Rudnytsky, *et al.*, editors, *Ferenczi's Turn in Psychoanalysis* (New York: NYU Press, 1996).

Throughout *Cherishment* we allude to recent psychoanalytic

studies of infants, and more can be learned about these from Joseph Lichtenberg, *Psychoanalysis and Infant Research* (Hillsdale, NJ: The Analytic Press, 1983) and A. N. Schore, *Affect Regulation and the Origin of the Self* (Hillsdale, NJ: Lawrence Erlbaum, 1994). The work of the Budapest School has been described briefly by Susan Deri, "Great Representatives of Hungarian Psychiatry," *Psychoanalytic Review* 77(4) (1990), 491–501 (with a bibliography). There are three important Michael Balint books in English: *Thrills and Regressions* (New York: International Universities Press, 1959), *Primary Love and Psycho-analytic Technique* (London: Tavistock, 1965), and *The Basic Fault* (London: Tavistock, 1968). John Bowlby wrote many books, but *A Secure Base* (New York: Basic Books, 1988) succinctly presents his ideas, which are being developed currently by Peter Fonagy and Mary Main. Rene Spitz wrote *The First Year of Life* (New York: International Universities Press, 1965), and his essays have been selected in *Dialogues from Infancy* (New York: International Universities Press, 1983). Spitz's student Robert Emde, who is well aware of Doi's work, too, continues this tradition (see his "The Prerepresentational Self and Its Affective Core," *Psychoanalytic Study of the Child* 38, 165–92). Much work on infants was spurred by Daniel Stern's *The Interpersonal World of the Infant: A View from Psychoanalysis and Developmental Psychology* (New York: Basic Books, 1985). Our Chapter 5 on adolescence is influenced by *The Collected Writings of Anna Freud*, V (New York: International Universities Press, 1969), and Peter Blos, *On Adolescence* (New York: The Free Press, 1962). D. W. Winnicott's work is often in our minds, especially the papers in the following volumes: *The Maturational Processes and the Facilitating Environment* (Madison, CT: International Universities Press, 1965); *Playing and Reality* (Middlesex, England: Penguin, 1971); *Through Paediatrics to Psychoanalysis* (New York: Basic Books. 1975); and *Psycho-analytic Explorations* (Cambridge, MA: Harvard University Press, 1989).

Suggestions for Further Reading and Acknowledgments

The many citations from the *I Ching* in our book are from the Cary F. Baynes translation into English of Richard Wilhelm's German *I Ching*, which is published in the Bollingen Series by Princeton University Press. In Chapter 4 we cite Wilhelm's *Lectures on the I Ching* (Princeton University Press, 1979). Stephen Mitchell's version of the *Tao Tê Ching* is from HarperCollins (1988), and Robert Fitzgerald's *The Iliad* and *The Odyssey* are now volumes 60 and 94 in Everyman's Library (Knopf). The two French essays on Homer mentioned in Chapter 1 are Simone Weil, "The Iliad: A Poem of Force" and Rachel Bespaloff, "On the Iliad." In Chapter 6 we quote from Theodore Zeldin, *An Intimate History of Humanity* (New York: HarperCollins, 1995).

Our gratitude to all our patients, who have taught us so much about cherishment. We would also like to acknowledge here good conversations about *Cherishment* with our friends Wendy Garthwaite, Ying Li (who did the cover painting), Sally and Joseph Russo (who kindly supervised our Greek language forays), Ernest Sutton, Katherine Dalsimer, Sara Kay Smullens, Susan Dean, Susan Coates, Shelly Hall, Jerome Kohn, Maureen MacGrogan, John Roger, Maxine Haft, Elizabeth Frumin, Eileen Casaccio, and David Rackow and Jack Solomon. Our thanks to Takeo Doi, our friend by correspondence. Students at Haverford College and The Graduate Faculty of the New School were wonderful collaborators in a course called "The Well-Cherished Ego and Its Development." Thanks also to Philip Rappaport, our editor at The Free Press, and his excellent co-workers.